Themistocles

The Powerbroker of Athens

Jeffrey A. Smith

Pen & Sword
MILITARY

First published in Great Britain in 2021 by
Pen & Sword Military
An imprint of
Pen & Sword Books Ltd
Yorkshire – Philadelphia

ISBN 978 1 52679 045 3

A CIP catalogue record for this book is
available from the British Library.

Typeset by Mac Style
Printed and bound in the UK by TJ Books Ltd,
Padstow, Cornwall.

Pen & Sword Books Limited incorporates the imprints of Atlas,
Archaeology, Aviation, Discovery, Family History, Fiction, History,
Maritime, Military, Military Classics, Politics, Select, Transport,
True Crime, Air World, Frontline Publishing, Leo Cooper, Remember
When, Seaforth Publishing, The Praetorian Press, Wharncliffe
Local History, Wharncliffe Transport, Wharncliffe True Crime
and White Owl.

For a complete list of Pen & Sword titles please contact

PEN & SWORD BOOKS LIMITED
47 Church Street, Barnsley, South Yorkshire, S70 2AS, England
E-mail: enquiries@pen-and-sword.co.uk
Website: www.pen-and-sword.co.uk

Or

PEN AND SWORD BOOKS
1950 Lawrence Rd, Havertown, PA 19083, USA
E-mail: Uspen-and-sword@casematepublishers.com
Website: www.penandswordbooks.com

Contents

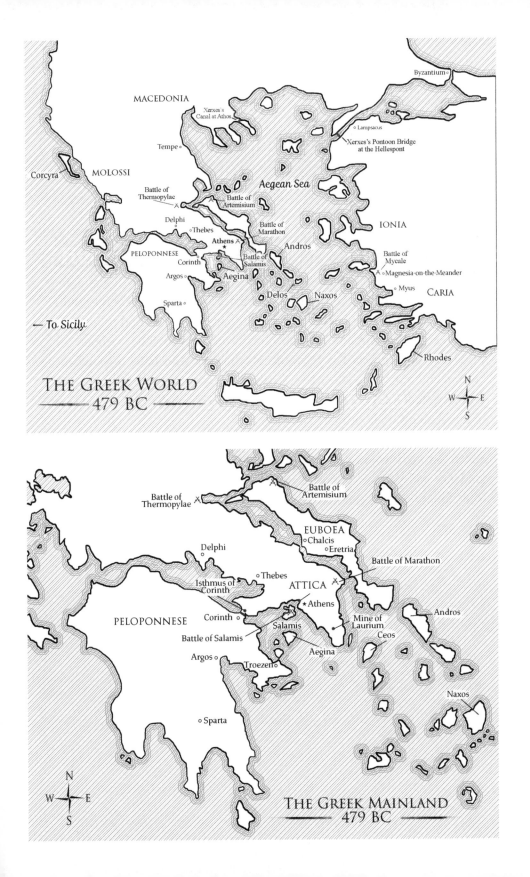

Acknowledgements

I am indebted to many for the production of this book. Firstly, I would like to thank my wife Majida for her support, encouragement, and willingness to let me pursue this project for many, many hours. I am deeply grateful for her consummate patience with my endless questions and discussing this book in greater detail than one might find tolerable.

The origins of this book would not have been possible without the wonderful students at The Stony Brook School, who have inspired me both in and out of the classroom. I would also like to thank my colleague Dr Jason Radcliff for his wisdom and expertise, especially in his assistance in translating Greek primary sources.

I would finally like to give my deepest gratitude to the entire team at Pen & Sword. I would particularly like to thank Phil Sidnell for his expert guidance and patient support. I would also like to thank Chris Trim and Matt Jones for their careful, excellent feedback and their professionalism.

Thank you, all.

A Note on Sources

The primary sources on Themistocles paint a consistent but incomplete picture. The core ancient sources from his life come from the Greek historians Herodotus and Thucydides, each writing within a generation or two of Themistocles's own life, and the Greek historian Plutarch, who lived during the early Roman Empire in the 1st century AD – nearly 600 years after the life of Themistocles. One more Roman-era Greek wrote a comprehensive history of his world during the 1st century BCE, Diodorus Siculus, and included new depth for some events in Themistocles's life but overall his history squares nicely with the other three.

Other sources are brief references or quotes across Classical literature, philosophy, and plays – including Simonides the poet, Aristophanes the playwright, Plato and Aristotle the philosophers, Xenophon the warrior-philosopher, and Cicero the emperor-philosopher. None dedicate more than a few lines to Themistocles, and most are in reference to his heroism in the Persian Wars or impressive rule over Athens. The four sources of Herodotus, Thucydides, Plutarch, and Diodorus Siculus have little in the way of disagreement and, by necessity, form the backbone for all studies about Themistocles.

* * *

Herodotus and Thucydides had access to eyewitness accounts, but they focus chiefly on the course of their respective subjects – the Persian Wars and Peloponnesian Wars, respectively – and do not expand on Themistocles beyond his contributions to the war efforts and related narratives. This is not to mention the fact that they are two of the world's very first historians, and the emerging craft of historical writing had not yet reached biography. Nevertheless, Thucydides had access to several historians whose writings no longer survive, and he references and quotes them to bolster and even contrast with his own analysis.

Themistocles is, however, prominently featured in Plutarch's *Parallel Lives*, a monumental contribution that wove together Greek and Roman history by writing comparative biographies between two great men from each civilization. Themistocles's biography is paired with the 'Second Founder of Rome' Camillus, yet Plutarch's comparative analysis of the two is sadly lost. Plutarch's access to a half millennium of ancient historical writing on Themistocles is enviable to the modern historian, as well as his liberty to quote or critique them liberally – dozens in the *Life of Themistocles* alone.

The Themistocles of Plutarch and Thucydides is a dashing hero with few weaknesses, one who has an incredible gift for foresight and strategic manoeuvres. But Herodotus humanizes Themistocles, occasionally downplaying his accomplishments or attributing them to others. As Herodotus is the oldest source for Themistocles, this may be due to the relatively fresh ostracism of Themistocles and prior to the recovery of his reputation in Athens – but Plutarch is merciless in his criticism of Herodotus as a historian. Plutarch wrote a treaty entitled *On the Malice of Herodotus* and one of its foremost claims is that Themistocles was mistreated and his legend tarnished.

I have not been quite so naïve as to believe every word of these sources on the life of Themistocles. However, this book seeks to understand the mythos of Themistocles – a man who transcended a typical political career to enter into the Greek mythology as a hero in the vein of Odysseus, Achilles or Theseus. And more critically, it aims to investigate how that mythos mobilized his political career and shaping of Athens, Greece and the West.

Chronology

Fall 480 BCE	The Battles of Artemisium and Thermopylae occur on the same day; a few weeks later Themistocles engineers a stunning naval victory at the Battle of Salamis, which turns away the Persian navy and Xerxes along with it
Fall 479 BCE	The Persians are defeated at Plataea and Mycale; Themistocles does not partake in either as he is nearly exiled from Athens
479 – 478 BCE	Themistocles negotiates a truce with Sparta as tensions between Athens and their former ally increase; the Themistoclean Wall and major fortifications are built
478 BCE	The formation of the Delian League and the advent of the Athenian empire
476 BCE	*Phoenician Women* by Phrynichus debuts, with Themistocles as *choregos*
472 BCE	*The Persians* by Aeschylus debuts, with Pericles son of Xanthippus as *choregos*
471 BCE	Themistocles is ostracized from Athens
469 BCE	Themistocles arrives in Persia and is accepted into the court of the Persian king
468–459 BCE	Themistocles serves as governor of Magnesia-on-the-Meander in Persian-controlled Ionian Greece
459 BCE	The death of Themistocles, potentially of his own volition, in order to avoid fighting for the Persians against the Athenians in Egypt

Introduction

If they live long enough, I suppose there is a moment in the life of every great man of history when they doubt their legacy. Most of the great world-changers had their pits of despair, after all. Winston Churchill was voted out of office after saving his nation and defeating the Nazis. Napoleon was imprisoned on an island. Even the Biblical King David was overthrown by his own son for some time.

But it is hard to imagine how this particular man felt as he was huddled alone on a ship, hiding his famous face from his fellow passengers for days on end. It would have been easier to spend most of the journey alone in a cabin to avoid recognition, but such luxuries would not be available for a few hundred years at the earliest. In a Greek ship, his best option was a communal room for quick rests, if this galley even had such a luxury.

Somehow, he was able to conceal his identity from everyone else on this trading ship for the first days of the journey. But the ship's captain had announced the next, unscheduled stop was to be Naxos and our protagonist panicked when he heard the news. If the trading ship stopped at Naxos, then he would not be able to hide his face any longer. Naxos was the home of the Athenian navy and any Athenian naval officer would surely recognize the man who had built the entire Athenian navy almost single-handedly.

His name was Themistocles and he found himself, perhaps for the first time, without a real plan. He had made a reputation for always having an ace in the hole. His clever strategies – and their backup plans – had won wealth and power for himself and his home city-state of Athens. In politics and in warfare, he hadn't had a shortage of cards up his sleeve: if he faced political pressure, he simply had his rivals blackmailed, bribed, or exiled. If he needed a navy to defeat the world's largest military, he simply used his eloquence to persuade an entire city's voters to vote for the redirection of their hard-earned wages to build more ships. If his navy faced certain defeat by the massive Persian forces, he simply tricked the most powerful king alive into employing the worst possible strategy. And if he needed to create a new career after being finally exiled from Athens, he simply talked his way into positions of authority in other city-states.

But there simply wasn't such a Trojan Horse this time on this trading ship as it crept closer to Naxos, where the Athenians would surely recognize their ostracized leader Themistocles and put him to death. He wasn't foolish enough to board a ship bound for Athenian territory but the storm winds had blown them so off course that they needed to stop at the closest major port. Themistocles was on his way to join his bitter rival the Persians and the Athenians at Naxos would piece that together. Even if they had supported him before, they wouldn't now.

His beard was fully grey by now. In his past life, it would have nicely matched his brightly coloured tunic with elaborate patterns on its edges. But during this journey whilst incognito, Themistocles would have needed to dress more plainly to blend in with the common crowds. It is hard to imagine him deigning to dress as a lower-class citizen in a simple off-white robe, and so it is more likely that he returned to the middle-class attire that he had been reared in. Themistocles had lived these past ten years with quite a bit more luxury and comfort than his first four decades.

Even as he rose through the political ranks of Athens, he never held wealth in any especially high quantity. He hadn't been born into the upper-classes but his father did make enough to afford the necessary equipment for his son to fight as a hoplite: shield, spear, helmet, short sword, and armour. He had maintained his warrior physique which he cultivated during his seasons training in the *phalanx* formation – a tight military formation shaped by Greek heavy soldiers standing shoulder-to-shoulder and overlapping shields and spears. Hoplites were universally middle-class; the nobility would ride on horseback and the lower class would be light infantry or rowers on triremes. As such, Themistocles's origin represented the core of the Athenian identity: a middle-class soldier who earned a reputation for fighting with excellence in both the *phalanx* and the political assembly.

Of course, Themistocles's journey to Persia wasn't his first time as a political refugee. Since his exile from his hometown of Athens, he had travelled to almost a half dozen locations in northern Greece – typically met with fanfare and accolades. But the cheers had faded a bit more with each new location.

Before this expedition to the modern-day coast of Turkey, his most recent stop had been Sicily. He had travelled to the Greek colonies there to offer his much-heralded political acumen in their incessant wars with the Carthaginians. These were the very same Carthaginians who the Romans would later fight with in the Punic Wars – known for Hannibal's elephants and the root of many pithy quotes on the Roman Senate floor.

In Sicily, he had the gall to not only ask for refuge but to take the hand of the princess in marriage and all the rights that come with it. He was refused, of course, and was wise enough to leave town shortly thereafter. He had clearly worn out his welcome among the several dozen independent Greek city-states.

The people of Naxos were headstrong and proud of it. They also had an irksome habit of throwing a monkey wrench in the established political order of Greece. Twenty-five years before, a ruler from the Ionian coast of Greece had the bright idea to borrow Persian troops and ships to invade Naxos and bring it under Persian control (with him as its ruler, naturally). When this ruler, Aristagoras, arrived at Naxos he found that the tall cliffs, fortified walls and experienced soldiers of the island made for an unfortunate situation. When he failed to conquer the island, Aristagoras did the next best thing and revolted against Persian rule which the Athenians quickly aided. One burned Persian capital city later and both Naxos and Athens found themselves in the midst of a formal rebellion against the most powerful empire on the planet. The Great King of Persia, King of Kings and Lord of Lords, subsequently invaded all of Greece but was turned away by a series of events characterized by the incredible luck of both these city-states and their bold military strategy. But more on that later.

In 471 BCE, Naxos continued in its maverick ways and were the first city-state to challenge the authority of the Athenians, who had bent the Greek world to its will for the past decade. The Athenian response was merciless. They immediately besieged the island with the strongest navy in the world in order to make sure no other city-states would look towards rebellion. It was directly out of the Themistocles playbook – exploit any opportunity to crush the opposition and then use it as an advertisement for the benefit of any others who might be considering a challenge.

Themistocles had taught Athens well. The same style of hegemonic leadership that he had brought to the Athenian democratic assembly was employed by Athens over the rest of Greece for the next century. It ushered in the Golden Age of Athens and created the most potent cultural revolution of perhaps all time. And yet Themistocles would never see his beloved Athens thrive in this way. His fate would not be in the emerging Athenian Empire but instead in the country that he had dedicated his life to defeating, and in servitude to the man who he had tried to kill many times over.

*   *   *

But for this statesman-turned-refugee, the task now at hand was to convince the ship's captain to bypass Naxos and push for Persian-controlled Ionian Greece. Themistocles opted to solve the problem in the manner he always had. Approaching the captain, Themistocles made two items directly clear. First, he confessed his identity. The master of the ship may have recoiled slightly at hearing the news and he would have certainly known exactly what it meant and exactly what Themistocles would say next.

Themistocles then delivered his second point, which was a detailed description of the consequences of going any closer to Naxos. Included among them was the revelation that Themistocles had bribed the captain with Persian gold and the uniquely painful death that such a treacherous ship's captain would face. All of these threats were eloquently wrapped in Themistocles's signature charm and cunning – the shipmaster might've almost felt complimented as Themistocles enchanted him with the blackmail-laced flattery. One ancient historian, Thucydides, also notes that Themistocles offered a hefty bribe to the captain should he survive the ordeal.[1]

The ship raced past Naxos and directly to the Ionian coast. In entering Persian territory, Themistocles was leaving independent Greece for the first time in his life. He was leaving a Greece that would never have been independent and would have surely succumbed to the massive Persian forces that he had so passionately fought against.

*   *   *

Indeed, Themistocles had been responsible for the salvation of Greece on at least three occasions. He fought as a hoplite at the Battle of Marathon, which held back the first Persian invasion of Greece in 490 BCE. He was later solely responsible for two logistical feats that ensured Greek survival during the second Persian invasion: the construction of the Athenian navy and the evacuation of Athens. All ancient sources give Themistocles sole credit for both events, and the importance of both events in tandem cannot be overstated.

He then, finally, engineered what is perhaps the greatest military victory in Western history at the naval battle in the straits of Salamis. The Battle of Salamis, in 480 BCE, was the turning point in the war and turned back the invading Persian emperor, Xerxes the Great. Victory at Salamis ultimately created an ascendant Athens, an influential Greece and the foundation of Western civilization.

If any of these had gone sideways, then the Persian conquest of Greece would have changed the complexion of Western civilization as we know it.[2] And had Themistocles measured even an ounce less talented in his rhetoric or cleverness then democracy might not be the Western ideal, Rome might not be that gold standard of Western accomplishments, and the Enlightenment might not have happened as we know it. For better or for worse, Greek history would have been just another footnote in the vast Persian empire that was never overthrown by Alexander the Great or brought Rome so many headaches and remained far more interlinked with the East.

But it was Themistocles's incurable drive to succeed that pushed the Greeks towards victory. There is rarely an instance in history of a single man – especially a man who is not an absolute monarch – orchestrating the political, economic, cultural and military means necessary to achieve victory and prosperity no matter the cost.

Themistocles certainly would not be a hero by modern standards. He personally committed human sacrifice. He betrayed his homeland of Athens. He accepted and made bribes regularly. He blackmailed rivals, framed colleagues, and lied ruthlessly and regularly.

And yet he has a story worth telling. Not only because of the consequences of his actions – the salvation of Greece, democracy, and perhaps even Western civilization – but also because of the clear fact that Themistocles was, more than anything else, *Greek*.

* * *

The Greek language is far more precise than our clumsy English, and they have a succinct word to describe a concept that we can only partially understand. The word is *arete*, and its meaning gives us a helpful summary of the entire Greek worldview.

Arete means 'excellence in all things' or 'effectiveness at everything a man pursues'. For the Greeks, *arete* was intertwined with the effectiveness of any person or thing. Examples might include the *arete* of a horse is to run fast and the *arete* of a spear is to cut through enemies. A swift runner holds *arete* of the feet while a brave warrior has obtained *arete* of victorious combat. When applied to a human being, *arete* becomes primarily concerned with maximizing the effectiveness of each and every action. The man who had truly obtained *arete* would have all the stereotypical qualities of an excellent person: intelligence, honour, and eloquence. But the Greek idea of *arete* took the notion of 'excellence in all things' very, very literally.

You would also need to be impressively athletic and accomplished at music, theatre and speech. You would need to be wealthy, or at least of middle-class status, and be so effective at rhetoric that you could convince any group of men to follow your lead. This rhetoric would be rooted in persuasion through both logic and craftiness – the effective debate and the effective blackmail have the same success, after all. In your pursuit of *arete*, you must also pursue excellence in religious devotion, poetry, and artwork. And we mustn't forget that you need to be exceedingly beautiful, tall and of impeccable reputation. Your glory and renown need to precede you; introductions should hardly be needed as everyone will know your name already. And finally, but perhaps most importantly, you absolutely must be distinguished on the battlefield for your bravery, fighting skill and kill count.

Its etymological root, *aristoi,* translates as 'the best'. This is where the term aristocrats originates as it translates to 'the best men' – or those men who had apparently been so effective and successful at all of their physical and intellectual pursuits that they stood head, shoulders and wallet above ordinary men. The *aristoi* were perennially brimming with a sort of kinetic energy of effectiveness and were always ready for every variety of potent, successful action.

This prevalent idea of *arete* became so influential that the Greeks deified it in the goddess of virtue, Arete. She was the sister of the goddess Homonoia, who was in charge of order and unity. These two goddesses formed the core of what the Greeks named the Praxidikai: the elite group in charge of exacting justice and punishment in the pursuit of virtue and order. We see here the Greek emphasis on living a life overflowing with *arete* . To miss the mark is to risk not only the wrath of the gods, but also the shame of your fellow men and the ruination of your reputation.

Later philosophers like Socrates, Plato, and Aristotle took the Greek understanding of *arete* in a deeper but often more abstract direction, as they pursued virtue through ethics and the good life. Indeed, its definition and pursuit become a bedrock of the Platonic dialogues. Like any good Athenian, these questions would interest Themistocles but for the Greeks who lived during the Persian Wars, the man who wished to display *arete* in spades had a much more practical model to pursue.

This model was the hero found in the epic poems of Homer: *The Iliad* and *The Odyssey*. If we consider the overwhelming impact of the Bible in medieval and modern thought, we begin to understand the role of Homeric poetry in the Greek world. For the ancient world, no single text was remotely as impactful; most dramas, comedies, poems, and histories of the Classical world burst with Homeric references and ancestries.

We call this era of Greek history the Heroic Age and it climaxed with the Trojan War in approximately 1100 BCE. The semi-fictional war, of course, began with the theft of the beautiful Helen and saw a civil war between the Greeks. The Achaeans, the attacking force from modern day Greece who were led by the power-hungry tyrant Agamemnon, invaded the territory of the Helen-thieving Trojans (now modern-day Turkey) for a decade long war that both devastated the landscape and provided ample opportunities for glory in combat.

In the course of the Trojan War and the journeys home from it, heroes like the wrathful and brave Achilles, the cunning and eloquent Odysseus and the noble and reverent Diomedes exemplified the ideal form of *arete* in all their accomplishments. The mythos surrounding these men plays a cultural role akin to the stories from King Arthur's court or the Wild

West. As Stephen Fry recounts in his telling of heroic mythology, the Heroic Age was when 'men and women who grasped their destinies, use their human qualities of courage, cunning, ambition, speed and strength to perform astonishing deeds, vanquish terrible monsters and establish Greek cultures and lineages that changed the world.'[3] The actions of these heroes had shaped Greece and given the Greek people a sense of meaning and purpose in life, answering the enduring questions of 'Who am I? What is the good life for human beings? What is the nature of a good society?'

The main characters of each poem, Achilles in *The Iliad* and Odysseus in *The Odyssey*, are especially profound for the Greeks. Achilles represented the Greek idea of perfection in combat and reputation, despite his massive flaws. Although he is heralded as a nearly flawless hero and saviour of Greek culture, the opening word of the poem in its original Greek – wrath – is a more apt description of Achilles through a modern lens:

> Sing, O goddess, the anger of Achilles son of Peleus, that brought countless ills upon the Achaeans. Many a brave soul did it send hurrying down to Hades, and many a hero did it yield a prey to dogs and vultures, for so were the counsels of Zeus fulfilled from the day on which the son of Atreus, king of men, and great Achilles, first fell out with one another.[4]

In Greek, sound grammar allows nearly any word of a sentence to begin that sentence, and often the first word contains the message that the author wanted to emphasize. Homer's *Iliad* is about this fateful wrath of Achilles and, if the first line is any indication, then the rest of the story should be about the hardships and losses suffered by the Achaean army as a result of Achilles's immature anger. But that is not quite the case. Instead, as Achilles fights without mercy and massacres his way through many honourable soldiers, he forges an even greater reputation because of his effectiveness in two particular climaxes of the story.

The first is the famous duel between a vengeance-seeking Achilles and the noble prince of Troy, Hector. Hector's reputation is as the greatest Trojan warrior and this moment for Achilles – defeating the other strongest fighter and getting vengeance for his fallen comrade Patroclus – is supposed to be his character's best and most successful moment, where he solidifies his reputation for the ages to come. This moment, called the *aristeia*, is another motif of Homer's writing: great heroes produce great results in great moments, and effect reverberating consequences for the rest of history. The Greeks would later use *aristeia* as the title of the prizes of valour, a democratically settled honour given to great heroes of great battles and athletic games.

Achilles will of course go on to ruthlessly slaughter Hector and defile his corpse, denying him a proper burial and journey to the afterlife. It is only his emotional encounter with Hector's father, King Priam of Troy, who pleads for Hector's body returned by asking Achilles to think of his own father, that abates Achilles's wrath and brings him peace. Modern society can't quite grapple with this scene – two men in a tent crying over their deceased family and friends – as the culmination of the story. But to understand the Greek audience, we return to the idea of *arete* as effectiveness. It is this moment for Achilles that allows him to finally put aside his wrath and anger and become an even more formidable warrior on the battlefield as he storms the gates of Troy. The result is a more victorious and effective Achilles. He becomes an even greater hero by using his anger, at both its height against Hector and its abatement with Priam, to create more opportunities for glory and reputational gain. Achilles is without peer as the prime example of Homeric *arete* for the Greeks.

It is a similar tale with the hero of Homer's *Odyssey*. For Odysseus, his success at the battlefields of Troy is remarkable, but far surpassed by his talents at devising clever schemes and persuading his peers to follow him. Odysseus designed the famous Trojan Horse that won the Greeks the war, after all. Over his winding journey home from the war he regularly uses his ability to quickly diagnose and solve problems. He avoids the sirens' call, he used trickery to escape the Cyclops's lair, he sees through the gambit of the lotus-eaters, he uses the fullness of his silver tongue to convince Circe to release him from captivity, and then he finally wins back his family from the threatening suitors first through trickery and then through bloodshed. He even takes a pitstop to the underworld along the way.

Like Achilles, his path to heroism is littered with the bodies of both enemies and companions, but his reputation stands all the taller for it.

Where Achilles used his spear and bloodthirstiness to become the unparalleled hero of the Greek army, Odysseus earns devotion from all of Greece for his weapons of shrewd strategizing and eloquence.

Even when his tricks are unsuccessful, the Greeks still gave him accolades for an admirable attempt. When the Achaean army was assembling before the war, Odysseus foresees the challenges ahead and tries to avoid the fighting by feigning madness. He ploughs his fields incessantly and mutters to himself. The Greek emissary that was asking him to fight sees through this – knowing Odysseus's reputation – and places his newborn child in front of the plough. Odysseus of course stops his ruse and agrees to fight at Troy, but the Greek audience would have interpreted this scene as pragmatism, not cowardice or dishonour.

And so the character of Odysseus is uniquely interesting for understanding the Greek worldview because he is brimming with traits that we would consider disqualifying of hero status: deceit, guile, a willingness to murder children and a penchant for either abandoning his friends on desert islands (as was the fate of his friend Philoctetes), and even fiercely competing with them for Achilles's armour so that they eventually take their own life (in the case of Ajax the Greater).

The Roman world didn't value these traits quite so much either – they found Achilles to be too bloodthirsty and Odysseus too dishonourable. Perhaps in agreement with modern Western standards, the Romans thought such vices simply could not be outweighed by their *arete*. Honour was not something to be found in our climatic moments, but in the sum of all aspects of a man's life from the doldrums of daily life to the reputation he forged through his public and private actions. This is partially why they promoted one Trojan refugee, Aeneas, to the Roman version of an epic hero; he maintained all the *arete* that meshed with Rome but was still Homeric enough to earn the necessary Greek credentials. In an intentional pattern, the same poem, Virgil's *Aeneid*, routinely labels Odysseus as 'cruel' and 'deceitful'.

But the Greeks prized the end result far more than the process itself, so much so that they constructed temples and religious cults around many of the heroes from Homer's poems. The worship of Achilles was prevalent across Greece, especially after the conquests of Alexander the Great. Local communities looked to the Homeric heroes from their geographic areas as patron deities, as evidenced by temples built to Ajax the Greater at Salamis, Menelaus at Sparta and Agamemnon at Mycenae. It seems some Greeks took a later philosopher quite literally when he said that Homer sought 'to degrade his deities, as far as possible, into men, and exalt his men into deities'.[5]

* * *

So what does this all have to do with the titular Themistocles? Well, everything. The very reason why Themistocles rose to prominence and led the Greek alliance was because of the overlapping traits he shared with the Homeric heroes, especially Odysseus. Themistocles relied on his carefully cultivated reputation as a cunning hero who – often through trickery and extreme measures – earns victory for his nation, consequences be damned. And like those heroes, it was the fatal flaw of *hubris* and exalting himself above the gods and his city-state of Athens that led to his downfall.

A survey of the astounding accomplishments of Themistocles gives us a better picture not only of his Homeric arc but also of just how enduring the actions of this one individual have been for our modern world:

Themistocles was the first populist in the first democracy and moulded the role of a political fixer who opportunistically used public support to his advantage. As democracy was in its infancy, he was perhaps the first to learn how to exploit it and maximize the impact a single man can have on a nation. It's a model we will see again and again throughout history. If we were to teleport Odysseus to the Athenian democracy of the early fifth century BCE, it's hard to see him behaving much differently than Themistocles. It was ruthless political lever-pulling that relied on a silver tongue and a thick wallet. And it was highly effective. Themistocles went from a middle-class nobody to a maverick whose decisions shaped the world. Politically, he was a Churchill or a von Bismarck against the backdrop of the ancient Mediterranean.

His striking prophecies about politics and foreign policy nearly always came true. He was essentially the sole Greek who had the foresight to see the looming invasion of Persia after their first invasion of Greece. His solo mission to prepare Athens and Greece for the second invasion by Persia allowed them not just a fighting chance but eventually victory. And after he defended Greece, he defended Athens. He was again the sole Athenian to truly foresee impending war, this time the Peloponnesian War between Athens and Sparta. Like the sage Nestor or seer Calchas who counselled the Greek army in the Trojan War, Themistocles had the uncanny ability to see around corners and place his people and pawns in the perfect position for even the unlikeliest victories.

He was also a brilliant military tactician who took a three-year-old naval fleet – which he created – to victory over the largest combined navy the world had ever seen. The fleet that Xerxes brought into Greece in 480 BCE was the cream of the ancient world already constituted with the finest warships of naval superpowers such as Phoenicia, Egypt, Cyprus and a host of Greek cultures in modern Turkey: Cilicia, Ionia, and Caria. But Themistocles took a small, undermanned fleet against a force quadruple its size and systematically and repeatedly delivered strategic draws and stunning victories. He was like Achilles or Diomedes on the plains of Troy – a single man changing the tides of the war by himself.

Themistocles was also the man who pushed Athens into the limelight of the Western world. His resolve to develop Athens as the epicentre of Greek commerce and naval power rocketed Athens into a leading position not only in the Persian Wars but subsequently as an imperial power bending the Aegean world to their will. Without his monumental efforts to prepare Athens for war against Persia and then Sparta, the democratic, artistic, theatrical, mathematical, scientific, poetic and philosophical advances of Classical Greece might look far different or undeveloped. Themistocles would have no hesitation in taking the credit for the incredible accomplishments of Classical Athens. In this, his actions harken back to the *arete* of the epic heroes in earning a reputation for exceptional achievement, akin to Achilles's all-consuming drive for glory.

And in the moments of his *aristeia* he always produced great results when the spotlight shone on him. In so doing, he did not shy away from extreme actions – he championed them. He ordered the mass evacuation of Athens, orchestrated a longstanding scheme to feed advantageously false information to the king of Persia and he convinced the Athenian assembly to vote for his outrageous plans through blackmail, populism, and even divine revelation. Like Odysseus slaughtering the suitors to win his family back or Achilles in his fabled duel against Hector, Themistocles used his *aristeia* to cement his reputation that was already worthy of the greatest epithets and titles that Greece could offer.

And yet every good Homeric hero has a tragic fall from grace. Perhaps I whitewashed the picture of a Homeric hero earlier when I made it seem as rosy and perfect. In reality, nearly all of the heroes of Homer's epic faced a ruinous end regardless of their status. Despite all his heroic accolades, Achilles was killed in battle by the cowardly Paris when his bloodthirstiness allowed him to become careless. Odysseus met a bitter fate when his bastard son murdered him over a livestock quarrel, with neither knowing the identity of the other. Jason died unremarkably when the mast of the *Argo* fell on him.

Themistocles's death had a somewhat similar Homeric quality. He was exiled from Athens in an astonishing fall from favour and eventually 'medized,' the Greek term for collaborating with the Persians. But even in his banishment from Athens, Themistocles was highly effective in his political intrigues and military pursuits. His well-known reputation for making things happen gave him several opportunities in city-states across Greece as an advisor, general, and governor. But the combination of his naked ambition and his constant targeting by political enemies wore out his welcome everywhere. It was time to go to Persia. Themistocles's journey to Persia (and the opening scene at Naxos) is Odysseus's odyssey manifest – the hero of the war to save Greece cannot truly return to the home that he rescued.

He rose to prominence as a trusted advisor to the new Persian king and became governor of several important cities on the Ionian coast. When he eventually received orders to attack Greek and Athenian ships with his new Persian fleet, Themistocles took the path of Ajax and decided to die with honour. In his Homeric pursuit to protect his reputation unto death, Themistocles threw a grand party with his closest friends and then drank poison – dying the hero's death in the Greek worldview. Even the Persian king Artaxerxes, upon hearing the news, 'admired the man yet more, and continued to treat his friends and kindred with kindness.'[6] He died the death of an epic hero, his glory untarnished and on his own terms.

Nearly all of the ancient historians who chronicled his life were enamoured with the gifts of cunning and intellect with which he had been endowed.

Thucydides, Plutarch, and Diodorus Siculus shower him with praises and count him among the greatest of all Greeks. He forged such an impressive reputation that his name was essentially etched into the lore of the Classical world among the heroes of mythology and of Homer.

* * *

Of all the influential Greeks whose actions formed Western civilization, Themistocles's story is the most intertwined with the virtues of the Greek worldview. Themistocles is the Homeric hero manifested – in virtue, in action, and in consequence for both himself and Greece. He is the closest historical figure to the very incarnation of an epic hero.[7] As we unpack his story in the coming pages, it is clear that nearly every category of *arete* that the Greeks prized is exemplified by Themistocles. He is far from perfect – indeed he is disqualifyingly immoral in our modern worldview – but he is in so many ways the pinnacle of the Greek identity.

Despite this, the literary spotlight hasn't shone much on Themistocles. He certainly isn't the most famous Athenian – Socrates or Plato take that mantle. He isn't known as the foremost Athenian politician; that role surely belongs to Pericles. His reputation for political subversion and extreme measures is overtaken by Alcibiades, who also overshadows other Greeks who medized and joined forces with Persia. And although his military prowess changed the fabric of the ancient world and kept the East from gaining a major foothold in the West, later Greeks like Alexander the Great are far more famous. But it is quite fair to say that none of these men would have had the chance to flourish had Themistocles not been overwhelmingly successful in transforming and defending Athens and each man emerged from the political, military, and rhetorical models first constructed by Themistocles.

A hundred years ago, Edith Hamilton wrote the quintessential books to introduce the ancient world to the twentieth century. Her works *The Greek Way*[8] and *The Roman Way* became standard classroom reading for secondary and college students in the English-speaking world. Yet Themistocles is only mentioned four times and only then as an example of the excellent historical writing of Herodotus. Nowadays, he is mentioned nearly exclusively by military historians enraptured by the romantic

Western victory in the Greco-Persian Wars. His contribution to saving Greece from the Persian threat was an admirable feat but it was only one moving piece of his substantial influence on Athens and democracy.

Although he does not get much of the modern limelight, some of the most formative players in world history recognized his lasting significance through the ages. Cicero called Themistocles 'the greatest man that Athens produced.'[9] Napoleon invoked Themistocles's name in his legendary surrender to the British. Socrates often used Themistocles's name in his dialogues while discussing the formation virtue. J.C. Bach wrote an opera chronicling Themistocles's exile from Athens.

But it was the Athenian historian Thucydides who gave Themistocles the most credit, just a generation later. Perhaps due to their shared Athenian citizenship and heritage, Thucydides understood the role that Themistocles had in shaping Athens, Greece and democracy and, in turn, defending them against the greatest threat to their existence. Thucydides was a fellow general and politician and would have doubtless followed the political and military model for success forged by Themistocles – perhaps too closely, considering both ended their days in exile.

Thucydides famously eulogizes his fellow countryman after settling his story:

> Themistocles was a man who exhibited the most indubitable signs of genius; indeed, in this particular he has a claim on our admiration quite extraordinary and unparalleled. By his own native capacity, alike unformed and unsupplemented by study, he was at once the best judge in those sudden crises which admit of little or of no deliberation, and the best prophet of the future, even to its most distant possibilities. An able theoretical expositor of all that came within the sphere of his practice, he was not without the power of passing an adequate judgment in matters in which he had no experience. He could also excellently divine the good and evil which lay hid in the unseen future. In fine, whether we consider the extent of his natural powers, or the slightness of his application, this extraordinary man must be allowed to have surpassed all others in the faculty of intuitively meeting an emergency.[10]

And yet the modern world is mostly unaware of his incredible and enduring impact on the world in which we live. It is time to change that.

Part I

The Dark Horse Who Moulded Democracy

Chapter 1

From Obscurity to Marathon

They looked like screaming madmen to the Persians. Looking from behind their wicker shields, the Persians' first true sight of Greek resistance was a force of 10,000 men, all heavily armoured and all shrieking a war cry, with the Athenian owl painted on their shields, sprinting for a full mile to fight a force up to ten times their size. The owl was supposed to symbolize the favour of Athena, goddess of wisdom. Yet there did not appear to be anything wise about this approach.

Indeed, almost no part of the Athenian battle planning had been wise or successful so far. They were only supposed to be one small part of a greater Greek army called to fight off the massive Persian forces that had, so far, swept through the north of Greece with effortless conquest. The coast here at Marathon – about two dozen miles north of Athens – was designed to stage a dramatic final stand by the Greeks against the powerful invaders from the East. But despite a call for aid sent to every Greek city-state that somehow still remained outside of the Persian king's pocketbook, it was only the mediocre and undistinguished hoplites of Athens that had bothered to show up.

Well, not quite. The Plataeans had sent a force of 1,000 men. But against a force of up to 200,000 Persians and their 600 ships,[1] it was unlikely to be of much help. The Spartans were the truly powerful Greek infantrymen and their presence at Marathon would go a long way towards levelling the playing field. But Sparta was fiercely religious and their king had delayed their arrival to finish a sacred festival. That was the official excuse, at least, but the reality is they were likely excited about the opportunity of Persia wiping out their lingering opposition to Greek dominance. They would arrive soon after the battle was over but were to be astonished at what they found.

Sprinting a mile is never an easy feat, but these Athenians made it more arduous by running under the additional weight of forty to fifty pounds of hoplite armour. Given its difficulty, many historians do not believe Herodotus, our main primary source, that this sprint occurred – or at least for the full length of eight furlongs. But it is nearly certain that the Athenians would have at least finished their assault with a sprint. We know this because a core strategy of ancient Greek hoplite warfare was to slam into the opposing force at full speed, breaking their ranks and forcing an opening in the shield wall of their opponents. This shield wall, famously known as the *phalanx*, was the singularly Greek military formation and its heavily armoured hoplites trained each year to assemble and fight with the *phalanx*. It was the hallmark of Greek military tactics.

But Persians did not fight like the heavy infantrymen of Greece and, instead of a *phalanx*, the Athenians would have slammed into a mixture of heavy cavalry, light infantry and archers – lots of archers. For the last 200 metres of their charge, the Athenians would have had to close the ranks of their *phalanx* and raise their shields. At this final range, the Persian archers would have been deadly effective. They would have sent a hail of arrows so heavy that Herodotus famously said, 'the sun would have been darkened by their multitude.'[2]

At this point in their assault, the Athenians would have heard a call by their commander Miltiades to tighten formation and raise their shields. In the heat of battle, this order would need to be repeated by the vice commanders. For the middling tribe of Leontis, that general barking orders to this crazed, foolhardy army was a 34-year-old Themistocles. The young Themistocles was a rising star in the Athenian democratic assembly and had recently been elected to the position of *strategos* – one of ten military commanders elected annually by the Athenian assembly of citizens. But Themistocles's days of fighting via political debate or backroom dealing were, for this pivotal moment in history, irrelevant. It was time to wed his political prowess to battlefield glory.

In a closely organized formation that was barrelling at top speed, Themistocles and his fellow commanders led the Athenian hoplites underneath the never-ceasing barrage of Persian arrows and maniacally aimed straight for a full-speed crash into the Persian forces. The Persian shields were made of thickly woven wicker in contrast to the bronze, wood, and leather composite of a Greek hoplite's shield. Wicker shields are good at stopping arrows, as the Persians designed them to do but they were not quite as good at stopping an eight-foot-long spear that had a considerable head start behind it.

There must have been a thunderous crash as the Greek soldiers made violent contact with the Persians. When a *phalanx* met an opponent, their shields interlocked and pushed into the enemy as hard as possible. The first line of men was tasked almost entirely with this push of shields, while the lines behind them thrust their spears into the openings in the shield wall, typically above the shoulders of the first line. These were quick and repeated thrusts early on, with the goal of exploiting any available opening in the enemy's front line. The middle of the fighting was merciless and messy. Men shouted orders, they pressed against their shields with their full weight, and stabbed almost blindly at anything near the opponents. They would pray to the god Apollo the Far-Striker for victory and aid – hoping their pleas would encourage him to come down and join the fray. And at the centre of the formation, where the two armies met on the most equal footing, the fighting was a bloody mess of men clamouring to survive, or at least die a heroic death. Even if they were unsuccessful, the glory won on this battlefield in a desperate attempt to save Greece would cause men to whisper their name as they walked the streets of Athens. They would be heroes worthy of mythology and epic poems – if only they could survive.

And Themistocles's tribe was located right in the centre of this Athenian formation. Herodotus tells us that the centre of the fighting was the 'hardest pressed'[3] this day and they faced the longest and bloodiest fighting. The Greeks traditionally placed the most revered commanders and fighters on the wings of their attacking forces, but today Themistocles was paying his dues and cultivating his future political reputation. He and his tribe faced the fiercest fighting in the centre. His days at the right wing would come but only because of the actions put in motion today. If he could lead his fighters to glory in the muddy, arrow-saturated fields of Marathon then his career would be on the trajectory for power and wealth in Athens. He knew the rewards and the great risk it was to achieve them. Themistocles resolved that it was Marathon where he would prove his mettle.

* * *

The Bay of Marathon was situated on the northern coast of Attica between two marshlands, with the actual city of Marathon about four miles inland. The Persian fleet had harboured around a cape that protected them from the devastating winds and storms of the Greek coast. That same wind had wrecked their first invading fleet and the Persians were careful not to repeat such mistakes. Their commander, Mardonius, was led this time by Greek and Athenian expatriates who were careful to give their best advice on navigating the treacherous coast of Greece. Most guides were quick to lose their lives if the Persians felt that poor directions or advice was given and so they were sufficiently motivated to guide the Persian fleet to the calm waters of the Bay of Marathon.

The Persian Empire was the largest the world had ever seen at this point, stretching from the northern parts of Greece to Pakistan, from Egypt to modern Kazakhstan, and from modern Romania to parts of the Arabian Peninsula. The kings of these lands had all, either by force or diplomacy, submitted their 'earth and water'[4] to Persian ambassadors as a show of deference to the King of Kings, Darius the Great. It was a symbolic act where soil of their land was mixed with that of the Great King's homeland, thereby uniting the nations. At the turn of the fifth century, Persia was at the height of its power – the entire civilized world was interconnected through the political and economic nerve centre that was Persia.

Darius led his massive empire with equal parts political savviness and brute force. The traditional Persian style of conquest was to seduce a nation's leader with offers of money, power and commerce as well as relative political freedom, assuming devotion to the Persian king. If the leaders did not accede, the Persians would then make the same offer to the leaders' inferiors, most commonly to the generals and governors. This next offer would also include a promotion to king or ruler, assuming a deep loyalty to the Persian state. This was a model perfected by the first great Persian rule, Cyrus the Great.

Cyrus had used this approach alongside two other essential diplomatic strategies: a meritocracy in leadership and kind treatment of conquered peoples. By including new peoples and giving them the relative liberty of self-governance, the Persians won loyalty, land and a powerful military. The Persian military was strong in numbers from its vast landholdings, experienced in leadership given its generals hailed from all over the empire regardless of ethnicity and had a formidable navy under the Phoenicians, Egyptians, Cypriots and the Greeks who dwelled in modern Turkey. However, the King of Kings would still demand tribute. For Cyrus's client kings, this was typically an annual pilgrimage to Persepolis, the ceremonial capital of Persia, to physically prostrate and submit their tributary taxes to the Great King of Persia.

The Greek view of humanity was rather binary. Men were either Greeks or they were barbarians – civilized or uncivilized. The word 'barbarian' itself was a Greek name for those who spoke a foreign language, usually from the Persian empire, as it sounded like gibberish, 'bar bar bar,' to the Greek ear. Yet many, many Greeks were part of the greater Persian empire, especially those around the Black Sea and the western coast of Asia Minor. The conquest of these Greek lands in the latter years of the sixth century cemented both Persian dominance and the resilience of the Greeks on the mainland. The common thread connecting their Greek identity was the emphasis on freedom: the Greeks despised monarchy and found the autocracy of the King of Kings oppressive and absent of *arete*. An oligarchy, aristocracy, democracy or tyranny were the preferred Greek style of government and they felt that, even in a tumultuous city-state, the Greeks had ascended beyond the primitive model of kingship.[5]

While some of these conquered Greeks detested the Persians, many of them nevertheless participated in Persian high culture, especially in mathematics, science, and philosophy. It is also apparent that the Persian tradition of promoting local rulers and generals was readily embraced, as many of the generals and soldiers who fought at Marathon or in later invasions were themselves Greek. Chief among them were those mainland Greeks who had been exiled from their own city-states, such as the deposed Spartan king Demaratus and the exiled Athenian tyrant Hippias. Each sought to rule their homeland in submission to Darius the Great.

Darius himself knew a thing or two about Homeric cunning. Like Themistocles, he was from a humble origin – by no means the legal heir in line of Cyrus the Great. But by trickery, blackmail and assassination he had fought his way to the height of the Persian empire and ushered in a golden age for his people. His economic and commercial policies made Persia wealthier than any previous empire by a large gap. His political organization of Persia into territories governed by local rulers who submitted to a Persian-installed *satrap* governor gave his empire stability and pragmatism on a scale never seen before. His vast empire functioned more smoothly than any previous authority ever had.

This was why the burning of the Persian capital city in their Greek territories was so surprising. In 499 BCE, a Greek tyrant named Aristogoras tried to invade Naxos on the Persian tab. His Persian troops, ships and gold were lent to him on the condition that he would capture Naxos, a valuable port perfectly placed in the centre of the Aegean trade routes, for Persia. His ambition was doubtless to be promoted to *satrap* governor eventually and this was a risky but feasible endeavour. Unfortunately for Aristogoras, it was an utter failure and no land was conquered. In lieu of returning to Persian-controlled Asia Minor, where he was certain to face death, he sailed his ships to the mainland of Greece and began a diplomatic tour of the most powerful city-states.

His goal was to convince them to lead a revolt of Persian-controlled city-states on the Ionian coast against Darius. He was a clever politician who pressed on the Greek love of freedom and their hatred of submission to the barbarians. While many Ionian states joined him and his city of Miletus in the Ionian Revolt for the next decade, only two mainland city-states answered the call: Athens and the small Athenian-allied Eretria. Athens, hungry for a place in the world to further their new democratic system and interested in maintaining some colonial interests, sailed to the Ionian coast and promptly marched to Sardis, the Persian capital city. They burned it to the ground in 498 BCE.

And so Darius the Great, who had essentially never lost as much as a small city during his reign, found himself facing a veritable rebellion by a ragtag force of upstart democrats on the very fringes of his empire. He had to make an example of these Athenians and show that Persian power must not be challenged. And so his response was to swiftly punish the rebels, with Athens as the targeted crown jewel of his revenge. After re-subjugating the Ionian Greeks by 492 BCE, he sent both a naval fleet along the northern coastlines of Greece and a land force under the leadership of Mardonius, a Greek-born commander whose father had been loyal to the Persians since their conquest of Asia Minor.

Had Mardonius had a better knowledge of his homeland, where he had spent very little time, he would have known to listen to the warnings about the treacherous waters around the cape near Mount Athos. The fleet sank, with Herodotus recording 300 ships and 20,000 men lost. The army, meanwhile, had more success after adding Thrace and Macedonia to the Persian empire, but Darius nevertheless recalled Mardonius and his army. Darius sent a new invasion force two years later.

This new invading fleet was also amphibious. The army counted 25,000 soldiers including the 10,000 Immortals, the elite special forces unit that the Persians never risked unless it was a necessity. Their naval fleet numbered 600 triremes, the largest fleet ever assembled. After adding Naxos – finally – to their empire, they sailed to Eretria, who had joined Athens in the Ionian Revolt, and burned the city and its remaining inhabitants to send a message about those who rebelled against Persia. Athens was next on their list.

*   *   *

It was in the sweepingly beautiful Bay of Marathon, some twenty-six miles from Athens, that the Persians moored on the beach and gave the Persian fleet the chance to unload troops and supplies for their invasion of Athens. The beach flowed into a large plain – almost two miles at its width – that was itself between two rivers that were each surrounded by thick marshlands. The beach was accordingly the only flat, serviceable ground for the thousands of Persian troops who would march across it. The main fleet of Persia was about two nautical miles away, where they were guarded by land via the densest marsh. That plain also became the famous battlefield at Marathon.

The Persians had chosen Marathon for its smooth footing for horses. Persians typically sought out the flattest land possible for battle in order to accommodate their most effective fighters: the cavalry. The Persians had invented the heavy cavalry, a tactic their ancestors refined in their constant battles with invading horsemen from the Caucasus Mountains. Both horse and rider were covered in heavy leather (and, later, metal) armour, later to be called a cataphract, and the rider wielded a lance. When backed by a fleet of expert archers who rained arrows from the sky, a charging Persian cavalry was the most fearsome sight imaginable for those outside of the Greek peninsula. The armies of Alexander the Great, Caesar Augustus and the entire medieval world would adopt variations of the cataphract as their main fighting contingent. What's more, Persian cavalry were traditionally the upper classes. At Marathon, they would be fighting to earn recognition and favour from their *satrap* governor and, in the ideal scenario, Darius himself. The Persian army was – perhaps paralyzingly – made up of individual commanders and fighters who were looking for the honours bestowed by the Great King after victory. Like Themistocles, this was a political and career opportunity that simply could not be passed up. Great men needed these great moments to earn their prize of valour.

The Persian plan was straightforward enough: unload their overpoweringly massive army and march the two dozen miles or so to Athens. They were aware they would encounter resistance, but the plan was simply to overwhelm the opposition with their raw numbers. After all, the Persian army had not feasted on Greeks in combat yet. There was no reason to believe this backwater micropolitan city of Athens would put up a serious resistance.

*   *   *

For the Greeks, Marathon was a perfect fit for their symbolic stand against the invaders. Marathon was in the north-eastern portion of Attica, a region of Greece dominated by Athens that was steeped in mythos and cultural significance. It was the very same bay where Theseus had captured and then sacrificed the Marathon bull, who sired the famous Minotaur of Crete. Marathon is even mentioned in Homer's *The Odyssey*, securing its position as profoundly Greek and bound in sacred Homeric tradition. Theseus of course was the legendary king of Athens and gave the Athenians a link to this heroic past; he modelled the *arete* necessary for survival against the overwhelming Persian forces.

Themistocles would have been keenly aware of this. Thus far in Athenian history, his tribe and its politicians had not yet earned any significant reputation in the assembly of voting citizens. Indeed, almost the only substantive reference to the Leontid tribe is to Themistocles in both politics and military prowess. Like Theseus capturing the bull that plagued Greece, Themistocles was hungry for a chance to place his name and identity on the map. It would have certainly been near the front of his mind as the Greeks sprinted towards the Persian beachhead.

This was the first time Themistocles met the Persians in diplomacy or in combat but it would not be his last. In fact, these Athenians were apparently the first Greeks to even see Persian soldiers in the flesh. Herodotus tells us that before Marathon, 'the Greeks were affrighted by the very name of the Medes.'[6] The Persian soldiers were clad in much lighter armour than the heavily-armoured Greeks. Bright colours and golden jewellery were common, with leather scales and helmets sometimes underlaid with iron. The aforementioned wicker shields, square in shape and coming up to shoulder height for most soldiers, were complemented by a short spear by most infantry.

A Persian front line of *sparabara*, the Persian infantry who also formed a shield wall, met Themistocles and the Athenian charge. The key difference in the Persian tradition was that the shield wall was formed in order to protect the far more important fighters behind them: the archers. A typical arrangement was a single row of *sparabara* providing covering for nine rows of archers who shot as many arrows as they could. Persian archers did not need to be expert marksmen as the goal was to cast the opposing forces into disarray under a barrage of arrows, weakening and demoralizing their front.

At first, when the *phalanx* met the *sparabara* for the first moment in history, it was something of a stalemate. Each side pushed mightily but the strength of the Persian numbers and archers proved impregnable for the centre of the Athenian lines. Themistocles and his Leontids were caught sinking ever backwards despite his command. But the Leontids were not the only Greeks holding the centre. Another Athenian tribe, the Antiochis, were also charged with the impossible by fighting with half a *phalanx*. This tribe was led by the *strategos* Aristides – a man so brimming with square-jawed honour that his name is always followed with the epithet 'the Just'. Aristides's legendary virtue made him a reliable, noble general but it was those same qualities that made him Themistocles's greatest rival. Themistocles and Aristides represented the poles of a functioning Athenian democracy: power by effectiveness at any cost or honour by virtue. In the Greek worldview, these *arete* were not exclusive.

On this day, Themistocles and Aristides laid aside their grievances and were in the midst of an unsuccessful push into the Persian lines. As the hours dragged on, the *phalanx* lagged in its effectiveness and the Persian troops began to push them back. The *sparabara* and their archers eventually moved the Athenian line back about a hundred yards and was surely beginning to break through the shield wall of the Greeks. But, of course, that was the plan.

From the time they first saw the charging Athenians, the Persians arranged themselves in conventional, equal formation. The *sparabara* groups of ten were evenly distributed across a half-mile straight line. The Persians surely expected the Greek formation to be comparably even, with the *phalanxes* balanced across the field. And from their perspective, it looked that way. There was no reason, visually, to assume that the Greeks were fighting in anything other than a conventionally symmetrical formation that distributed the hoplites straight across in a rectangle. Their lack of high ground meant that they could only see the Athenians at eye level; no proper scouting appears to have taken place. And so the Persians assumed that *sparabara* and *phalanx* would be evenly organized and rely on their numbers.

On this day, however, the Athenian general Miltiades was anything but predictable. The Greeks' mile long sprint was not their only ingenuity. Miltiades had devised an unorthodox plan to weaken the centre of Athenian *phalanx* and bolster the two wings. This meant that the centre of the Greek lines, led by Themistocles and Aristides the Just, would have *phalanxes* that would only be four men deep, as opposed to the standard eight men. Even with the medising Greeks advising the Great King's forces, this was a subtle enough change that it would not be recognized until the centre line was adequately pushed back.

With the centre thinned, Miltiades placed on the left wing the 1,000 Plataeans who had answered Athens' call for aid. On the right wing, the most esteemed of the *strategos* at Marathon took charge. Callimachus was no mere general like Miltiades or Themistocles. Callimachus held the traditional role of *polemarch*, the democratically elected *archon* of Athens specifically tasked with the role of senior military commander.

The right wing was the position of reverence where the best fighters were traditionally placed; with Callimachus's experience and leadership this right wing was the most critical part of the Athenian strategy. And as such, Miltiades took the displaced hoplites from Themistocles's and Aristides's tribes and placed them on the left and right wings. These *phalanxes* were now four men deeper than normally at twelve hoplites.

Miltiades's plan was for the strengthened flanks to hold their ground or press the Persians back. Meanwhile, the centre tribes were pushed back. The trap was set – and the Persians fell for it perfectly. Themistocles and his tribe fought valiantly but with the depleted numbers his *phalanx* was pushed back, exactly as intended. Herodotus recounts the tides of battle turning when the Greeks 'drew their wings together to fight against those that had broken the middle of their line'.[7] The Athenian hoplites were able to form a U-shaped formation that slowly encircled the bulk of the Persian fighters, despite their greater numbers. The pincer manoeuvre, as it came to be called, would be a hallmark of later warfare by Alexander the Great, Hannibal and Genghis Khan and was even used in the American War of Independence.

The Persian line soon broke and they retreated to their ships. Some even ran through the marshlands, sinking in and drowning in their panic. But the drama was far from over. The Persians and their Greek advisors realized something that they perhaps should have seen earlier during the four day standoff preluding the battle. If the Athenians mustered 9,000 hoplites at Marathon, then there were very few left in Athens. Athens' citizenry was only about 30,000 and most of those men were too old to fight. This left Athens vulnerable.

The Persian fleet sent off a contingent of ships straight to Athens in the hopes of capturing the city quickly and efficiently. And so the Athenians at Marathon had precious little time for the customary looting and pillaging. After their mile-long sprint under arrow fire and then an hours-long battle, the Athenian hoplites were off running towards Athens to save their home. Again.

Plutarch, a Roman-era historian who wrote accounts of Themistocles and Aristides, emphasizes the gallantry of the centre-aligned tribes on this occasion that they were used as the bait. It was perhaps for this reason, and certainly for Aristides the Just's reputation for honour, that Aristides was asked to remain behind and manage the hostages. This was high praise, for the Greeks had yet to count the gold and supplies they had won. But their hope was well placed, and neither Aristides nor his troops skimmed off the top. The quick decision to place Aristides in charge of this and not consider Themistocles is quite telling – Themistocles's reputation for bribery and quick fingers clearly stretched back to his earliest days in politics.

Themistocles and his tribe ran the full 26.2 miles from Marathon to Athens and managed to reach the city-state before the Persian fleet was able to disembark. Seeing the hoplites on the horizon, the Persians – deflated, embarrassed, and angry – sailed back across the Aegean Sea. The Great King Darius had, for the first time, failed in conquering a new land. At Marathon, the Athenians had lost only 192 men while the Persians had lost several thousands. Athens had officially delayed its doom and had saved Greece. The men at Marathon set Greece on the course to become the bedrock of Western civilization, with Athenian democracy and hoplite warfare inspiring all Greece. Heroes had been made, reputations had been earned and the prizes of valour had been distributed.

*   *   *

And such was Themistocles's first *aristeia* – his great moment of earning renown, glory and, most critically, a name for himself. The men who survived Marathon lived the rest of their days as celebrated defenders of Greece; for the Athenians, they were the most heroic Greeks since the Trojan War. The Battle of Marathon was joined into Greek mythology as emblematic of the shining pinnacle Athens was ascending to. A later ancient writer described how at Marathon 'every night you can hear horses neighing and men fighting.'[8] Most Greeks thought that this would the end of the Persian threat, or that their return was so distant that any preparation didn't matter. Themistocles was the only one both wise enough and effective enough to see that Persia's return was imminent.

For Themistocles, the Battle of Marathon supplied a political opportunity, a lifetime in the making. It was, finally, inclusion in the highest social echelon. The heroic status of a commander at Marathon cemented Themistocles's future political career. Although he was a *strategos*, his youth and rivalry with Aristides the Just had held him back. But no longer.

When he was born in 524 BCE, Themistocles ranked near the bottom of the Athenian citizenry. In fact, he barely – if at all – met the requirements of a citizen. An Athenian citizen had to be the native-born child of two Athenian citizens. His father Neocles met the requirement easily, though was apparently so unimpressive a man that Plutarch snipes him as 'no very conspicuous man at Athens'.[9] He lacked money and status but lacked ambition most of all. Nevertheless, the family of Neocles was linked to the Lycomidae, a priestly family in Athens that held modest influence at best. Their worship was to Demeter, goddess of the harvest and fertility and, when Themistocles reached the apex of his power in Athens, he constructed a temple to her honour in the Acropolis complete with a mention of the Lycomidae family in its entrance.

His mother, however, is of unknown origin. Most ancient sources chronicling Themistocles's early life are lost to history, but Plutarch identifies her as a foreigner from Caria, across the Aegean Sea. This meshes well with the fact that the small village that they called home, in the Phrearrhian region of Attica about twenty miles outside of Athens, had a reputation for immigrants and foreigners.

Whether it was another ploy of Themistocles to hide his dubious citizenship is unknown, but it is reported that his earliest political struggles were to overcome his lack of truly Athenian blood. Themistocles's resourcefulness appeared when he was only a small boy when he convinced the nobly born Athenian youths to join him at the gymnasium of Heracles – that demigod himself of mixed heritage – which was located, quite intentionally, right outside the city gates. This daily messaging was obvious and very public. Even as a youth, Themistocles turned his weakness into an opportunity and blurred the class divisions, conveniently positioning himself as their ringleader and of distinctly Athenian birth-right. The young Themistocles left a mark not only on Athens but in the history books. The historian Plutarch invokes Themistocles's approach to his rivals in a philosophical dialogue on the utility of jealousy when one has successful or undeserving peers: 'Don't envy them, surpass them.'[10]

Despite his ignoble family life in an obscure village outside Athens, his education was spent in the company of those upper-class youths he had brought to the gymnasium. He was, as Aristotle might have said, a political animal from the onset. Plutarch describes him as 'a boy he was impetuous, by nature sagacious, and by election enterprising and prone to public life'.[11] For the boyhood Themistocles, everything was about politics and victory. Even education.

An Athenian education focused on the comprehensive virtues wrapped up in a life of *arete* and so covered topics such as athletics, literature, mathematics, philosophy, music and theatre. It simply would not do for Themistocles to be outmatched in any of these fields – or rather, the ones that he found pragmatic. He was consummately utilitarian; education was a tool to cultivate the skills that would best bring him tangible gains and best position him for success, without any regard for the students and tutors who stood in his way. He was pragmatic above all else – even in his hyper-competitiveness.

The scant stories for his school years show this repeatedly. He was described as constantly working to outwit his peers. Plutarch tells us that he never permitted himself leisure during free time, but 'would be found composing and rehearsing to himself mock speeches. These speeches would be in accusation or defence of some boy or other.'[12] His earliest teacher realized his unrelenting drive and prophetically said that he was destined for greatness – 'either for good or evil'.[13]

In fields he deemed impractical, such as virtue ethics or liberal arts, he cared little and tried less. He was able to skate by in those areas by natural talent – or a lack thereof – to the extent even in his adulthood at the height of his political power, he was publicly ridiculed in the Athenian assembly for his lack of musicality. This seems an odd criticism for a policy debate, but remember that, for the Athenians, artistic excellence was every bit an element of *arete* as battlefield glory or political dexterity. Themistocles deftly pivoted this insult in his signature style, saying that while playing a lyre or acting in a tragedy were not his gifts, his specialty was a better pursuit: 'taking in hand a city that was small and inglorious and making it glorious and great'.[14]

* * *

Like any good Greek, Themistocles and his fellow students studied the quintessential Greek reading list of Homer, Hesiod and mythology.

They read about the heroes from the Trojan War, about Achilles and his battlefield fearsomeness, about Odysseus and his cunning effectiveness and about Hector and his unflagging nobility. They read from mythology about Theseus and his heroism in saving Greece, about Jason and his singular quest for glory and power with the Argonauts and about Heracles and how his labours changed the future for himself and for Greece. And they read about the basic condition of humanity in Hesiod, who shows humanity as the playthings of the gods and who are prone to being cast aside – unless we can take charge of our own destinies through raw ambition and effectiveness.

It all blended in a sort of propaganda focusing on raising Greek men that practised virtue in all pursuits. For Athenian males under the age of about fourteen, their education usually meant being tutored and chaperoned to lessons by a *paidagōgos*, a servant or slave that raised upper-class children in a role that mixed teacher, au pair and mentor. A close relationship was often formed between *paidagōgos* and student and, while we do not know who Themistocles's *paidagōgos* was, we do know that his future children's *paidagōgos* became his most trusted servant and confidant, Sicinnus. The role was clearly influential and essential to Themistocles's formation as a Greek leader.

As Themistocles entered adolescence, his education became more formalized as his secondary education focused on logic and rhetoric under the tutelage of one or a few specialized teachers. These wise men were later labelled the Sophists and, a hundred years after Themistocles's education, were renowned for teaching rhetoric and virtue – though often without much regard for morality, if Plato and Socrates are to be believed. But Themistocles's education was more closely linked to the political tradition of Solon, the Athenian who created the first version of democratic reforms a half-century earlier.

This style of education, Plutarch contends, was less focused on eloquence and more on civic participation in the quasi-democratic government of Solon's day, when the non-aristocratic classes had their first, imperfect role in shaping policy. By the time Themistocles was schooled, many Sophists had abandoned such practical civic education and instead 'blended it with forensic arts, and shifted its application from public affairs to language'.[15] Themistocles however already had admirable persuasive and rhetorical skills and his unswerving vision of dominating politics – and not a philosophy dialogue – drove him to one Mnesiphilus,[16] a Phrearrhian like Themistocles, for his education.

Although we have scant sources on him, we do know Mnesiphilus was a very experienced politician who had an impressive ability to navigate Athenian politics as a fellow non-aristocrat. A member of the same *deme*, or population group, as Themistocles, Mnesiphilus had apparently survived multiple attempts at his ostracism. The Athenians annually ostracized a few citizens who were, ostensibly, a threat to the purity of their democracy. In practice, of course, this was politicized and influential men could persuade the masses to vote out their rivals. That Mnesiphilus avoided ostracism several times indicates a rare and refined savviness and the ability to pull political and social levers.

That acumen was exactly what Themistocles needed to be a political force and a successful part of a generation that was upending the previously dominant noble class. But although some students might have focused only on the pragmatic sagacity of politics, Themistocles did not entirely neglect the traditional Greek teachings of logic and rhetoric. In rhetoric, Themistocles found the perfect outlet for his passion to be the best. Themistocles knew it was these rhetorical skills that would be recognized as virtues and allow him to grasp his destiny in the fledgling democracy of Athens, where any citizen could rise to power if they could be persuasive and effective enough.

His passion for rhetoric apparently was quite forceful in his earliest writings. In his youthful works, he 'gave his natural impulses free course, which, without due address and training, rush to violent extremes in the objects of their pursuit, and often degenerate; as he himself in later life confessed, when he said that even the wildest colts made very good horses, if only they got the proper breaking and training.'[17] It seems that Mnesiphilus the Phrearrhian was able to smooth out these rough edges and redirect Themistocles's rebellious streak towards Athens's well-being.

Themistocles trained under Mnesiphilus for years, likely until his early thirties and shortly before – or even during – his fighting at Marathon. At some point during this time he married his first wife Archippe, daughter to Lysander of Alopece, and had at least three sons. All told, Themistocles would have two wives (the second wife's name long forgotten), five sons and five daughters. One son, named Neocles after his father, died tragically after being bitten by a horse as a child. Another son was raised by Themistocles's father-in-law Lysander. Although his son Cleophantus is lauded by Plato himself as an excellent horseman, the only son who followed his father's footsteps into politics was Archeptolis. Archeptolis inherited his father's skill for government, evident in the translation of his name ('magistrate of the city') and also, many years later, when he took his father's governmental post upon Themistocles's death. Archeptolis was not the only child of Themistocles named after his own great deeds; his daughter's name Nicomache translates as 'victory in battle' – a reference to Themistocles's most famous moment at the Battle of Salamis.

Mnesiphilus's influence on Themistocles was evident in the name of his favourite daughter, Mnesiptolema. In an odd twist, Archeptolis used a loophole in the Athenian marriage code to marry his half-sister Mnesiptolema, Themistocles's daughter by another wife, yet was still his father's favourite son given his involvement in Athenian public life.

Even in the naming of his children, his passion for politics was evident. The practicality of political education Themistocles received was a natural fit for him. After all, *themistocles* translates to 'glory of the law'. And his education paid off, as he was elected *archon* of Athens around 493 when he was about 31. *Archons* only served for a single year, and very little is known of Themistocles's year in the role, but it is clear that, after he served, his political influence dramatically increased – especially after the heroism at Marathon.

*   *   *

But as his habits became more focused on rising through the ranks of Athenian politics, despite his non-aristocratic birth, Themistocles's father grew concerned. Politics was not the path his father wanted him to take. When Themistocles was just a boy, his father Neocles summoned him to go for a walk on the beaches of Phrearrhi. Along the way, Neocles pointed to a row of rotting, dilapidated triremes that the Athenians had deserted after deeming them too costly to fix, despite their loyal service in warfare. Neocles warned Themistocles that this was the fate of all Athenian politicians: to be discarded and neglected when deemed past service.[18]

It makes sense that Neocles the commoner would feel this way about the politicians from the city centre who, during his day, traditionally came only from the nobility. Neocles had not seen a particularly successful version of democracy yet. For perhaps this reason, Plutarch actually repeatedly disparages Themistocles's father in order to emphasize the romantical origin story, calling his father 'too obscure to further his reputation'.[19]

But even as a boy, Themistocles was unswayed; he surely understood the message but did not heed it. The heroes of Homeric and Hesiodic tradition had not necessarily required the noblest birth or the fanciest education – just an opportunity to immortalize their honour and name through their actions. For Themistocles, the battlefield to earn glory was not just at Marathon, Artemisium, or Salamis against the Persians, it was in the assembly of Athens where his reputation and immortality would be forged. Later in life, he might have reflected on this lesson from his father and considered the broken-down triremes – the Athenians did of course reject him eventually. But Themistocles, in the style of a true Homeric hero, would have considered it worthwhile to etch his name in the history books for eternity. Themistocles engaged this directly when he was asked whether he would rather be Achilles or Homer. His answer revealed his great ambition: 'And pray…which would you rather be, a conqueror in the Olympic games, or the crier that proclaims who are conquerors?'[20]

*   *   *

When the Spartans finally arrived at the plains of Marathon, they were stunned at the sight of Athenian dominance. The Athenians had never lagged too far behind other city-states in warfare, but Marathon changed the complexion of Greek politics and military. With Athens ascendant, the policy they made would shape Greece and prepare them for the return of Persia – if the Persians were to even return. And Themistocles was now equipped, by education, connections and experience, to transform Athens to his vision. The only thing that stood between him and his goal for Athenian – and his own – supremacy was navigating the straits of direct democracy. He dived headfirst into this challenge immediately after Marathon and began a passionate campaign to prepare Athens for the return of the Persians. He knew that the fate of Athens, democracy, and Themistocles hinged on the success of his plan, if he could pull it off.

He would pull it off, of course. And along the way, he discovered populism.

Chapter 2

The Rise of the Subtle Serpent of Athens

Despite its fame, democracy in Athens did not exactly emerge in linear fashion. It is true that Athens invented the first democratic system and allowed even its basest citizens to have an equal say in all policy under a direct democracy. But that freedom was ultimately short-lived, and its development was punctuated by tyranny, despotism and corruption. And Themistocles was a product of both political worldviews.

The experiment began as many political revolutions do: over money. The middle-class Athenians, who since the end of the Greek Dark Ages had served as hoplites for a season and farmers for a season, faced a persistent debt crisis. The nobility ruled Athens with an iron fist as an oligarchy – where only a small few held power. But these middle-class citizen-soldiers had earned their keep in Athens, what with controlling the precious resources of food and protection. But the aristocracy held the purse strings and made routine loans to the middle-class so that their farms could operate each year.

After successive years, these loans compounded and the debt became unpayable for an overwhelming number of the middle class. They faced a predicament with three morbid outcomes. Their first option was to simply starve. Their second was to declare bankruptcy and sell themselves and their families into debt slavery, typically with interest rates that would never allow their freedom. And their third was to pay the debt, but then be left without enough money for purchasing farming seed or supplies for the following season – thus delaying their starvation and/or slavery. When the aristocrats stopped getting their loans repaid, change finally occurred.

Somewhere around 574 BCE, the Athenians agreed to place one Solon in charge of rewriting the constitution to incorporate the middle-class and to ease the crippling debt. Solon was a highly respected statesmen in Athens and renowned for his integrity and skill at poetry. This endeared him to both the upper and middle classes, and they empowered him to create a new governmental model from scratch. The result was the establishment of some essentially Athenian institutions: the assembly of voting citizens to pass or veto laws, the *boule* or Council of 400 (later 500) citizens that determined the voting agenda for the assembly, and the assembly serving as a jury for major trials including ostracism. Solon also limited the power of the traditional governing roles of Athenians nobility: the nine *archons* and the council of former *archons*, the *areopagus*, both of which had been operating without account for some time.

Solon also organized the entire citizenship into four distinct tribes, allocated by social class. This was an important feature that would have been a cause for concern among the middle classes, but they were likely too preoccupied with Solon's economic reforms. Solon made the dramatic decision to forgive or restructure nearly all debts which was coupled with an injection of trade outside the boundaries of Attica and even Greece. The Athenian economy quadrupled quickly and, for once, all social classes were relatively happy. In order to prevent corruption or tyranny, Solon sailed off into the sunset – determined not to return for a decade, after which time he would come back, fix any lingering issues with his new government, and then leave again.

But Solon failed. His vision did not even last half the decade before major cracks began to show in the assembly. It took only a few years until a tyrant took command in Athens. Unlike our modern understanding of the term, a tyrant did not necessarily mean a despot. It referred to a person who took control by force, usually the wealthiest man who could muster enough sellswords. In 561 BCE, Peisistratus became that man.

Solon's first phase of democracy did not last long, and it may have never returned with such a vengeance had Peisistratus been a better mentor or father. Peisistratus's reign last about three decades and was generally peaceful and happy for all social classes. Like Themistocles, whose father Neocles would have been born during his reign, Peisistratus had a knack for balancing political tact with shows of force. Peisistratus's tyranny was far from tyrannical – he was vigorously popular with the middle-class due to his debt relief and with the upper-class due to his allowing loans again and giving back their voice in policy.

But for all the good he did, Peisistratus's sons managed to undo most of it. Shortly after his death, his two sons Hippias and Hipparchus each took a turn as tyrant of Athens. They may have ruled simultaneously for a time, but it is quite clear they lacked the elan and leadership of their father. Hipparchus was murdered in 514 BCE and Hippias was exiled a few years later. Hippias went straight to Persia – where he advised the Persian army in their first invasion at the Battle of Marathon.

While the Persians were trying to reinstall Hippias as a new tyrant of Athens (and perhaps Greece), the Athenians made a triumphant return to the democratic roots of Solon. In 508 BCE, they employed Cleisthenes – another aristocrat with a good reputation among the middle-class – to redesign the constitution once more. Cleisthenes's reforms gave him the moniker 'the Father of Democracy'.

Themistocles was around fifteen years old when Cleisthenes organized the Athenians into ten tribes based on geography instead of four tribes based on social class. This not only allowed the middle-class to rival the traditional aristocratic powers, but also gave a middle-class nobody – like Themistocles – the chance to rise to the highest positions: as an *archon* in politics, as a *strategos* in combat or in the *areopagus* for judicial influence. If one could manipulate the Athenian assembly to vote in one's favour, one could exert one's influence over the entirety of Athens.

And when they became a true democracy, the Athenian influence in Greece vaulted almost instantly. Herodotus points to the democratic impact on morale and enthusiasm, saying that the Athenians became better warriors, better merchants and better citizens simply because they now had the opportunity to advance in society. Herodotus describes the ramifications of Cleisthenes's democracy in his *Histories*:

Thus grew the power of Athens; and it is proved not by one but by many instances that equality is a good thing; seeing that while they were under despotic rulers the Athenians were no better in war than any of their neighbours, yet once they got quit of despots they were far and away the first of all. This, then, shows that while they were oppressed they willed to be cravens, as men working for a master, but when they were freed each one was zealous to achieve for himself.[1]

*   *   *

Themistocles represented the new template of success for an Athenian: ruthless cunning in navigating the assembly and new democratic practices. He was a new breed that Athens had not yet adjusted to. He had used his personality and talent to become the consummate populist. Themistocles was the first member of any democracy to realize the potential of middle- and lower-class voters, and he made himself masterfully known to them and them alone. No aristocrats needed.

His ignoble background resonated with the lower-classes, who felt the aristocrats – even in the new democracy of Cleisthenes – disregarded their struggles. Themistocles did not just rely on his raw talent, he married personal relationships and politics in a profound new way. He made sure that he really knew the men, and the women who influenced those men, that voted in the Athenian assembly.

His fame soon set the tone for his interactions with the common man of Athens. Each and every conversation became a chance for Themistocles to cultivate a particular image. He sought out opportunities to deliver a quip or to insult a particularly renowned member of Athenian culture. Simonides of Ceos, a famed poet, was one such target. When Simonides made an illegal request of Themistocles when Themistocles served on a magisterial council, Themistocles publicly gave his admonition, 'You would not be a good poet if you should sing contrary to measure; nor I a clever magistrate if I should show favour contrary to the law.'[2]

When Simonides later insulted Corinth in his poetry, Themistocles continued his public assailing of Simonides, though this time with less subtlety. Themistocles proclaimed that he should not 'abuse the Corinthians, who dwelt in a great and fair city, while he had portrait figures made of himself, who was of such an ugly countenance'.[3] Since the Greek emphasis on *arete* was not confined to intellectual and athletic excellence, but also included physical beauty, Themistocles was simultaneously stepping on a public rival and also loudly entering public discourse and culture through the arts – a practice that Themistocles would soon make a habit. There was no better way to get headlines than to insult the trendiest poet in Athens and then not-so-subtly imply that you maintain the beauty that he lacks.

He also made certain that the Athenians, and the rest of Greece and Persia knew that, in order to further his political career, he was open for business with like-minded people. When advertising for employees, Themistocles publicly quipped, 'I would rather...have a man that wants money, than money that wants a man.'[4] He was always on the lookout for deals and bribes, no matter the subject, and he made sure that potential partners and customers were aware. Even in dull matters, he never relented; he once sought to sell a parcel of farmland and advised the crier to 'proclaim also that it had a good neighbour'.[5]

Such a persona mixed well with his humble origins and political skill. The name he had made for himself in Athens was now formidable with both the aristocrats and the commoners. He was 'on good terms with the common folk, partly because he could call off-hand the name of every citizen, and partly because he rendered the service of a safe and impartial arbitrator in cases of private obligation and settlement out of court.'[6] Nobody had done the baby-kissing, personal touch political approach yet. The Athenians felt known and cared for, and they repaid Themistocles by voting for his laws and by elevating him to *archon* at the earliest eligible age of thirty.

By 493 BCE, he was elected to *eponymous archon*, the highest position in Athenian government where one leads the city-state for the next year. This was no small feat for anybody, but Themistocles was one of the very first non-aristocrats to ascend to the role and certainly had the humblest origins of any member of the *areopagus*, the council on which he would serve as a judge after his time as *archon*.

Little detail of Themistocles's tenure as *archon* survives in the historical record, but we do know of one major accomplishment: a vast expansion of the Athenian navy and harbours. Themistocles always looked to the sea. He saw the future of Greek supremacy – and Greek independence against Persia, for that matter – as directly linked to naval dominance. While some city-states like Corinth and Samos had relatively strong navies, the evidence of any serious naval powers in the Greek peninsula is fragmentary at best. In the Archaic era, city-states still relied on hoplites and traditional land armies. The Corinthian and Samian navies would not be considered particularly strong if they had matched up against the truly dominant naval powers under Persian rule: the Phoenicians, Egyptians, Ionians, and Carians.

Athens had, at best, a modest navy with triremes either a recent development or not existing at all. A safe estimate would be no more than two dozen Athenian triremes in 493 BCE, with most Athenian ships being the smaller, cheaper *pentekonters* like the twenty ships the Athenians used at Marathon. But the trireme was the gold standard of naval warfare by the 480s and Themistocles knew that if Athens was going to have any say in Greek policy, they needed to build triremes and harbour them at Athens.

His first step was to construct a new port to harbour the future navy. Athens lies about seven miles from the coast, and the historical harbour for its ships was the port of Phaleron. Although Phaleron was closer and had far more infrastructure ready for expansion, Themistocles eyed Piraeus as the future of Athens' navy. Piraeus was only three miles west but had a natural peninsula that guarded the harbour from the fickle winds of the Saronic Gulf. Moreover, it was far larger and could be more easily defended or blockaded, if need be, and even allowed a faster escape route towards the island of Salamis.

Before choosing Piraeus, Themistocles – no natural seaman himself – would have done his homework. Themistocles likely walked down to Piraeus himself to talk with its fishermen, merchants, and traders in an effort to learn as much as possible about the harbour. In those talks, he would have learned about the shallow waters of Phaleron and how they wouldn't support the many ships Themistocles envisioned, and how the deep waters of Piraeus allowed for a greater scope of ships.[7] He would have asked about the morning and evening winds and if they would take ships off course. And he also would have made promises of jobs in the construction process, or of lucrative trade deals, and made the requisite bribes to local magistrates. All of these were essential not only to creating the best harbour, but also to solidifying Themistocles's voting blocs – as Piraeus was a new citizenry with new voting rights who now appreciated Themistocles's support and would repay him at the voting booth. He would have been keenly aware of the impact of the project for lower- and middle-classes of both Piraeus and Athens, whose lower- and middle-class citizens would populate the ships as rowers.

There was more to his prescription of a new harbour. Themistocles valued the symbolism of a strong Athenian harbour and navy: it could be a rallying cry for resistance against Persia and even provoke rebellion among the Persian-controlled Greeks. Recruiting others to this vision was no small task, and Themistocles had to be creative in reaching his domestic and foreign audience. To that end, he took up patronage in the theatre. During his archonship in 492 BCE, Themistocles bankrolled a play entitled *The Capture of Miletus*. *Archons* were tasked with selecting cultural and artistic productions to celebrate the Festival of Dionysus, called the Dionysia, which held at its core a competition of tragic and comedic plays. Whichever productions were selected were given considerable influence with the population that season – an opportunity Themistocles could hardly squander.

The Capture of Miletus was Themistocles's strategic method of depicting the Persian menace to the Athenians. Its plot followed the sacking of Miletus, a key Athenian ally, in 494 BCE in the brutal Persian punishment for the Ionian Revolt which had sparked war among the Greeks of the Ionian coast and Darius the Great's Persian army. Although little record remains of Themistocles's archonship, he apparently used his position to fully support Athens' Ionian allies against the Persians – and used the theatre to persuade the voting assembly of Athens that it was in their best interest to act quickly and decisively against the looming Persian threat. Phrynichus is credited with introducing historical content to Greek tragedies and theatre productions, which had previously been mythological and religious in content. Themistocles, in his grand style, reconfigured the arts to serve his political purposes. The tactic had success, though perhaps not in the style Themistocles had envisioned. Herodotus recounts that, upon the first production of *The Capture of Miletus*, 'the whole theatre broke into weeping; and they fined [the playwright] Phrynichus a thousand drachmae for bringing to mind a calamity that touched them so nearly, and forbade for ever the acting of that play.'[8]

This only shone a greater spotlight on the rising Persian threat for Athens. Now, no Athenian was unaware of the extent that Darius the Great would go to in order to keep power – even if it remained unpopular to voice such an opinion. But by Themistocles's calculations, if Athens could help the Ionians break their Persian chains then it could be the beginning of a new generation of Athenian influence across the Aegean world, especially when paired with his ship-building ambitions. After all, Themistocles's grand vision was for all of the Greeks to be so 'immensely impressed by the magnitude of their naval strength [that they] would readily align themselves with the people which had the power both to inflict the greatest injury and to bestow the greatest advantages'.[9]

Those people, of course, would be the Athenians. Themistocles noted the great influence that the mighty Spartan army had over the Greek city-states and that their reputation alone could motivate Greeks and strike fear in the enemy. Themistocles wanted the same for Athens and, since the Spartans had no military peer, it was the navy where they could best transform the Aegean region. And perhaps most of all, as illustrated by his propagandistic theatre productions, a great navy might be the only chance Athens and Greece had against the Persians.

Unfortunately, building enough new triremes to actualize that vision was not financially possible during his archonship. Themistocles hoped that 'the city would be able to compete for the hegemony at sea'[10] but recognized that bankruptcy was counter-productive. He could also not autocratically redirect funding for the project, given the checks and balances of Athenian democracy. His harbour project was too ambitious to complete during his archonship, but it became a lifelong project for him.

Nevertheless, Themistocles was able to substantially build up Piraeus and make it a workable and profitable port in just one year. The lion's share of Athenian ships began to use Piraeus and commerce steadily transitioned from the old harbour at Phaleron to Piraeus. Creating a world-class harbour is no small feat and the assumption was that it would take Themistocles's crew years to complete the project. But Themistocles 'devoted himself to that work'[11] and won over the crewmen, politicians, bankers, and construction workers. The harbour was completed in a fraction of the expected time, since everybody 'enthusiastically co-operated it was speedily done and the harbour was finished before anyone expected'.[12]

The manoeuvre made him a darling of the non-privileged *demes* and gave him a bedrock of political support that he would rely on throughout the next decade. It was not only the new *thetes* – lower class trireme rowers – who found employment and a steady wage through Themistocles's harbour project. Themistocles also had the savviness to remove taxes on foreigners, merchants, and artisans who moved into Athens to invigorate the new harbour. Policies such as this were introduced 'in order that great character crowds of people might stream into the city from every quarter and that the Athenians might easily procure labour for a great number of crafts,'[13] but, of course, their newfound loyalty to Themistocles was a helpful bonus.

Finally, Themistocles was able to convince the Athenians to begin construction on new triremes to improve their diminutive navy. It was a modest fleet at first, with funding set aside for twenty ships built annually. But within half a decade, these added up to make Athens a sizeable naval force. Themistocles was keen to manage his image when it came to the triremes and the harbour: all of Athens knew that Themistocles had staked his reputation on the naval future of Athens. And it worked well, as Piraeus shortly became the commercial and economic nerve centre of the Aegean Sea. It was the crown jewel that Themistocles had hoped it would be.

Themistocles fortified Piraeus as well, constructing modest walls around the port to complement the natural rocky landscape. Although Themistocles may have modelled the new Piraeus after the heavily defended port in Corinth, Piraeus had significant geographic advantages in its protection from invaders, namely the bottlenecking of ships entering the port and the difficult geography deterring any landings outside Phaleron or Piraeus. Themistocles capitalized on the strategic benefits of Piraeus and began building walls around the port, but had to halt the project before completion due to funds and logistical challenges. He would return to the project nearly two decades later and fully fortify Piraeus, making it nearly impregnable.

He notably expanded the fortress at a nearby hill named Munichia. Munichia had been originally fortified by Hippias but was drastically developed by Themistocles who redesigned it to be used as a watchtower and refuge if the city were ever conquered. From the top of the hill, the Athenian troops could see over the entire Saronic Gulf, towards the island of Salamis and further to their near-constant enemy Aegina, as well as watch the comings and goings in Piraeus.

In fourteen years, this hill would be the place where the Great King of Persia sat while watching Themistocles and his Athenians defeat the largest navy ever assembled. And seventy-five years after that, the location of the last stand of Athens against Spartan invaders restored Athenian democracy for another few generations. The king of the hill at Munichia was truly a symbol for the future of Athens.

Themistocles also ordered the construction of new ships to populate his new harbour at Piraeus. While some were surely built, it wasn't until 483 BCE that Themistocles's naval construction truly began. But the ships he made during his archonship certainly bolstered Athens enough to supply ships at Marathon.

Themistocles had an endgame for Athens: a naval superpower, dominating politics and commerce, that would overwhelm Greece in the aftermath of fighting back the invading Persians. Athens wasn't there yet and wouldn't be there during his time as *archon* in 493 BCE. But, by the end of the next decade, Athens would have the largest naval fleet in Greece that would allow it to hegemonically control the Greek peninsula. All because of Themistocles's first steps.

*   *   *

When Themistocles entered into leadership in the city-state, he had a clear vision of the type of leader he wanted to emulate. Surprisingly, it was not his mentor and fellow countryman Mnesiphilus, with whom he was still apparently very close. It was instead his former commander at Marathon, Miltiades. Plutarch does not cover much of Themistocles's service at Marathon, but he makes sure to emphasize to his readers how Themistocles fixated on Miltiades's renown for *arete* and became determined to exceed it. Shortly after Marathon, Themistocles become a recluse, declining dinner and drinking invitations and losing sleep over the fact that 'Miltiades' was the name on every Greek tongue. When asked about his change, Themistocles replied that 'the trophy of Miltiades would not let him sleep.'[14]

And although Themistocles was not a fan of Miltiades in the least – he found him to represent the tyrannical underbelly of Athenian politics – he certainly attempted to emulate Miltiades in disposition and political prowess. Indeed, while many found Themistocles to be charming and persuasive, politics has always been a divisive game. One didn't need to look much further than how the other heroes of Marathon – supposedly demigods now among the Athenians – were treated in the political arena. While their lionheartedness against the Persians won them many political advantages, many men had pushed it too far.

Chief among them was the commander himself, Miltiades. Just one short year after victory at Marathon, Miltiades had already worn out his welcome in Athens. He had first attempted to take a cadre of seventy Athenian ships and conquer Paros and its Persian-allied city-states in the Aegean islands. The expedition was a catastrophe.

It was catastrophic enough that the Athenian assembly immediately put Miltiades – the saviour and defender of Greece – on trial with the threat of death. As one does in one's trial, Miltiades attempted to persuade his followers of his own worth. His camp's propaganda was that this Athenian hero and former Olympic chariot champion was the consummate Athenian and has earned a place in Athens by his *arete* and effectiveness. But the prosecution was led by another influential aristocrat, Xanthippus. Xanthippus was a clansman of Cleisthenes and typically represented the aristocratic interests; in this case, they were to rid Athens of the populist threat Miltiades represented. Miltiades could not overcome the eloquent prosecution of Xanthippus and he was exiled only eighteen months after saving Greece at Marathon.

But if you take into account the embryonic state of Athenian democracy, Miltiades's penalty might make some sense. When he left Athens originally, it was a tyranny under Peisistratus. And, until a half decade before Marathon, Miltiades was a tyrant in Chersonese. Following his father's leadership of a colonial experiment to this peninsula near the Hellespont in Thrace, he and his father had ruled there for many years on behalf of their native Athens. But on Miltiades's return to Athens, the democracy he found was alien and unaccommodating. Further, the assembly of citizens – zealous to protect their democratic project – likely saw Miltiades and the reputation he earned at Marathon as a major threat to democracy. They could not have him tyrannizing Athens, and the weakness displayed in his failed campaign (and his leg injury, to boot) was the perfect chance to rid Athens of a potential threat.

But there were more juicy details. In about 496 BCE, Miltiades had astonishingly fought in the service of Darius the Great of Persia. That's right: the Greek hero at Marathon was a former Persian soldier. In the typical fashion of the Persian King of Kings, Darius had called up all the local armies in order to expand his empire, this time against the horseback warriors of Scythia, on the northern banks of the Black Sea. The legend is that Miltiades not only abandoned the Persians but marooned them in Scythia by cutting the pontoon bridge they had constructed to travel there. This merited enough of a reputation to return to Athens and rapidly rise to *strategos* by Marathon in 490 BCE.

But regardless of the verdict's legitimacy, Miltiades had become yet another rotting Athenian trireme on the beach – the inevitable fate of Athenian politicians, according to Themistocles's father. Miltiades went on to die of gangrene while in prison, another anticlimactic end to a Greek hero. If you believed the Athenian aristocrats, Xanthippus had heroically dispelled a threat to democracy and all Athenians should heed the lesson of overweening.

* * *

We have no historical record of Themistocles becoming involved in the trial of Miltiades and, though he was certainly heartbroken by the hero's demise, Themistocles had no time to grieve. Themistocles was nearly the only Athenian who had not been wrapped up in the romance of the Greek victory at Marathon. In the aftermath of Marathon, Themistocles had become transfixed on preparing Athens and Greece to defend itself against any future attacks. He considered Marathon to be merely the first Persian invasion and he was confident that Darius the Great would be back, armed with a better strategy and vastly more powerful army. After all, Persia had not lost any land and could easily weather the troops and political impact that their surprise defeat had caused. The rumours circulating from across the Aegean were that Darius was devoted to destroying the meddlesome Athenians who had the audacity to stand in the way of the Great King's conquests, and he was allegedly recruiting a massive military to avenge his humiliation.

By 491 BCE, the Persian king had sent envoys all over Greece demanding 'earth and water'[15] in a show of submission to Persia. Many Greek city-states had accepted willingly and some with great enthusiasm. In fact, even some city-states near Athens had accepted. Themistocles was one of several in the assembly to take a hard line against Persia and advocated Athenian intervention and the launching of attacks on these states. When Persia had enough support, they invaded in 490 BCE, failing to capture

Athens due to their loss at Marathon but still taking many parts of northern Greece along the way.

Themistocles did not think Athens – never mind the rest of Greece – was ready to handle another Persian threat. It would take a miracle to convince them to think seriously about Persia and to look past their petty squabbles. Athens, rather short-sightedly, was already back to warring with its neighbour Aegina and the Athenian assembly had no interest in talking about what they considered the old news of Persian invasion. It would take a miracle to change their minds. Or maybe some silver.

In late 484 BCE, the Athenians had the most improbable and utterly beneficial stroke of luck, and it literally changed the complexion of the Western world. They struck silver. At an Athenian silver mine in Laurium, they had been slowly milking the last of two veins of silver for a few decades. Right at the point where their silver was nearly depleted, they discovered a rich new vein that was previously unknown, given its location under the surface and hidden from generations of previous miners. This gave Athens a sudden and massive injection of wealth and gave them the best of problems in the entire world: trying to figure out what to do with all the extra money.

Two camps quickly emerged and each persuasively presented their case to the Athenian assembly over the next year. The first group made an argument that hardly anybody has ever argued against: free money. They did the maths and figured that they had 100 talents of silver, about hundredfold the annual wage of an average Athenian. A single talent paid the monthly wages for the entire crew of a trireme. In modern currency, it would be surplus of roughly £1.9 million (or $2.6 million). If it were equally distributed among the citizens, it would be a nice bonus, if not a life changing amount. There was precedent for this as well, as previous, though smaller, amounts of silver had been democratically shared with all citizens over past decades.

One influential citizen, Aristides the Just, led the first group advocating to share the wealth among the Athenian citizenship. Aristides's reputation was extraordinarily helpful to his case: his nickname 'the Just' was earned by his deep commitment to rule Athens with a view to justice and *arete*. He had been the other *strategos* from the centre lines at Marathon – alongside Themistocles's tribe – and had been made *eponymous archon* shortly thereafter. His archonship was successful by nearly all accounts, but especially from the nobility who appreciated his work as a Solon-like figure in uniting the upper-class desire for financial security with the middle-class desire for political representation.

Aristides gave an eloquent speech proposing the bonus payments to all Athenian citizens and at first there seemed to be little disagreement. But then Themistocles the Populist proposed a different idea, that on its face went against everything populism should be: he convinced the people to turn down free money and instead invest it. Specifically, Themistocles wanted to invest it in a massive construction project of ships, ships, and more ships. His ambitious plan was to build over 200 triremes and catapult the Athenian navy from a middling power to the strongest in the Greek world – the fulfilment of the vision from his archonship. His motivation was the same as then, and it was a simple one. He knew the Persians would return and that Athens, in order to have any true hope of survival, had to become not just proficient at naval warfare but dominant.

And when Themistocles addressed the Athenian assembly, he knew that such a sales pitch had no hope and he instead channelled his Odysseus-like persuasive skills. Themistocles's speech to the Athenians first chastised Aristides and then invoked the great enemy of Athens that he knew would scare the Athenians into supporting his naval vision. And it wasn't Persia. Themistocles intentionally avoided any and all references to the Persians, since he knew his political opponents would cast him as paranoid and foolish if he did so. Plutarch says that, to the Athenians in 483 BCE, the Persians were 'too far away and inspired no very serious fear of their coming'.[16] Instead, Themistocles deftly pointed to the 'true' Athenian rival that they could only overcome with a new navy: Aegina.

Aegina was a medium-sized city-state right across the Saronic Gulf from Athens and there had been constant rivalry with Athens during the 480s over control of the region. Solon's reforms had actually severely limited all economic interaction with Aegina in order to cripple them but it hadn't worked. Aegina was, by all accounts, a major naval power in Greece, ranking somewhere below Corinth but above Athens. They were no pushover and, if Themistocles had been less successful in building his navy, could have overtaken Athens as the Attican power.

Themistocles knew the common folk of Athens would see Aegina as a far more immediate threat to their daily life, and that the establishment of Piraeus as a commercial and naval hub had shown the people that the future of Athens was on the sea. Aristides fought back, arguing that the rich tradition of Athens had been in hoplite warfare and that becoming a naval power was a departure from the Athenian identity. But Themistocles, no doubt, was able to turn such an argument around with his populist backing: the aristocrats always wanted tradition and couldn't handle the reality that creating a powerful navy might give more power to the lower classes.

Many Athenians might have seen right through Themistocles's cloak, but he even had a strategy to convince these opponents as well. If the triremes were constructed, they would need to be manned. Triremes held almost 200 men who had to be paid for the work, and it was a wonderful way for a lower-class man to earn a steady wage. Unlike hoplite warfare, where you needed to buy expensive equipment that prohibited anyone from a lesser background, the trireme rowers simply needed to purchase a seat cushion. Themistocles's speech made sure to emphasize that the lower-classes would be given a handsome salary if 200 triremes were constructed – a far better investment than the one-time payout from Aristides.

And the cunning ploy worked. The Athenian assembly voted to build at least 100 new triremes, and soon thereafter up to 200. It was the first step in a grand vision for Athens to dominate the seas and so dominate Greece. As the Roman philosopher Cicero later has it, in a pithy summary of Themistocles's dream of a dominant Athenian navy: 'he considers that the master of the sea must be master of the empire.'[17]

Themistocles even employed some creative accounting to support his marketing about the threat of Aegina. Aristotle, when he describes the unique democracy of Athens, dedicates significant time to explain how Themistocles used the silver from Laurium:

> Themistocles…not saying what use he would make of the money, but recommending that it should be lent to the hundred richest Athenians, each receiving a talent, so that if they should spend it in a satisfactory manner, the state would have the advantage, but if they

did not, the state should call in the money from the borrowers. On these terms the money was put at his disposal, and he used it to get a fleet of a hundred triremes built, each of the hundred borrowers having one ship built, and with these they fought the naval battle at Salamis against the [Persian] barbarians.[18]

The new triremes of Athens were the sleekest, most formidable warships available at the time. The shipyards at Piraeus worked day and night to build the three-level galleys which sat 180 rowers, each on their own oar. Within four years, Athens' seemingly miraculous fortune at Laurium allowed the Athenians to build the largest navy in Greece, dwarfing the previous powers of Corinth and Samos. In this short time, they had become the dominant political force in Greece and had a shred of hope in the case of a Persian naval invasion.

It is hard to imagine anyone other than Themistocles successfully convincing the Athenian citizenship. His singular focus on Persia might come across as obsessive, but its accuracy could not be denied, considering Xerxes the Great would lead a massive invasion in just three years. But it was also a masterpiece of Homeric eloquence delivered with just the right clever strategy to convince a group of middle- and lower-class citizens to vote against their own ostensible advantages. Odysseus would have been proud, especially with Themistocles's cloaking of the true enemy Persia.

Interestingly, Themistocles is even said to have defeated the arguments of Miltiades, potentially returned from exile by this point. Plutarch quotes the ancient historian Stesimbrotus (of whom we now very little, given his works are long destroyed) saying that Miltiades fought against Themistocles's naval vision for Athens and instead pushed to reinvigorate the hoplites and prepare for a land war akin to Marathon. It's unclear how the chronology for this might work, if he is even accurate, but it is possible that this was an older argument dating back to Themistocles's construction of the port at Piraeus – which would have clearly indicated the long term plan for the Athenian naval project. Either way, Miltiades and his sizable influence was another obstacle that Themistocles overcame to push Athens into military preparedness. Nothing came easy for him.

Yet Themistocles's debate with Aristides and Miltiades did not just represent a political future, it was a linchpin for the non-aristocratic classes.

It was the first true test of the democratic experiment that Cleisthenes (a close friend of Aristides, ironically) had created. Never before in history had the citizens of a sovereign state *voted* to go to war. Themistocles did not just add accomplishments to his resumé, he orchestrated the first trial run of democratic foreign policy. Athenians were not just voting to raise or lower taxes, their votes were also now shaping diplomatic relations for Greece.

The vote to create a navy also laid the foundation for Athens to become an imperial democracy. Themistocles knew that by dominating the seas, Athenian ships could do much more than win battles: they could trade better than ever before, blockade their weaker enemies, give the lower-classes more political power given the critical role of *thetes* – the rowers of a trireme, win votes from those same *thetes* in assemblies, and ultimately bully their way to the top of the Greek food chain. By making Athens a seafaring state, as Plato describes, Themistocles 'robbed his fellow-citizens of spear and shield, and degraded the people of Athens to the rowing-pad and the oar'.[19] It was a radical departure from their traditions, but it was a necessary one for Athens to repel the Persians and take the lead in Greece.[20]

For Themistocles, the decade after Marathon saw a dramatic rise in his political influence and his hegemonic vision for Athens' navy was typified by his heavy-handed leadership of Athenian politics. He wielded the power of the middle- and lower-classes that adored him. Xenophon, a famous commander and philosopher trained by Socrates himself, would later write of Themistocles in a Socratic dialogue:

> Crito: And how did Themistocles win our city's love? Socrates. Ah, that was not by incantation at all. What he did was to encircle our city with an amulet of saving virtue.[21]

Chapter 3

Of Rivalries and Ostracisms

But every good hero needs an antagonist, even if our antagonist is an exemplary person. Aristides the Just, Themistocles's fellow general at Marathon and rival in the debate over the silver of Laurium, also eyed political dominance in Athens. Aristides had more than a few advantages over Themistocles. For one, he was an aristocrat from an ancient and respected Athenian family. He had a reputation for honour, justice, and integrity that was unparalleled in Athens. He was a patron of arts and culture and eschewed all opportunities for individual wealth or power.

He, alone among all the famous fifth century Athenians, was thought to be of such excellence and *arete* that the historian Herodotus said he had 'come to believe that he was the best and most just man in Athens'.[1] And, more importantly for any political rival, he was 'an intimate friend'[2] of Cleisthenes and very possibly helped design the democratic system itself. But dangerously, Aristides also had an affection for order and justice that flew a bit too close to the Spartan worldview. He was most influenced by Lycurgus, a semi-mythical forefather of Sparta who had designed the ruthless governmental and cultural system that turned Sparta into a perpetual military state. The Lycurgan Reforms were brutal but effective: Spartans had their own identities ironed out beginning at age seven in boot camp, held no true property, were cut off from the outside world and devoted their whole selves to the prosperity of the city-state. But that process also created a distilled form of justice and honour admired by many other Greeks, who often considered the Spartan to be the truest form of *Greek*.

Aristides brought the same ironclad justice and honour to Athens, and his accomplishments at Marathon propelled him into the leadership he been trained for since birth. His ancient biographers point to numerous anecdotes illustrating his political skill and unwavering honour. He once so eloquently prosecuted a trial that the judges asked not to hear the defence's case whatsoever, yet Aristides intervened and demanded that all court procedures be followed to dignify the justice system. He was often hired to privately mediate disputes between citizens where he categorically refused any personal offence and focused only on determining the cold, emotionless integrity of the case. In one such case between two aristocrats, he interrupted the plaintiff when the discussion focused on how Aristides had been dishonoured – and he ordered that the proceedings return to the facts of the case without any regard to his own stature.

For these examples and many more, he was lionized as Aristides 'the Just' and the name became an intrinsic part of his reputation and vocation. His renown was so solidified in the community that when he attended a reading by the famed poet and playwright Aeschylus, all eyes in the theatre turned to him when the poet read the following esteemed words:

> His shield no emblem bears; his generous soul
> Wishes to be, not to appear, the best;
> While the deep furrows of his noble mind
> Harvests of wise and prudent counsel bear.[3]

Aristides's sterling reputation and aristocratic pedigree allowed him to be voted *eponymous archon* of Athens in 489 BCE, shortly after Marathon, and he led Athens with an emphasis on respecting its traditional institutions and virtues – especially giving more authority back to the aristocratic class. He was careful to be seen as beyond reproach, apparently refusing all attempts at subterfuge and bribery. He even eschewed many political alliances, since he felt that 'power derived from friends incited many to do wrong, and so was on his guard against it, deeming it right that the good citizen should base his confidence only on serviceable and just conduct.'[4] But by all accounts in Athens, he was the consummate Athenian aristocrat.

Yet Themistocles would not have seen it that way. To him, Aristides was a stubborn remnant of the old ways, and so lacked the awareness that his influence in the city-state threatened its survival. By this point, Themistocles had become the champion of the lower-classes and framed his meteoric rise as the truest form of democracy's power – any man can accomplish anything with enough *arete*. But the aristocrats stood in his way.

Aristides and Themistocles represented the height of Athenian democracy – the good and the bad. Aristides was a stalwart representative for the aristocrats in Athenian democracy; he always leveraged his impeccable reputation and influence to support the aristocratic agenda and foothold on politics. Although he skirted personal gain, his worldview was firmly anchored in a strong, traditional aristocracy strengthened by a subservient middle- and lower-class. Democracy was a vessel for aristocratic power, given that the aristocrats were the most honourable and traditional Athenians.

Themistocles obviously disagreed. His vision was a radical reconfiguring of the Athenian power structure with democracy as the catalyst. For Themistocles, the democratic experiment in Athens was a rejection of aristocratic influence and the first step in the power being placed in the lower-classes – with himself as their advocate, of course. Both Aristides and Themistocles had ample defence for their positions, as Athenian democracy was still finding its own identity. The two, therefore, found a rival in the other.

This rivalry was integral to the formation of Themistocles as a hero of Athens. In the Homeric and mythological legends of Greece, the greatest heroes all had an adversary worthy of their competition. The glory and honour won by defeating such a villain, usually with the world watching and their future on the line, solidified characters like Achilles, Odysseus, Heracles, Theseus and Jason as the true Greek champions and culture-makers.

Plutarch had a similar idea in mind as he summarized the rivalry of Aristides and Themistocles:

> However, the dissimilarity in their lives and characters is likely to have increased their variance. Aristides was gentle by nature, and a conservative in character. He engaged in public life, not to win favour or reputation, but to secure the best results consistent with safety and righteousness, and so he was compelled, since Themistocles stirred the people up to many novel enterprises and introduced great innovations, to oppose him often, and to take a firm stand against his increasing influence.[5]

And fittingly, the two men had a mutually averse history that stretched back to their youth. If you recall Themistocles's distaste for the privileged youth and determination to outdo and prove his own worth, then it is easy to see why Themistocles and Aristides were never friendly.

> Some say that even as boys and fellow-pupils, from the outset, in every word and deed, whether serious or trivial, they were at variance with one another, and that by this very rivalry their natures were straightway made manifest, the one as dexterous, reckless, and unscrupulous, easily carried with impetuosity into any and every undertaking; the other as established on a firm character, intent on justice, and admitting no falsity or vulgarity or deceit, not even in any sport whatsoever.[6]

The rivalry between them was ingrained in the identity of each man by time they entered public service. This makes their past service at the Battle of Marathon, where they each led their tribes in the centre ranks, that much more remarkable. Themistocles and Aristides had together taken on the fiercest fighting and risked the most at that battle, and therefore should have forged a camaraderie, or at least a tolerance, with each other. But that was far out of the question at this point.

Childhood rivalry matured into bureaucratic brawling as the two men entered adulthood. When Aristides was elected as the main treasurer of Athens, a position which had lacked serious oversight given that previous office holders had redirected its funds into their own pockets, he publicly challenged his predecessors for their embezzlement. And after examining the accounting, Aristides called out Themistocles for his corruption and famously quipped, 'The man was clever, but of his hand had no control.'[7]

Theft, bribery, and blackmail were the hallmarks of Themistoclean governance, but Themistocles had no patience for the public embarrassment that Aristides had now delivered to him. Athenians would often tolerate and even expect such behaviour from a politician, as long as it didn't clearly undercut any policy or visibly harm the citizenship. But Themistocles could not tolerate such an overt insult and Aristides's comments could have cast aspersions on the carefully cultivated and marketed civic support that Themistocles had worked so hard on. And so his retaliation was swift and merciless.

Themistocles leaned heavily into the social class conflict between aristocrats and the lower-classes, consolidating enough lower-class voters to prosecute Aristides for an allegedly illegal audit, and even secured a conviction.[8] This infuriated the upper class who were astonished that any aristocrat could be prosecuted for corruption, especially their most virtuous. Aristides's response illustrated his worthiness as the foil to Themistocles. He immediately abandoned his typically honourable ways and began distributing Athenian funds to all manners of people, whether they deserved the money or not. As word got out, he was catapulted past even Themistocles among the lower classes as he allowed them any funding they wanted. For a short time, he was as corrupt as the shadiest of democracy's politicians.

But it was all a ploy to show the Athenian voting assembly how much Themistocles had been manipulating democracy and its bank accounts. As they moved to re-elect Aristides the Just to treasurer, he revealed himself:

> When I served you in office with fidelity and honour, I was reviled and persecuted; but now that I am flinging away much of the common fund to thieves, I am thought to be an admirable citizen. For my part, I am more ashamed of my present honour than I was of my former condemnation, and I am sore distressed for you, because it is more honourable in your eyes to please base men than to guard the public moneys.[9]

The message was crystal clear to Athens. Aristides was unimpeachable in office and Themistocles and his ilk aimed to please 'base men' and accumulate power for themselves at the great cost of Athenian stability and security. Aristides the Just won praise and influence among the Athenian voting assembly and Themistocles's reputation took another hit. No Athenian could now stay neutral in the proxy war between the aristocrats' Aristides and the common man's Themistocles.

In fact, the rivalry grew so red hot that Plutarch, in his compilation of Classical biographies, frames nearly all of Aristides's story through the lens of the political conflict with Themistocles. The very existence of Aristides was as a foil to Themistocles. Aristides was a deeply traditional aristocrat who better matched the Western or Roman definition of honour as both personal and communal ethos demonstrated in action. Themistocles, however, was consummately Greek: the only thing that mattered was the end result, and honour came from being highly effective in heroic situations. The two worldviews were oil and water.

The Athenian voting assembly, where laws were proposed and debated, became ground zero for the intricate political battles between the two. Themistocles, his desire for influence combined with his dislike of the ruling class that Aristides represented, essentially refused to support any measure the Aristides proposed or endorsed. And with his ever-increasing influence among the non-privileged voters, especially after 489 BCE and the exile of Miltiades, a massive chunk of voting Athenians similarly denied Aristides any political accomplishments.

Themistocles was so successful in stunting Aristides's career that, even when Aristides was on course to pass a vote, it could be derailed by exploiting loopholes and procedural minutiae. On one occasion Aristides proposed a law and it was smoothly moving towards passing, but Themistocles agitated his followers to speak out against it and slow down the final vote, and so frustrated Aristides that he simply 'withdrew it without a vote'[10] in order to avoid the pain. Aristides the Just left the assembly soon after declaring that 'there was no safety for the Athenian state unless they threw both Themistocles and himself into the death-pit.'[11]

Aristides was forced to introduce measures through middlemen in order to keep his name hidden, else the supporters of Themistocles would suffocate his policies. The increasing influence of each man set them up for a dramatic showdown – under the current circumstances, the two men simply could not coexist in Athenian politics.

*   *   *

To find resolution for this conflict, we must remind ourselves, at this point, of the story from Themistocles's youth, where his father Neocles pointed out the ruined triremes along the beaches near Athens. Neocles had said that such abandonment and decay was the inevitable future of all Athenian politicians: the city-state eventually used up its leaders and spat them out. Even during Themistocles's adulthood, there was ample evidence to support this: Miltiades, Hippias, Solon, and others had all fallen out of favour to some degree.

But Themistocles's father was even wiser than we give him credit for, and it is clear to see where Themistocles inherited some of his acumen. One of the major reforms of Cleisthenes, who (if you remember) had transformed Athens into a democracy by 510 BCE, was to formally institute a practice known as *ostracism*. Ostracism was the process by which the Athenian assembly could vote to exile any member of the city-state for ten years. Although it was a new law, it was essentially the formalization of a practice that had already existed: kicking people you disliked out of town.

In theory, it allowed for the citizens to band together and fight back against tyranny, oligarchy and corruption, and to vote out the members of their community who most threatened the health of their fledgling democracy. In practice, however, it often became a political tool to banish rivals and sway public opinion.

The name derives from the *ostraka*, broken pottery pieces that the names of citizens would be written on and accordingly placed into piles. Of course, since we are in the ancient world, the majority of the citizenship couldn't read or write and so pottery sherds with names pre-inscribed could be strategically distributed as the assembly filed in to conduct a vote. At the voting assembly, people could publicly propose first that an ostracism should take place, with no specific candidates being named. Two months later, the assembly reconvened and then the votes would be cast for individual candidates for exile until 6,000 *ostraka* were counted in that person's pile. Once you reached 6,000 votes, you were sent away for the next decade. There were no formal allegations, no formal defence and no deliberation whatsoever. These would of course occur but they happened outside the assembly, often in the form of information warfare, propaganda, and bribery.

The first formal ostracism occurred in 487 BCE with Hipparchus, a relative of the previous tyrant Peisistratus (of whom little is known except his apparent desire for tyranny), almost twenty years after the process was first created by Cleisthenes. Ostracism had a slow start, it appears, and was apparently used more as a distant threat than an actual civic procedure. A later Greek historian remarked that the Athenians instituted ostracism 'not for the purpose of punishing wrongdoing, but in order to lower through exile the presumption of men who had risen too high'.[12] It is clear that for the first generation of Athenian democracy, this bar was too high for the voting assembly and that ostracism was best used as an insurance policy and not a habit.

But within seven years of Hipparchus's ostracism, four more ostracisms would occur – with two very prominent names on the list. Clearly something happened in Athenian politics during the 480s that increased the political utility of ostracism. We could surely point to the Persian threat, to the war with Aegina or to the rise of Athenian colonial and commercial power as factors that transformed the political landscape. But the reason was most likely the Assembly's shift towards weaponizing ostracism. Ostracism became a Sword of Damocles that was a constant threaten to all in power. At any moment, the tides could turn and the power of populism and demagoguery could be unleashed on any Athenian politician who accumulated too much influence or too many enemies, or at least appeared to.

The Greek historian and general Thucydides labelled this a *stasis*, an ancient Homeric term describing a struggle to be the best. Thucydides emphasizes that this concept evolved to be a competition among leading aristocrats in the oligarchies of Greece and between the social classes in the democratic city-states. Even today, most democracies inherently have a tension between those parties who want oligarchic rule and those who want populist rule. Athens was no different except in the critical fact that they were the first. The two Athenian forces pulled equally and accomplished enough to keep democracy functioning but not lurching too far in either direction – illustrated by the literal definition of *stasis* as 'a standing still'. But the ostracism explosion in the 480s was a phenomenal push in the populist direction because of Themistocles's political challenge to the fixed social order.

And so we again see democracy figuring itself out. As the first democracy matured and experienced growing pains, its participants slowly but effectively learned how to pull the levers of government, how to best convince or blackmail or bribe its voting bodies and how to stimulate and weaponize its processes. The most cunning of politicians realized that the clever pragmatism of populism and ostracism were a nice way to consolidate power. It was also very helpful to otherize any potential rivals

And our cutthroat protagonist Themistocles is a reasonable suspect in this reshaping of ostracism. He was, at the bare minimum, a contributor to making ostracism a strategic apparatus instead of a democratic failsafe. We do not have a detailed record of Themistocles from 489 BCE to 483 BCE, but it is clear that he was involved in all of the ostracism debates, even if peripherally. That is because of two major issues: the ostracism of two of his political rivals and the prevalent social class conflict which Themistocles was typically puppeteering.

This created a precarious climate for those politicians from conservative and aristocratic classes. The social class conflict reached a crescendo in the mid-480s as the chief aristocratic clan, the Alcmaeonids, were targeted for their great wealth and traditional influence. Many of the most prominent Athenian statesmen and politicians had come from this family including Cleisthenes and Megacles, and eventually Alcibiades and Pericles would be among their number. They were one of the most ancient and respected houses of Athens.

They had an impactful but chequered past. The Alcmaeonids had financed the construction of the temple for the Oracle of Delphi, the holiest place in Greece and the home of the seer and priestess of Apollo. But they also were cursed. In the seventh century, a would-be tyrant of Athens named Cylon attempted to conquer the city with mercenaries borrowed from the nearby rival Megara. Cylon failed but left a major impression on the Athenians who desperately tried to avoid falling victim to any future tyrant – a process that ultimately led to the democratic reforms of the Alcmaeonid Cleisthenes. However, during the battle that defeated Cylon, the Alcmaeonids stormed the Temple of Athena and slaughtered the soldiers of Cylon while they begged for mercy.

Destroying a temple and those who plead for compassion therein was a grave offence for any Greek. Homer had illustrated this clearly to the Greeks when Achilles and Agamemnon did the same in the events leading to *The Iliad*, incurring the wrath of Apollo and curses laid upon the Greek army. The same happened to the Alcmaeonids: they were cursed by the priests of the temple and banished from Athens for a century. Upon their return, the lingering effects of this curse remained in political and social endeavours, but the deep pockets and cunning political practices of the family allowed them to regain their influence and power, if not the admiration of the Athenians.

But Marathon was to change their fortunes again. While most Athenians benefited from the liberty and prosperity that came from the Greek win at the Battle of Marathon, the Alcmaeonids had lost a calculated gamble. Prior to the battle, they had bet on the Persians to win and had apparently sent a signal to the Persians directing them to sail past Marathon and towards the unguarded city of Athens. This signal was made with shields on top of a nearby mountain, and so the entire Athenian army had a view of the treachery. This was quite typical of the Persians: they always made it known they would accept and reward traitors, and the Alcmaeonids must have sought to govern in Persian-ruled Athens.

Megacles, the leading Alcmaeonid at the time, was seen as the orchestrator of the Alcmaeonid duplicity and although he remained a very influential politician, his apparent Persian sympathies and his cursed family were a political liability. He was ostracized in 486 BCE, just one year after Hipparchus, as the lower-classes increasingly pushed back against 'the presumption of men who had risen too high'.[13]

And his ostracism set off the firestorm of strategic exiling by the lower-classes. Athens had now ostracized two aristocrats in two consecutive years, sending the clear message that all aristocrats and politicians had to carefully manage their reputation or else face judgement. Each of the leading politicians endured a referendum on their service to Athens. Even Themistocles most likely could not be as abrasive and strong-willed as he was accustomed – ostracism was too sharp of teeth. He is conspicuously unaccounted for in many sources from 489 BCE to 483 BCE, when his fortunes after Laurium skyrocketed his reputation. But this also placed him on the shortlist for ostracism and left him consistently on a political knife edge.

*   *   *

Two other men found themselves alongside him on the edge of that knife: Xanthippus and Aristides the Just. As his stock rose and the target on his back grew bigger, Themistocles capitalized on the newfound political climate by orchestrating a three-way ostracism duel between the three statesmen. Xanthippus, Aristides and Themistocles were all heroes of Athens who had served with distinction at Marathon and in the democratic assembly. But the social class conflict set the three against each other in a fashion that illustrated three major cultural currents of Athens in the 480s. And ultimately, beginning in 484 BCE, the three men would be the victims of the next three ostracisms in Athens.

Xanthippus represented the traditional aristocrats desperately trying to maintain their influence against the background of a fledgling democracy. Aristides exemplified the Spartan strain of the Greek worldview that emphasized justice, honour and a consummate commitment to the community. And Themistocles, of course, was the incendiary populist aiming to mobilize the lower-classes to take democratic control of their own destiny by overwhelming the upper-class grip on political power.

First on the docket was Xanthippus. We know little of his background except that he was a ranking member of the Alcmaeonids and likely fought at Marathon, though not as a general. However, he was not an Alcmaeonid by birth; he married into the family during the height of his career. He came to prominence, politically, just one year after Marathon when Xanthippus led the aforementioned prosecution and imprisonment of Miltiades.

Xanthippus argued persuasively and eloquently to prosecute Miltiades and it secured his position as one of the most influential Athenian statesmen. Despite his aristocratic agenda and connections, he was seen as a populist leader that had 'saved' the Athenians from the tyranny of Miltiades. In his history of Athenian democracy, Aristotle names Xanthippus as the lower-class populist struggling against Miltiades, the aristocratic champion.[14] Immediately afterward, Aristotle says that social class struggle – the *stasis* – was inherited by Themistocles and Aristides the Just.

And so how does a popular man, with strong links to both the upper- and lower-classes, become ostracized so quickly after his rise to power? The answer might lie in a set of governmental reforms in 487 BCE, two years after the political rise of Xanthippus. These reforms ostensibly limited the political power of aristocrats because the nine *archon* positions were now chosen randomly from a predetermined list created by each tribe.[15]

Historians differ on the exact intention behind this law. Perhaps it genuinely was a move by the lower-classes to ensure that the aristocrats would not stack the councils. Perhaps it was a pushback against the tyranny of past rulers like Peisistratus who had skirted accountability by installing loyal bureaucrats. Perhaps it was the result of a conflict between the generals and the politicians. Or perhaps it was Themistocles strategically eliminating younger politicians who could seize influence as successful *archons*.

But regardless of what the goal of the reforms actually was, Themistocles was able to paint a vivid picture of what it *seemed* to be. In 484 BCE, the Athenian assembly voted to hold an ostracism in two months' time, the fourth ostracism in as many years. The three leading candidates were, of course, Xanthippus, Aristides and Themistocles. And during those two months, a propaganda campaign took place between the three.

Themistocles, often the main agent of the rumour mill, spread stories of Xanthippus's aristocratic connections and a disingenuous agenda built on lying to the lower-classes in order to strengthen the upper-classes. Themistocles specifically would have pointed to the reforms of 487 BCE as a stratagem in the game of thrones played by the aristocrats, saying that Xanthippus had no real intention of diluting his upper-class power. And Xanthippus's marriage into the Alcmaeonids became a scarlet letter for him; he began to haemorrhage non-aristocratic supporters over the two months before the ostracism vote.

In the face of this threat, Xanthippus and Aristides teamed up and built an alliance focused squarely on the aristocratic interests. Aristides's position was unchanged but Xanthippus cast aside many of his populist ideologies in a bid for survival. But this also meant that the lower- and middle-classes were less interested in his continued residency in Athens. The two men tried to use the weight of their influence against the surging Themistocles.

The move backfired, as no man exemplified the aristocracy more than Aristides the Just. Themistocles was able to continue to paint Xanthippus as duplicitous and self-serving, running into the arms of the aristocrats when in need of power or refuge. The name Xanthippus carried too much weight and Xanthippus lost the ostracism of 484 BCE and was exiled. Themistocles's campaign was so brutally effective that when one surviving *ostrakon* was found, the Athenian who had voted to exile him had not just written the name Xanthippus but had even provided a commentary:

The cursed Xanthippus, son of Arriphron, has done more harm than any other politician.[16]

*   *   *

It turned out that the ostracism battle of 484 BCE was simply a warm-up for what occurred between Themistocles and Aristides in 482 BCE. It was now a year after the fierce debate over the silver of Laurium and, after a lifetime of opposition, their rivalry reached a boiling point in a backbreaking political struggle where the winner took the reins of Athens and the loser was ostracized. Laurium had changed the complexion of Athenian politics.

It is clear, now, why Aristides fought for the ostensibly populist position of redistributing the silver of Laurium. Although he packaged his argument as in line with Athenian traditions, which was true, it is more likely that he was hedging his bets and appealing to the voting base that had ostracized each of the aristocratic champions that preceded him. Aristides knew his reputation and valour alone would not save him, and actions to excite the lower-class voters would be necessary for survival. He positioned himself as 'the Just' for all social classes, and his passionate case over Laurium was meant to endear the public on his integrity and honour.

But Themistocles used those very strengths against him. In the debate over Laurium, emboldened no doubt by the exiling of Xanthippus, Themistocles began to characterize Aristides the Just in a new way: the future tyrant of Athens. The epithet 'the Just' was a built-in weapon in Themistocles's rhetoric, as he was able to weave a narrative that Aristides considered himself to be above the lowly Athenians and desired to 'save' the unenlightened by seizing power. He tightened the screws even further by pointing to the arrogance of a man who embraced a title such as 'the Just', effectively sowing dissension among the electorate until they were 'therefore vexed with those who towered above the multitude in name and reputation'.[17]

After laying this foundation, Themistocles began to spread more specific rumours that Aristides had 'done away with the public courts of justice by his determining and judging everything in private, and that, without anyone perceiving it, he had established for himself a monarchy, saving only the armed bodyguard'.[18]

One might wonder how Themistocles, by now a wealthy and upper crust aristocrat, maintained his influence with the lower classes during this time. But we must not forget that the thousands of *thetes*, the lower-class who rowed triremes, were loyal to Themistocles after the employment they found through the construction of his triremes. As it was now about a year after the vote on Laurium's silver, many of those triremes would now be at the point of completion and would need crews to be hired. With their stable employment and regular wages, they thanked Themistocles with political allegiance.

In 482 BCE, the Athenians voted to again ostracize a citizen. It had been two years since Xanthippus's departure and one year since Laurium, but the ostracism of 482 BCE can be seen, without doubt, to set the course for Athens over the next decade. The ostracism vote of 482 BCE, therefore, became what the Romans would later call a plebiscite, where the entire electorate votes on a question critical to the future of the state. No Athenian cast his *ostrakon* without a strong opinion on either the political future of Athens, the two rivals Aristides and Themistocles, or a mixture of both positions.

The two months between any vote to ostracize an Athenian and the vote to ostracize a specific Athenian must have been a storm of polemics and division, and 482 BCE was more contentious than any before it. We have no record of Aristides fighting back in any other way than his typical eloquence and public statements. He relied heavily on his Homeric reputation for justice and honour. Meanwhile, Themistocles used the propaganda campaign and the rumour mill to paint Aristides not as a Nestor-like sage, but as an Agamemnon-like tyrant.

When the final vote came, a legend is told by Plutarch of the far-reaching effects of Themistocles's marketing and image management. The story goes that an illiterate peasant from a distant region of Attica travelled to Athens to make his vote. When it came time to write his target's name on the potsherd, he realized he needed assistance and asked a nearby man, who just happened to be Aristides.

An unlettered and utterly boorish fellow handed his *ostrakon* to Aristides, and asked him to write Aristides on it. He, astonished, asked the man what possible wrong Aristides had done him. 'None whatever,' was the answer, 'I don't even know the fellow, but I am tired of hearing him everywhere called "The Just."'[19]

Without hesitation, Aristides wrote his name on the *ostrakon* and returned it to the man. He no doubt realized at this point the extent to which Themistocles had outmanoeuvred him and that the Athenians would surely vote for his ostracism. Plutarch says that Aristides then offered a prayer to the gods that Athens would never face such a crisis that would necessitate his return after his ostracism. He knew his time in Athens was over for now, and prayed, with some foreboding, that it would be over for good.

The Athenians voted to ostracize Aristides in 482 BCE. The referendum on populist democracy versus traditional aristocracy was over, with the democrats and Themistocles taking the day. The voting assembly was too deeply indoctrinated by Themistocles's machinations and whisper campaign, and exiled the most honourable man in Athens due 'to their envious dislike of his reputation in the name of fear of tyranny'.[20] Aristides the Just left Athens for parts unknown, to join Xanthippus and the other champions of conservative Greek values in the scattered refuges of city-states loyal neither to Persia, Sparta, nor Athens.

* * *

How Themistocles evaded ostracism himself is not entirely a mystery. The silver of Laurium won him great public security, but his opponents still characterized him as a demagogue and a conspiracy theorist obsessed with the distant Persian threat. But Themistocles prepared thoroughly for all political dangers, especially ostracism. He spent much of his time fostering relationships with lower-class men he had arranged to be promoted to bureaucratic councils, famously quipping, 'Never may I sit on a tribunal where my friends are to get no more advantage from me than strangers.'[21]

His hegemonic takeover of Athens was complete. He exerted all control over Athenian politics, with the social class conflict coming to a ceasefire in 481 BCE and no new ostracisms for a decade. Yet men like Themistocles always do better with a foil, however, so that they may be constantly compared and opposed to a greater foe. Populists, especially, crave the siren song of an oppressive or traditional government. With Aristides gone, Themistocles needed a new rival to oppose in order to keep his finger on the nerves of the lower-classes. Thankfully for him, a new, old rival emerged: the Persians invaded Greece again, beginning in 481 BCE.

The hero in Homer's epic poems has an expert sense of timing, always balancing action with patience. Achilles refused to fight for much of *The Iliad* which only solidified his position as the army's true leader. And when Odysseus 'smote his breast and thus rebuked his soul,'[22] he showed his self-control by waiting for the perfect timing to enact his trickery instead of murdering all the suitors the moment he first saw them.

Half of the battle is proper timing. And after all, every Homeric hero attained his greatest glory on the battlefield, and one needs a great war to fight in to gain the immortal reputation of a hero. For Themistocles, the Persian Wars were that opportunity, though that was not likely his agenda. He was concerned solely with the survival and prosperity of Athens – knowing that his strength, cunning, and foresight were the only things binding together the faint possibility of Greek, and not just Athenian, independence against the massive Persian threat. If Greece had any chance of survival, its best hope was with Athens – which now fully belonged to Themistocles.

Part II

An Amulet of Saving Virtue

Chapter 4

The Persian Invasion & the Hellenic League

In the Homeric epics, we find the term *doryktetos*. It translates as 'spear-won land' meaning that only the brute skill of military combat could conquer such land and seize it from the enemy. It drew its powerful symbolism from the spear as the crux of *arete* on the battlefield, without which no hero would earn their reputation and glory. 'Spear-won land' was never surrendered, knees were never bent. The only possible way to win the land was via the grit, struggle, and honour of the battlefield. If *doryktetos* was taken, then both sides won glory – either by defeating a valiant enemy or in the sacrifice of life for one's country.

The Persian empire found this a foreign concept. Their preferred model for conquest was diplomacy and bribery. The Persians always managed to pinpoint a likely traitor, and broadly advertised their willingness to reward and promote defectors from the nations they targeted. And behind the leadership of their new King of Kings, Xerxes I, their next target was the mainland of Greece. Xerxes had spent half a decade raising the largest fighting force in human history: up to two million men according to the ancient sources. With both a grand army and a navy double the size of the Athenian counterpart, the invading Persians had swallowed up all resistance in their path and were now beginning to cross the Hellespont and encroach into northern Greece.

But for the Greeks who gathered at the Isthmus of Corinth in the fall of 481 BCE, their homeland was *doryktetos*. It was a matter of honour and reputation that Greece never be taken by anything but military might, regardless of the size or strength of the Persian invaders. They were determined to have no traitors; if Greece fell, they would be sure to take out as many Persians as they could on the way.

* * *

To fully understand the desperation among the Greeks at the Congress at Corinth, we need to properly examine the scope of this second Persian invasion of Greece. Over the last decade since Marathon, Persia had changed mightily. Darius the Great, the architect of modern Persian prosperity and the King of Kings who had ordered the first invasion of Greece, was dead. His son, Xerxes I, now ruled and sought to eclipse his father in mightiness. Darius was an excellent king who had bound Persia together and set up the political and economic structure for their opulence, despite the origins of his kingship coming from a coup d'etat. He had pioneered many key Persian policies, including *satrapy* government organization, the construction of the Royal Road across the empire, a centralization of currency using the *daric* and the assimilation of conquered nations into his military and political leadership. And he had been further lionized in death.

It was impossible to stand outside of his shadow. Yet Xerxes was determined to succeed where his father had failed: to destroy Athens and Greece along with it. It was a remarkably single-minded vision for Xerxes: to target one single nation on the outcrop of its empire. But Xerxes saw the punishment of the Greeks as not solely a justification for his throne, but a legitimization of his lineage. Xerxes was not the original heir to the throne, as he was chosen by Darius over his brothers. Perhaps the core reason for this was he was the only one of Darius's many sons who came directly from the line of Cyrus the Great, founder of the Persian Empire. As such, he inherited the royalty of Cyrus, the pragmatism of Darius and the enormous pressure that came with both.

When he became King of Kings in 486 BCE, he ruthlessly put down a rebellion in Egypt when the Egyptians had falsely sensed vulnerability in his kingship. Two years later, Babylon suffered the same fate. Xerxes soon had an ironclad grip on the Persian empire and its vast subjugated peoples. He quickly turned his attention to punishing the Greeks who had given his father's reign such a blemish. Darius had in fact died in the midst of raising an army to invade Greece and Xerxes, now solidified in his rule, gathered his commanders to give a speech announcing his intentions:

> Ever since I came to this throne, I have taken thought how best I shall
> not fall short in this honourable place of those that went before me,
> nor gain for the Persians a lesser power than they; and my thought

persuades me, that we may win not only renown, but a land neither less nor worse, but more fertile, than that which we now possess; and not only so, but vengeance and requital withal. For this cause I have now summoned you together, that I may impart to you my purpose. It is my intent to bridge the Hellespont and lead my army through Europe to Hellas, that I may punish the Athenians for what they have done to the Persians and to my father. You saw that Darius my father was minded to make an expedition against these men. But he is dead, and it was not granted him to punish them; and I, on his and all the Persians' behalf, will never rest till I have taken and burnt Athens, for the unprovoked wrong that its people did to my father and me...

We shall make the borders of Persian territory and of the firmament of heaven to be the same; for no land that the sun beholds will lie on our borders, but I will make all to be one country, when I have passed over the whole of Europe. For, as I learn, there will then be left neither inhabited city, nor nation of men, that is able to meet us in battle, if those [Athenians] of whom I speak are once taken out of our way. Thus they that have done us wrong and they that have done us none will alike bear the yoke of slavery.[1]

Beginning in 483 BCE, Xerxes sent emissaries to demand 'earth and water'[2] from all Greek city-states – except Athens and Sparta. As the main target of the invasion, Athens would never be offered peace, but it is a mild surprise that Sparta was left out. But the Persians had good reason for this: Sparta had cast the prior Persian emissaries, sent by Darius, into a well. Athens had done the same, though less creatively, throwing another contingent into a pit for criminals. They were obviously not going to be the traitors that Persia was searching for.

But many Greek city-states did mix their earth and water with Persia's. Major players like the Thebans and the Thessalonians gave their allegiance to Xerxes, and other significant city-states like the Magnesians, Melians, and Achaeans later acquiesced. In fact, the entirety of Boeotia – an historic military power that directly bordered Athenian territory – medized, apart from Thespiae and Plataea. Macedonia, in the north of Greece, became a vassal state of the Persians. And Argos, a traditional power on the Peloponnese situated between Athens and Sparta, either played neutral or were tacitly pro-Persia – but either way benefited Xerxes.

The Persians, therefore, already controlled nearly all of Greece, from the entirety of the Ionian coast to the whole of northern Greece. Only about a quarter of modern Greece resisted and they were relegated to pockets of resistance in central Greece, the Peloponnese, and a myriad of Aegean islands that were not directly allied with Persia. The odds of survival were unfathomably low.

Those odds dip further when the vast army of Xerxes is numbered. According to Herodotus, Xerxes travelled to Sardis, the Persian provincial capital, and stayed for nearly a full year, assembling a massive army that drew from the breadth of his empire. In full, it took four years to assemble. At the time of the army's departure for Greece in 481 BCE, Herodotus numbers it at 2,641,610 men not including almost three million more members of the logistical support team: sappers, cooks, slaves, eunuchs and so forth. Never before had so many nations united under a single banner.

The Athenian poet Aeschylus paints Xerxes as 'filling his train and emptying of manhood Asia's vasty plain'[3] in order to create his multi-faceted army. The infantry alone was counted at 1.7 million from nearly fifty ethnicities. There were soldiers from Central Asia such as the Chorasmians, Sogdians, Bactrians, and Sacae. From South Asia there were Hindush, Pashtuns, Arians, Gandarians, Mycians, Paricanians and Dadicae. From the Iranian Plateau, Xerxes united his own Persians with Medes, Parthians, Cissians, and Hyrcanians. From Mesopotamia, the Assyrians and Chaldeans sent troops. Anatolia and the Caucasus Mountain region was well-represented with Cappadocians, Phrygians, Armenians, Lydians, Caspians, and colonial Thracians. Northern Africa also joined Xerxes with fighters hailing from Ethiopia and Libya, as well as marines and ships sent from Egypt. The aforementioned medized Greeks like Thebes, Macedonia, and Achaeans had already joined with Xerxes's army, and more Greek states like Thessaly would soon be conquered and forced to enlist. And this is not to mention the 80,000 cavalry that came from Persia, Cissia, the Medes, and India, with Arabian camels and Libyan chariots rounding out the ground forces.[4] Even if modern scholars shrink that number to a more realistic 200,000 soldiers, it still far outweighs any other fighting force of its day – even more than his father Darius's army that had invaded almost a decade prior.

The Persian-controlled nations from the shores of the Mediterranean Sea mostly sent ships. Given their naval empire and dominance of the Mediterranean, the Phoenician ships were the jewel of the Persian fleet and over 300 triremes from Sidon, Tyre, Byblos, and other major cities led the Persian navy. Egypt sent 200 ships packed with marines, each ship eager to impress Xerxes after he had mercilessly reconquered them five years earlier. Greek states in the Black Sea and modern Turkey sent scores of ships as well: the hundred ships from Ionia were the strongest Greek ships fighting for Xerxes. Pontus in the Black Sea sent another hundred ships. Culturally Greek regions and major political players like Caria, led by the warrior queen Artemisia, a close advisor to King Xerxes who would rise far beyond her station over the course of the Persian invasion, sent further triremes, numbering nearly a hundred. Cyprus, Cilicia, Aeolia, and Lycia sent more ships, up to a hundred each. Herodotus numbers the final naval fleet at 1207 ships. It was the largest and most powerful naval fleet ever assembled, eclipsing even that of the first Persian invasion, and would fight in the grandest naval battles the world had yet seen.

This leviathan invasion force gathered at Doriskos in Thrace in the north of Greece during the spring of 480 BCE to march and sail south, after Xerxes surveyed his force one final time. In the eastern Mediterranean, the summer is sailing season. The winds and storms were far too treacherous during the winter months, as evidenced by the sunken Persian fleet that had failed to reach Marathon a decade earlier. The Persian strategy was therefore to arrive in Greece in early spring to maximize their naval opportunities. The winter journeying to Doriskos also allowed the Persians final moments to solidify the supply chain of Xerxes's force. The Royal Road, stretching from the capital Susa in modern Iran to Sardis near the Aegean coast, allowed the quick and efficient movement of food, weapons, construction materials, and other supplies. This kept his monstrous army well stocked when coupled with the many ports on the Ionian coast. The only thing as impressive as the raw size of the invasion force was its robust and sophisticated logistical support.

* * *

After departing Sardis in early 480 BCE, Xerxes aimed his army towards Greece. Progress was slow, yet the army moved quicker than expected due to the advanced support structure and supply chains. As they moved, Xerxes relished the theatre of it all; he stopped to take in the battlefields of Troy, he met with local rulers to survey his empire, and he held lengthy strategy sessions with his generals and admirals. He also took up the habit of watching the battles from a throne overlooking the fields, rewarding or punishing his leaders based on his perception of their performance. Xerxes personally led this invasion force, as opposed to his father Darius who had not entered Greece, and he wanted the public to know this. They would adore him or fear him.

The army weaved its way up the Ionian coast until it reached its first challenge: crossing the Hellespont. This strait separates Europe and Asia and, at the port of Abydos, is about three-quarters of a mile long. Under Darius, the Persian army had mastered the crossing of straits by constructing pontoon bridges: a series of *pentekonter* ships arranged side by side over the water with wooden bridges built over them, forming a traversable path. The Persians had made this three decades earlier during Darius's invasion of Scythia, up by the Black Sea. It had been equal parts effective and intimidating, up until the moment that Miltiades betrayed the Persians and cut the tethers of the bridge,[5] forcing the Persians to return by another route and laying the foundation for the Persian hatred of Athens.

Yet Xerxes's original plan was more majestic in scope, given his reliance on the theatrical. Construction had already begun on a permanent bridge connecting Europe and Asia over the Hellespont, and each side of the bridge was coming along nicely until a storm destroyed both sides. Xerxes, always committed to the cultivation of his reputation, handled it as maturely as one would expect of the King of Kings: he executed all the engineers. He then famously ordered his men to wade into the water, whip the water for its disobedience and put tethers on the waves. As a final insult, the water was 'branded' with hot iron and publicly shamed.

Xerxes then, less humorously, ordered the construction of his own pontoon bridge. It was a marvel – constructed in astonishing time, with nearly 700 ships built from both sides of the Hellespont. The pathway had hardwood flooring and high walls so as to not scare the livestock. It took a full week of day and night crossing for his army to pass over onto a new continent. Perhaps more importantly, word of the feat travelled quickly across the Aegean and did its job of terrifying the lesser Greek city-states.

Xerxes went on to finish many wonderful construction projects, including palace complexes in Susa and Persepolis, the Gate of All Nations (which still stands today), a grand meeting hall named the Apdana and the Hall of a Hundred Columns. Yet none of these are half as famous as the vanity project that was the pontoon bridge. The Greeks would later see it as the pinnacle of hubris and a beacon of Greek superiority over the barbarians. The laureled poet Aeschylus includes a fascinating analysis of this from the perspective of Darius himself, appearing as a ghost in the play *The Persians*. The play was a celebration of Athenian ascendancy and the Greek victory over the invaders. When Xerxes's mother brings the Ghost of Darius back from the afterlife to inform him of Xerxes's invasion of Greece via the pontoon bridge, Darius gives an incisive judgment:

> But the event my son too rashly wrought
> In the blind arrogance of childish thought.
> He dreamed that he could chain, as men chain slaves,
> The holy haste of Hellespontine waves,
> God's flowing Bosphorus; another measure
> Presumed to teach its billows, at his pleasure
> Bound them in linkéd fetters hammered fast,
> Yea, made a high way, where his army passed.
> A mortal man on all the Gods that be
> He ventured war; the lordship of the sea,
> Poseidon's realm (he judged so much amiss),
> Challenged and thought to quell. And was not this
> The very madness of a mind diseased?
> Prosperity and power and wealth, which eased
> The lives of men, my long reign's rich reward,
> Is plunder now for some freebooter's sword![6]

This 'very madness of a mind diseased' continued the closer he got to Greece. Possibly Xerxes's chief logistical accomplishment was navigating the cape at Mount Athos. Jutting out from Macedonia is the three-pronged Chalkidiki peninsula, its easternmost cape the thin, long Mount Athos. The weather around this cape is infamously perilous, with stormfronts and fatal winds threatening all ships. Two ancient fleets were lost here, including those 300 ships led by Mardonius in the first invasion of Greece in 492 BCE. A Spartan fleet of 60 ships was lost during the Peloponnesian Wars in 411 BCE. Even today this cape is treacherous, accessible only by a ferry, even though it is linked to the land. The mountains are nearly untraversable and thus Persian land forces steered far clear of Chalkidiki peninsula.

Their naval fleet had less options: they could delay their invasion and wait for patches of clear weather to get their navy through piecemeal, or they could wheel the boats across on dry land. Both choices were relatively easy and logistically clever, yet Xerxes found them pedestrian. And so he chose a third option: to dig a canal. Herodotus says that this choice was 'out of pride, wishing to display his power and leave a memorial; with no trouble they could have drawn their ships across the isthmus'.[7] And quite the memorial he left; the canal is still present and visible today. At thirty metres wide, it cut through the base of the peninsula and provided a clear sailing course for two triremes at a time. The 1,200 ships were barely slowed in their passage towards Athens. It was also an example of the longevity of Xerxes's ambition to destroy Greece, given its construction had begun three years earlier and taken sizeable manpower and resources.

The earthmoving invasion force was a spectacle of human achievement and the pinnacle of power wielded by a single man. And since the Persians historically employed a meritocracy of leadership, each nation was vying to impress the king who had personally led the invasion. Moreover, scores of Greeks lined up to medize and be rewarded with money or power if they could somehow assist Xerxes's raw ambition. There were simply no categories in which the scales were not in favour of Persia, and the remaining Greeks knew this. If they had any chance, they must come together for a national *aristeia* – the climactic moment when a hero achieves such dramatic *arete* and excellence that their name is immortalized. It was either this longshot miracle or conquest: there would be no middle ground.

* * *

And so a desperate confederacy of Greek city-states gathered near Corinth to discuss their options in the face of the alarming and massive

Persian invasion. The location was deeply symbolic. The mythical hero Theseus had built a signpost at the Isthmus on his first journey to Athens, the site of his coronation. The sign had read 'Here is not Peloponnesus, but Ionia'[8] to the east, and 'Here is Peloponnesus, not Ionia'[9] to the west, symbolizing the joining of Greece's two major territories. Moreover, Corinth's Isthmian Games were part of the Olympiad cycle of games and represented one of the few times when all of Greece put aside their conflicts and differences to gather together for a greater purpose. Persia had now given them that purpose.

At the behest of Sparta, nearly 700 city-states had been invited to join this alliance of Greek states against the looming Persians. Only seventy answered the call. The rest either remained under Persian control or were keeping their options open, hoping for plausible deniability when the Persians seized the land. The rumours that sailors and merchants brought from Asia Minor were that the Persians were assembling the largest military force ever put together. Most city-states decided that even *doryktetos* was not worth it against the impossible odds. Herodotus conveys the despondency of the Greeks at Corinth: 'they who had refused tribute were sore afraid, since there were not in Hellas ships enough to do battle with their invader, and the greater part of them had no stomach for grappling with the war, but were making haste to side with the Persian.'[10]

In order to properly prepare for the Persians, the first order of business was to settle the existing disputes between the Greek city-states. Sparta took the lead at the assembly, given their mighty warriors and subsequent reputation. It was indeed Sparta, far more than Athens, that any of the other seventy city-states even considered resisting the Persians – the vaunted warriors of Sparta were the finest in the world. Sparta's hoplites trained endlessly, with the entire city-state having devoted itself to making their warriors the 'city walls' in lieu of physical defences. The Spartan virtues of sacrifice and unwavering commitment to fighting to the last man would need to be adopted by the rest of the Greeks if they were to maintain their *doryktetos*.

Themistocles led the Athenian delegation. This was his first political foray beyond the borders of Attica; his statecraft had not yet been tested on anyone other than his Athenian rivals. But at the Congress at Corinth, Themistocles would make a name not only for himself, but also for the upstart Athens and their newly minted navy, now far and away Greece's most powerful.

Under the leadership of the two Spartan kings, Leonidas and Leotychidas, the Greek council first sought to unify the seventy city-states that had been brave enough to show up. Athens and Aegina, whose conflict had served as the Athenian distraction from the Persian bogeyman before Themistocles's ascent, were immediately reconciled.

As the Congress pivoted to strategizing for the Persians, they received an update from three spies that had been previously sent to Sardis to survey the Persian military. All three spies had quickly been caught and sentenced to death. But Xerxes the Great, upon hearing the news, instead gave the spies a personal tour of the army's camp and answered all their questions about the army and its strategies. Xerxes's plan was intimidation and submission, as he remarked that 'when the Greeks hear of my power they will before the expedition surrender this peculiar freedom that they have.'[11]

This made the Congress at Corinth a sordid affair, and soon another new development changed the complexion of the assembly. This was, of all things, a religious prophecy spelling calamity and death for the Greeks, yet Themistocles quickly recognized it as an opportunity, not a curse.

This prophecy had been handed down by the Oracle of Delphi, the priestess of Apollo whose divine word was infallible and formative for all Greeks – regardless of allegiance. In fact, the Greeks at Corinth had already agreed to dedicate to her all the spoils of war, with all remaining city-states agreeing that 'they would dedicate to the god of Delphi the possessions of all Greeks who had of free will surrendered themselves to the Persians.'[12] Unsurprisingly, all major city-states had consulted her on the prospects of their own survival in the looming war.

Of all those omens, Athens and Sparta had received the most dismal news. The Spartan divination reflected their own worldview in its guileless message:

Fated it is for you, ye dwellers in wide-wayed Sparta,
Either your city must fall, that now is mighty and famous,
Wasted by Persian men or the border of fair Lacedaemon
Mourn for a king that is dead, from Heracles' line descended.
Yea, for the foe thou hast nor bulls nor lions can conquer;
Mighty he cometh as Zeus, and shall not be stayed in his coming;
One of the two will he take, and rend his quarry asunder.[13]

The choice was binary: either Sparta fell or one of their kings fell. The good news for the Spartans was that they always had a king to spare. Their government, obsessively arranged to avoid corruption by one constituency, made a complex set of checks and balances that included two kings from two separate noble families. Their rule was far from a monarchy, however, as Sparta was more probably an oligarchy run by a set of five magistrates and a senate of thirty elders. They could spare a king, but not a city.

The terms of this prophecy dominated the Congress at Corinth. Sparta was the heartbeat of Greece and their hoplites the only true hope for survival. Nearly every Greek, apart from Themistocles, believed that the spears and shields of Sparta's peers would be the mettle of the allied resistance. Leonidas, the Spartan king from the Agiad tribe, took this message quite personally and believed that he was – or at least would make sure to be – the king who was slain in lieu of Sparta herself. Leonidas further wanted to make this prophecy the cornerstone of the Greek resistance, yet he also 'desired that the Spartans alone should have the glory'.[14] His passion for this empowered him to demand full leadership over the allied Greek land forces.

That Leonidas would have such a position might have been assumed given the status of Sparta in the mainland of Greece, but another Greek ruler had a different idea. The tyrant Gelon ruled Syracuse and other cities in Sicily of modern-day Italy. Although this was quite some distance from Greece, the southern coasts of Italy were later called 'Magna Graecia' by the Romans as it was colonized by Greek expatriates from the eighth century BCE. These Greeks had a vast amount of resources and influences and wielded a substantial army and naval fleet; Gelon had amassed more political and military power than any single individual in the diasporic Greek world. Herodotus points out that he '[surpassed] by far any power in Hellas.'[15]

The Athenians had fervently recruited Gelon to their alliance, sending envoys to Syracuse to entice him. Gelon offered an ambitiously large fighting force to fight the Persians: nearly 30,000 men and 200 triremes. It would be a massive injection of much-needed manpower and ships against the endless waves of Persia's troops. Yet Gelon's leadership claim came with a catch: he would only supply the fighters if he was installed as the allied Greek's land and naval commander.

This was too much for both Sparta and Athens, who saw this as yet another outsider attempting to seize control of the Greek peninsula. Gelon's offer was rejected on this basis and not even supplies were given by the Sicilians. Gelon, though, exhibited some shrewd politicking by appeasing both sides in the aftermath. He donated substantial funds to the Oracle of Delphi, in an attempt to show respect to his fellow Greeks in their moment of need. Nevertheless, he kept lines open with Persia and prepared a series of gifts and tributes to Xerxes to be delivered after the Persians took Greece. Yet it was probably for the best that the Greeks refused Gelon. Within a few months, the Greeks of Magna Graecia were attacked by a confederacy of Carthaginians and Phoenicians, almost certainly in an attempt by Xerxes to subdue Greece on two fronts and divide their forces. The Sicilians were quickly preoccupied with the ensuing war. This war, eventually won by the Sicilians and leading to the priming of Carthaginian tension with Rome, took Gelon out of Greek affairs permanently.

With Gelon out, the military command was given to Leonidas of Sparta. Leonidas was relatively untested since he was a younger son who had never been expected to ascend to the throne. And, unlike his fellow monarch Leotychidas, he had not served as a king or general in the first Persian invasion, even though Sparta had never fought the Persians. Leonidas had a rare populist flair for a Spartan king; he had graduated from the *agoge,* the gruelling 'upbringing' of Spartan soldiers. Sparta was always in position to lead the allied Greek military and Leonidas was the beacon of resilience necessary to inspire the deep costs/heavy losses that would be incurred in fighting the Persians

* * *

As the Congress at Corinth turned to appointing the naval commander, the Oracle of Delphi's prophecies rose again to the top. Sparta was not the only city-state to receive the ruinous omens. Athens' divinations were similarly disquieting, although in their case there were actually two prophecies. The Oracle's first words were unambiguous:

Wretches, why tarry thus? Nay, flee from your houses and city,
Flee to the ends of the earth from the circle embattled of Athens![16]

The Athenian envoys who had first heard this message from the Oracle herself interpreted it and responded to it as one might expect: with panic and anxiety. The clear takeaway from her words was the destruction of Athens. The Oracle's advice was to run from Athens and leave it to burn at the hands of the Persians. Those Athenians most panic-stricken would soon take this as a call to evacuate Athens and migrate to parts unknown, beyond Persian reach. Sicily, North Africa, and beyond were offered as future settlements of the Athenian expatriates. To the Greeks, this clear word of the divine was a death sentence that simply could not be avoided.

Yet when some Athenians asked for a clarifying word, the Oracle of Delphi offered some obfuscated and veiled hope:

Pallas has not been able to soften the lord of Olympus,
Though she has often prayed him, and urged him with excellent
  counsel.
Yet once more I address thee in words than adamant firmer.
When the foe shall have taken whatever the limit of Cecrops
Holds within it, and all which divine Cithaeron, shelters,
Then far-seeing Zeus grants this to the prayers of Athena;
Safe shall the wooden wall continue for thee and thy children.
Wait not the tramp of the horse, nor the footmen mightily moving
Over the land, but turn your back to the foe, and retire ye.
Yet shall a day arrive when ye shall meet him in battle.
Holy Salamis, thou shalt destroy the offspring of women,
When men scatter the seed, or when they gather the harvest.[17]

These words caused a firestorm in Athens, especially in the context of the previous prophecy that promised the destruction of Athens. Did this mean Athens would truly fall? Would all of Greece be conquered? How would the island of Salamis, near Athens' port of Piraeus, destroy the offspring of women? Did that mean that the Persians would be turned back at Salamis? What safety was offered by the 'wooden wall'? How was it that the whole land of Cecrops, the first Athenian king, could fall yet Zeus would preserve a 'wooden wall' alone? And most critically, what exactly were these 'wooden walls'? The fate of Greece depended on these answers.

The precise definition of the 'wooden wall' quickly became the focal point of the discussion involving the independent Greeks leading up to the Congress at Corinth. Many believed the prophecy referred to the walls around the Acropolis in Athens, the fortress temple to Athena that was on a large hill and served as a refuge when the city was in danger. This camp believed these defences would never fail the Athenians who fought to the bitter end while the rest of the city burned – thus reconciling the two prophecies.

Still more Greeks interpreted the wooden walls as the shield wall of the *phalanx* repelling the Persians out of Greece. This was sensible given the *phalanx*'s success at Marathon in 490 BCE and the subsequent commitment to hoplite heavy infantry across Greece, but the Athenians had already dedicated abundant resources towards their navy, not their army. And so, while the Athenian army was still relatively strong, nobody seriously believed that the outcome of Marathon would happen again as a result of Athenian shields. The Spartans had a better chance of such a victory but the words of the Oracle of Delphi were clear that it was in Athens – not Sparta – that Zeus would preserve some hope of Greek survival.

It was at the height of this debate in Corinth that the historian Herodotus finally introduced Themistocles into the narrative of the Persian Wars. His entry into international politics was right up his alley, too, as the Congress at Corinth was essentially a democratic affair that was subject to the rhetoric of its speakers. Themistocles rightly saw that those who vaulted themselves to importance at this assembly would shape the future of Greece, should Greece survive. And so he positioned himself to persuade the Congress of his Athens-centric vision; the ambiguity of the 'wooden wall' prophecy provided the perfect opportunity.

Themistocles offered the assembly a different interpretation of what the wooden walls were. Focusing his attention on the final two lines about 'Holy Salamis', Themistocles emphasized the precise label the Oracle had given to the Athenian island as 'holy' or 'divine', but not as 'cruel' or 'accursed'. Themistocles contended that this meant that Salamis was the site of the final Greek stand, where they would destroy the Persian invaders in either the spring, when farmers 'scatter the seed', or the fall, when farmers 'gather the harvest'. This interpretation conspicuously ruled out the winter.

The location and timing were essential to Themistocles's divining of the Oracle's words. Salamis was an island so close to Athens that it was visible from the Acropolis on a clear day. The strait between Salamis and the port of Piraeus provided a logistical and strategic advantage for a naval battle, something that had been moderately tested during the war between Athens and Aegina. Moreover, the fall or spring timing meant that a winter conflict, when ships could not effectively sail in the Aegean and no naval battles could be fought, was off the table.

Themistocles's argument was clear. The Oracle of Delphi's words were a call to make the 'wooden wall', a fleet of triremes so large it swallowed up the strait of Salamis and the Persians along with it. It was this wooden wall that would save Greece, and it was this wooden wall that would come from Athens. Themistocles perceived the prophecy as a suitable moment for his grand Athenian strategy and his new armada, and so encouraged the Greeks at Corinth to 'make ready to fight by sea'[18] and form the wooden wall as a naval *phalanx* of sorts. Themistocles therefore pushed for a naval approach primarily, to strike fast and furious against the Persian armada which outnumbered the Greeks to a far lesser extent than on the land. He was unable to convince the Congress or even the Athenians of this strategy, although he certainly was able to improve their naval focus by convincing a considerable number of them of his position.

Thus, with the Greek land forces led by Leonidas and the Spartans, the Greeks needed to appoint a naval commander. Although it would have been natural to slide Themistocles into such a role, something the members of the Congress likely assumed would happen, he declined to even pursue it. In a clever show of deference, Themistocles yielded naval admiralty to the Spartan Eurybiades. This was an interesting move, in no small part due to the relative absence of a Spartan navy up until this point in history. Although it was not unheard of for Spartans to row on triremes or command ships, they usually only did so as mercenaries hired due to their renowned discipline and military virtue – not their seamanship. The standing army of Sparta had no triremes, and so Eurybiades would sail in Athenian and other Greek ships.

The decision to accede to this leadership model was not entirely Themistocles's. He had planned on assuming the role himself, of course. When a popular but strategically short-sighted rival named Epicydes had run for *strategos* in Athens, Themistocles had paid him off with silver to withdraw his candidacy. Leading the Athenians and Greeks against the

Persians was the singular goal of Themistocles and surrendering it ran against the grain of his character. Had he pushed for the post, a different type of Greek rebellion would have likely occurred, this time against the Athenians. The other city-states of the Congress at Corinth were said to believe that 'if the [Spartan Eurybiades] were not their leader they would rather make an end of the fleet that was preparing than be led by the Athenians.'[19] Eurybiades was therefore a default choice selected to limit Athenian influence and, although he was a worthy commander, his actual naval admiralty was now predetermined to be seen through a political lens. He would be second-guessed in his decisions and his successes would likely be attributed to the Athenian naval fleet, as the raw number of Athenian ships would give Themistocles ample opportunity to publicize Athens' contributions to the war effort. Themistocles nonetheless knew that Athens needed a seat in Greek war room, and he took on a role as subordinate to Eurybiades in the allied navy. He did, of course, maintain hegemony over the Athenian triremes.

Themistocles may not have taken the Greek world by storm at the Congress at Corinth, but he did make substantial inroads into the leadership of the Greek resistance. His reputation for guile and ambition worked both for and against him when creating the command structure. If Themistocles wanted clear-cut Athenian leadership over other Greek city-states, he would need to work within the established hierarchy to make a name for himself and for Athenian supremacy. That is why his appointment to lead the first major stand of the Persian invasion was so important.

*   *   *

Delegates from Thessaly beseeched the Congress to meet the Persians in combat at a narrow pass near Mount Olympus named the Vale of Tempe. The Thessalonians had not yet joined the Persians, but they made it clear that if the Greeks did not send significant military support that they would have no choice but to medize. Although this was a thinly veiled threat by Thessaly, the allied Greeks nevertheless saw the value in a stand at Tempe. The Vale of Tempe was on the major thoroughfare connecting northern and southern Greece, meaning the Persians were sure to travel through it at a predictable time. Moreover, it was infamously narrow – only twenty-five metres wide at some points – and easily accessible by sea. This would allow the Athenian navy to ferry a hoplite army there with enough time to survey and fortify the area. As the icing on the cake, the Vale of Tempe was renowned as a site favoured by Apollo and his Muses. In short, it was the perfect strategic setting and cultural symbol from which to resist the Persians.

This emboldened Themistocles who turned it into an opportunity for glory. He pushed the Congress to send a 10,000-man army to swiftly barricade the Vale of Tempe, and he personally commanded the force alongside a Spartan general named Euaenetus. To the independent Greeks, this was the moment of truth. It would be either their *aristeia* and the first steps to victory, or the beginning of the massacre of their culture. The pressure must have been overwhelming as the Athenian triremes carried the hoplites off to the Vale of Tempe to make the final, heroic stand for their nation. Themistocles would either win over the entirety of Greece with his gallantry and strength or die vainglorious.

But, unfortunately for both Greeks and Persians, the desperate last stand never materialized. When the Greek army set up camp, they were approached by messengers from the Macedonian king, Alexander I, an ancestor of none other than Alexander the Great. He was a known Hellenophile who had constantly pursued close relationships with influential Greek city-states and Athens in particular. Because of this passion, and despite Macedonia's position under Xerxes's thumb, Alexander I obliged the Greeks by advising them of the existence of a local path around the Vale of Tempe of which the Persians already knew. This suddenly made Tempe a useless strategic location and made the allied Greek army hopelessly vulnerable given their numerical disadvantage. Themistocles and Euaenetus had no choice but to withdraw to the south of Greece, dashing the morale and hope of many Greeks.

This led directly to the crumbling of the alliances made at the Congress at Corinth. With the Persian army intact and unimpeded, the allied Greek resistance, dubbed the Hellenic League by historians, dwindled to just thirty city-states as major players like Thebes and Thessaly joined the Persians after failure of Tempe. Crete opted to remain neutral and the Sicilians sailed back west to fight a different war. The paltry remnant of independent Greek city-states needed to formulate a war plan to repel the Persians. The Congress regathered in the spring of 480 BCE, a shadow of its former self, but with a more pressing purpose. After the disaster of Tempe, the Persians had crossed the Hellespont and began taking Greek territory piece by painful piece.

*   *   *

An earlier account in Herodotus's *Histories* tells us of the tyrant Anaxagoras who sailed to the mainland of Greece to recruit help in his fledgling Ionian Revolt. After failing to persuade the Spartan king, he succeeded in the Athenian voting assembly. Herodotus credits this to the flat reality that, for the right type of man, 'it is easier to persuade many than one.'[20] Themistocles appears to have been cut from the same cloth because he convinced the Hellenic League to, if not fully believe him, at least commit both to increasing their naval focus and to challenging Xerxes on the sea. This was a remarkable development; the Persians had essentially never been confronted in naval combat on a large scale.

With Spartan leadership of the Hellenic League, it was impossible to have a purely naval campaign, but Themistocles entreated the other Greeks to make a new plan. Despite not having any formal leadership in the Hellenic League, Themistocles proposed an audacious plan: a two-pronged, simultaneous stand on the land and on the sea.

He offered a new site for the land battle: another mountain pass named Thermopylae. The pass was a rocky coast situated between untraversable mountains and cruel rocky waters, and it was so named the 'Hot Gates' in Greek after the sulphur springs abundant in the area that were the mythological entrance to Hades. Thermopylae was meant to be what Tempe never became: the final stand of the Greek hoplites. The Persians absolutely had to travel through Thermopylae and their massive numbers would be bottlenecked in the narrows of the pass. This choice of location, with its rocky soil and small spaces, ensured the elimination of the Persian cavalry from the battle. It was, however, narrow enough for the shield wall of a Spartan *phalanx* to completely close it off and guarantee a lengthy delay for the Persians, even if they won. Leonidas famously led a fighting contingent of 300 *Spartiates* –

full Spartan hoplites – alongside several thousand slaves, other Spartan-controlled city-states as well as Thespians, and Tegeans. In sum, about 6,000 Greek warriors fortified the pass to be held against the Persians who outnumbered them by at least twentyfold.

Tempe had afforded Themistocles and the Athenians new prominence by reminding the Hellenic League of their mortality – something that enough members of the Congress valued more than the prospect of an Athenian-ruled Greece. Themistocles's counsel for a primarily naval strategy had gained enough traction to make the second part of Thermopylae's defence be on the waters. At Artemisium on the northern shore of Euboea, the long island directly east of Thermopylae and north of Attica, the Greeks would make a naval assault timed simultaneously with the defence of Thermopylae.

If even one of these two failed, it would spell catastrophe for Attica and Athens since the Persians would have a clear shot at getting their long-delayed vengeance. The Spartans and the rest of the Hellenic League would, if Thermopylae fell, regroup at Corinth to defend its Isthmus and seal off the Peloponnesian Peninsula. Defending the Isthmus was to become the cornerstone of the Greek strategy, but it would mean forsaking all territory to the north of Corinth which included Attica. While that plan could work for the rest of the Hellenic League, Athens and its citizens would surely be destroyed at Xerxes's leisure.

The ancient historians like Plutarch, Herodotus, and Cornelius Nepos skim over Themistocles's speech to the other Greek states at this spring Congress, but it might just be the most important speech he ever gave. The Spartans balked at the idea of leaving the Peloponnesian Peninsula again after the Tempe fiasco, having thrown all their efforts into constructing a wall across the Isthmus of Corinth to impede the Persians. Themistocles had the unenviable task of overturning the stubborn Spartan willpower and their influence on the other Greek city-states. We have no record of his words to the Congress in 480 BCE, but they were apparently penetrating. The only confirmed details are his commitment to send two hundred triremes to Artemisium, in a display of Athenian generosity towards the war effort. Relying on the rhetorical skills sharpened in the voting assemblies of Athens, Themistocles had a relatively easy time inspiring the non-Athenians to agree to his battle plans. The question of whether

Themistocles could lead the Greeks with the same perspicacity that he had led the Athenians was now clearly answered.

As such, Themistocles and the Athenian navy at Artemisium had to steer a course narrower than Thermopylae or Tempe. They needed to fight well enough to defeat – or at least delay – the Persians in order to save their own city-state when their Greek comrades may have been willing to sacrifice it. And they needed to also distinguish themselves in that effort from a subordinate position under Eurybiades the Spartan. Despite the hopelessness of the situation, and the desire of many Athenians to abandon the Hellenic League and return to defend Athens, Themistocles had laid an effective foundation by persuading the Athenians of the spoils of war if they were to find victory. He didn't sell them on the beauty of liberty or democracy, instead he promised them that 'if they would show themselves brave men in the war, he would induce the Hellenes to yield a willing obedience to them thereafter.'[21] Remember that for Themistocles, it was always a virtue to work the system to his advantage. He was willing to play along with the Hellenic League's terms as long as he could subvert their goals by laying the foundation for Athenian supremacy in the aftermath of the war. This vision was palpable enough to soothe the Athenian navy and convince them to make their stand at Artemisium and not return to defend Athens.

If Xerxes was annoyed with the 'peculiar freedom'[22] that motivated the independent Greeks, he clearly still did not understand that freedom's unique manifestation in the Athenian worldview. Themistocles's cleverness in interpreting the Oracle's 'wooden wall' had effectively prepared the Athenians to be ready for war both for their survival and for their ascendancy. Greece, after all, was *doryktetos*. It was only earned by the spear. Though perhaps now, Themistocles and the Athenians might add that it would also only be won, or lost, by the trireme.

Chapter 5

Artemisium: The Cornerstone of Democracy

There was no shortage of Greek heroism at Thermopylae, but it still ended with Leonidas's head on a pike. The endless waves of Persian soldiers eventually broke the Spartan *phalanx* after three days. By the end, the allied Greek troops had been whittled down to just the 300 Spartiates and a few hundred more Thespians, free Thebans, and slaves. Before his own death in battle, Leonidas had sent the rest away, hoping to send a message through the Spartans' glory-filled sacrifice. He no doubt also wished to see the Oracle of Delphi's double-edged prophecy fulfilled by offering his own life to save Sparta:

Mourn for a king that is dead, from Heracles' line descended.[1]

The fiercest fighting had taken place over the body of Leonidas, given the Greek custom of giving dead heroes an honourable burial. Xerxes, however, had grown to despise Leonidas and demanded no such honour be given to the Spartan king. For the King of Kings, Leonidas represented that Greek 'peculiar freedom' and spirit of resistance that had slowed his long-awaited revenge too many times. Perhaps this was why, on three occasions during the battle, Xerxes had so panicked that he jumped up from his throne in fear.

Consequently, as Xerxes surveyed the field after the battle, he ordered Leonidas's body to be decapitated and crucified. It was a far cry from the typical Persian treatment of valiant soldiers. Cyrus's empire would have showered Leonidas and the Spartans with tribute and given the Spartans the time and space necessary to bury him with full honours. But Xerxes's solitary passion to see a burning Athens had consumed him by this point. The cost was too high for the Persians to allow any Greek momentum whatsoever.

One Persian tradition proved fruitful at Thermopylae, however, as they succeeded in finding a traitor. A local Greek shepherd named Ephialtes

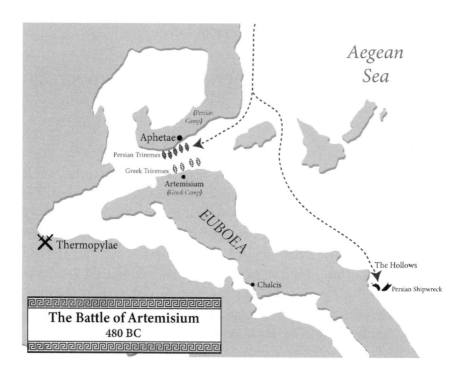

The Battle of Artemisium
480 BC

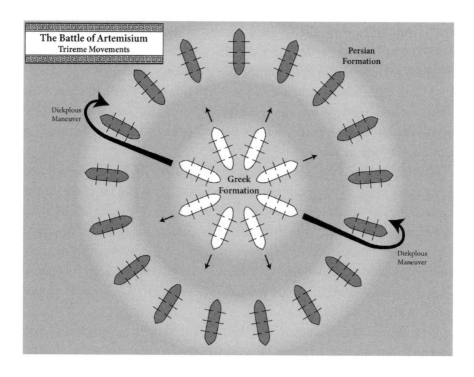

The Battle of Artemisium
Trireme Movements

had shown the Persians a path that allowed the Immortals, the strongest Persian soldiers, to outflank the Spartan hoplites. Ephialtes joined the swelling ranks of Greeks who fell for the Persian propaganda about rewarding those who willingly medized, and it cost Greece not only the battle but also the time necessary for preparing for larger stands at the Isthmus of Corinth or at Athens. This message of well-rewarded collaboration was clearly sent across the dwindling Greek independent city-states, and more would soon seek to help the Persians.

For now, though, it seems that Athens was not the only city-state that saw its politicians end up like the ruined triremes of Themistocles's youth. Just like Hector's noble but ill-fated final stand against Achilles, the moral victory of Thermopylae was not enough to overcome the loss of an inspiring and unifying military commander. Leonidas's fate, a flash of glory quickly usurped by indignity at Persian hands, was to be the fate of all the Hellenic League's leaders if Artemisium was unsuccessful.

* * *

Although the sailors at Artemisium would not find out about the loss at Thermopylae until after their own battle, the defeat should have spelled doom for Athens and its people. Even if Artemisium was a success, there was no way to stop the land army as the Greek forces had retreated to the Isthmus of Corinth. But Themistocles, by virtue of his impressive discernment, had counted on Thermopylae being little more than a postponement of the Persian advance. He prepared for this by laying an intricate groundwork across Greece and within Athens especially. The first stage was built on persuading the Hellenic League of a wrinkle in the battle plan, allowing the Greeks to fight hard at Thermopylae but not rely on it alone to save Athens. His grand strategy was bold and unsophisticated: he wanted to evacuate Athens.

This alleviated the need for a victory at Thermopylae by borrowing time for the evacuation of the citizens and their travel to two locations: Troezen and Salamis. Troezen made sense as it was located on the Peloponnesian Peninsula safely within the boundaries of the Greeks' remaining free lands. The women and children of Athens were therefore sent to Troezen as it was a far more secure option than Salamis. The Troezenians were handsomely rewarded with gold for their troubles and accepted the refugees with open arms.

The island of Salamis was only ten miles from Athens and was partially visible from the temple complex at the Acropolis. The cities on the island had tenuous diplomatic links with Athens and had allied themselves with historical Athenian rivals such as Aegina and Megara. Through the establishment of democracy in Athens, however, Salamis had been an Athenian subject for a couple of generations as they increasingly flexed their imperial muscles. Given its proximity to Athens, it was not a location safe from the Persians despite being an island. The distance from the mainland to the island was only one nautical mile, an easy distance to ferry plenty of Persian soldiers. As such, Themistocles ordered 'the older men and all Athenian property'[2] to Salamis. All capable fighting men would already be fighting or rowing with the Hellenic League, and so only a small contingent of elderly hoplites and priests remained at the Acropolis to fortify Athens. That only a few remained at the Acropolis showed that the 'wooden wall' had now truly become the triremes off Salamis.

Convincing the Athenians to abandon their city was no small feat, and they hardly went along with it simply because Themistocles recommended it. The voting assembly had denied him the evacuation plan already. The fashion in which Themistocles induced the evacuation of Athens presents a distillation of his moral and political philosophy. Firstly, Themistocles played on an old standby, the fundamentally Greek passion for manipulating religion. Plutarch characterizes him as 'a theatrical manager would for a tragedy'[3] when he supplicates the Athenians for a sign from heaven. Day after day, Themistocles publicly asked the gods for a clear sign that his evacuation plan had divine approval.

At the Temple of Athena atop the Acropolis, the priests kept a snake for soothsaying and rituals. The snake was an extension of Athena herself, and it was carefully watched as a divining rod representing Athens' position with the gods. When that serpent mysteriously disappeared one morning, its offerings left behind untouched, Themistocles made sure that a publicity campaign quickly proclaimed that the serpent had abandoned Athens because Athena had abandoned Athens. Men across Attica whispered about how the reports of the missing snake dovetailed with the Oracle of Delphi's prophecy about a burned and ruined Athens. These same men pointed to a solitary solution: voting in favour of Themistocles's evacuation plan. It was indeed a miracle that Themistocles was so fortuitously prepared for this unanticipated event.

Further, Themistocles's messengers made sure the citizens of Athens were conditioned to believe that the 'wooden wall' was, indeed, a wall of Athenian triremes at 'divine Salamis', and not 'cruel or dreadful' Salamis.[4] If Salamis was, as the Oracle had said, divine then that was clearly where Athena was calling her people, and she had removed her serpent from her temple in order to convince the Athenians to leave the city. The public relations push worked and Themistocles, using a middleman, proposed the evacuation plan again in the Athenian voting assembly where it passed overwhelmingly.

It also included substantial funding, from a conspicuously unnamed source, for the hire of new rowers for a few dozen new and unmanned triremes. Paying for all these new rowers was no small feat, and the highest political council, the *areopagus*, had to pass a special wartime budget to man the new triremes. One ancient historian name Cleidemus, however, provides a more colourful account of how Themistocles procured these essential funds. In this version, the golden Gorgon head from the statue of Athena in the temple mysteriously disappeared during the early phases of the city's evacuation. Normally, this could be attributed to standard looting during a disaster, but the Gorgon head was famously gifted to Athena by Theseus, the greatest defender of Athens. Its theft was a worse omen than anything the Oracle might say. Themistocles, suddenly finding a deep faith and piety in the gods, led a search for the Gorgon head. After several trips to local aristocratic houses and political council treasuries, he miraculously found the Gorgon head as well as complete funding for the new rowers.

Interestingly, there may be historical evidence of Themistocles's announcement of this evacuation plan to the residents of Athens. A monument engraved with the formal orders of the Athenian voting assembly called the 'Troezen Decree' chronicles Themistocles's instructions regarding the evacuation and arranging reinforcements to Artemisium.

And the 200 triremes will be manned by order of the Council of 500 and the *strategos*, who after making sacrifices to almighty Zeus, Athena Nike, and Poseidon the Securer and after manning their triremes, will send 100 of the triremes to Artemisium in Euboea to aid in the fight against the enemy. The other 100 triremes will remain at Salamis and in Attica to protect the land.[5]

The historicity of this inscription is doubtful at best, with many scholars saying it is a later forgery as part of a nationalistic campaign to make Classical Athenian leaders look better than they were. If this is true, then it would have made Themistocles proud to see his style of political machinations continue into the later generations. The Troezen Decree is deeply Athenian in its ethos regardless of its veracity.

Themistocles's religious commentaries about the wooden wall and 'Divine Salamis' quickly became the prevailing theology. As the Athenians departed the city one final time, the sight of an empty Athens, once so illustrious and proud, provoked 'pity in some, and in others astonishment at the hardihood of the step; for they were sending off their families in one direction, while they themselves, unmoved by the lamentations and tears and embraces of their loved ones, were crossing over to the island where the enemy was to be fought'.[6] It was increasingly clear to the Athenians and to the Greeks that the Isthmus of Corinth would not be the final stand – Divine Salamis would.

The Congress at Corinth ended its final meeting in the spring of 480 BCE but the battles at Thermopylae and Artemisium didn't occur until early September of that year. This gave Themistocles and the Athenians more than enough time to make the proper preparations and relocations. Within a few weeks of the formal start of Persian-Greek fighting, the city of Athens was abandoned, along with its people, property and luxuries – but not its spirit. The evacuation of Athens also fulfilled its diplomatic purposes as a way to fill the rowers' seats on the new triremes, and therefore show the Spartans that it was profitable to travel past the Isthmus one last time to Thermopylae. Had Athens not committed their full arsenal and fleet to Artemisium, the Spartans may have remained at the Isthmus and not seen the sacrifices of Leonidas and the 300.

Remarkably, all of this was envisioned and realized before the fighting at Thermopylae or Artemisium had even began. This Themistoclean prescience allowed Athenian strategies to become truly compatible with the twin battles at Thermopylae and Artemisium. It also gave the Spartans time to properly fortify the Isthmus of Corinth and construct a wall across it, in anticipation of what was indeed to be the final stand of Greece.

*   *   *

Themistocles had yet one more insurance policy to claim before the fighting at Artemisium began. He knew that to bolster Athens' dim hope of survival, they would need all the help they could get. He also knew that the Greeks rallied around heroic figures, men of great *arete* who took charge of their own destiny with overwhelming skill. The problem was that Themistocles had done his best to remove those men from Athens during his political ascent. They had been obstacles he had removed in pursuit of his destiny. But the Troezen Decree ended with a declaration of a dramatic policy that had not yet been tested in Athens: Themistocles ordered the recalling of any and all ostracized Athenians.

> And so that all Athenians may unite in the resistance against the Persian invaders, all ostracized Athenians are to journey to Salamis and remain there until the People make a decision about their future. All of those exiles who have had their civic rights stripped will now have them restored.[7]

And yes, this included his vaunted rivals Xanthippus and Aristides the Just. Moreover, his old nemesis Aristides was immediately given a considerable military command and a seat on the Hellenic war council. This was an astonishing reversal that demonstrated the desperation of both Themistocles and Athens. The move was of course aimed at strengthening the Athenian ranks with a handful of experienced, charismatic leaders who could quickly step into commanding roles. Themistocles knew that the two virtuous men would 'devote their best powers to the service of Hellas along with the other citizens'.[8] Both Xanthippus and Aristides would go on to lead the same Athenians who voted to ostracize them into battle – and they became key heroes of the Second Persian Invasion.

But the motivation to recall Aristides back to Athens was a bit different than for the other exiles. There were swirling rumours that Aristides had been considering medising. In his three years outside Athens, Aristides had apparently travelled Greece advising fledgling democracies, mediating aristocratic disputes, and cultivating his reputation for excellence in judgement. There was no greater target for Xerxes in his relentless pursuit to colonize Greece than Greek expatriates. The Persian rumour infiltrated Athenian courts quickly and the voting assembly moved just as rapidly to help Themistocles reclaim Aristides to Athens, 'lest he attach himself to the enemy's cause, and corrupt and pervert many of his fellow-citizens to the side of the Barbarian'.[9]

The former exiles spent little time in Athens as their primary task was to first lead the evacuation to Salamis. With Themistocles already well on his way to Artemisium, the storied reunion between Aristides and Themistocles would have to wait. The evacuation was swift and effective, especially since the women and children were already safe in Troezen. Although Athens was now empty and the Athenians enthusiastically committed to Themistocles's vision, there was no shortage of melancholy over leaving the city.

One memorable story illuminates the Athenian experience of giving over their home to Persian destruction. Xanthippus had brought his dog back with him from his exile and the two were famously close. A shining example of 'man's best friend', not even this dog's enviable political connections could save him from the same unfortunate destiny of the rest of the domestic animals of Athens: abandonment along with the city. The ships for Troezen and Salamis simply had no room for all creatures great and small. But Xanthippus's dog, upon seeing his master depart by boat to Salamis, jumped into the sea and swam behind the boat all the way to the island. The dog sadly succumbed to exhaustion seconds after reaching land but the memorial Xanthippus constructed on Salamis for him, the 'Dog's Mound', was still there in Herodotus's day.[10]

Athens was empty, the triremes were at Artemisium, the exiles recalled and the Persians were en route. All the chess pieces were in place to confront Persia. Themistocles's ability to take extreme measures, like the evacuation, and to then lay down personal rivalries and his own hubris when the moment demanded it shows his unique acumen in constantly advancing his cause and never becoming complacent. Like the Homeric heroes, Themistocles's abundant talents were a gift from the gods –

evidenced by his newfound piety – yet he was still without serious testing in combat as a commander. Artemisium would be that opportunity, and he would shine, but it was the groundwork he laid between the Congress at Corinth and the actual fighting that set up his future prosperity. The recalling of his rivals thrust him into new territory for a Greek hero. One can hardly imagine Agamemnon or Achilles doing the same. Themistocles was never afraid of venturing into unfamiliar territory and taking the extreme approach. But whether the Themistoclean leadership style could transfer to military success against Xerxes in open combat, and whether Themistocles could maintain his influence over the Hellenic League in the aftermath of Artemisium, would soon be decided.

* * *

The sailing misadventures of the Persians continued when another 400 ships were destroyed in the late summer of 480 BCE when they hit a storm sailing off the Magnesian coast. A third of the Persian navy was now at the bottom of the Aegean. This might seem a great boon to the Greeks, but in reality the Persian fleet had lost about a hundred more ships than the entirety of the Greek fleet itself, including the Athenian triremes. This was an extreme occurrence but this was always doomed to happen, given the massive size of the Persian navy. The ports around Greece were simply too small to accommodate all of the ships and this left dozens or hundreds of them outside the protected harbours. These Persian ships, anchored away from these secure waters, were continually exposed to the merciless winds and storms of the Aegean. Despite their phenomenal logistical planning and leadership, the sheer scope of the Persian military was causing it to become unwieldy as they entered further into Greek territory.

On their journey southward, along the Greek coast, the Persian fleet knew they would meet Greek resistance somewhere around Euboea. The Persian captains were careful along these treacherous shorelines, often bribing local fisherman to navigate their ships. These local Greeks were attempting to take advantage of traditional Persian hospitality towards medizers, yet they were often murdered when ships were damaged or when the Persians became sceptical of their unorthodox routes.

The Greek navy had, meanwhile, set up camp at Artemisium on the northern shore of Euboea. The island of Euboea had a rich history in Greece. Inhabitants of their main cities, Chalcis and Eretria, were found in the Catalogue of Ships as among those Greeks who sailed to win back Helen of Troy in *The Iliad*. Agamemnon's fleet had actually departed from a port on the southern part of the island, after he murdered his own daughter as a sacrifice to Artemis. Chalcis had sent twenty ships to Artemisium yet the Eretrians had sent none, although it was not due to a lack of patriotism. Eretria had been the only other city-state to assist Athens during the Ionian Revolt in the 490s and they had participated in the burning of Sardis. The Persians, on their way to the Battle of Marathon, had retaliated by destroying Eretria and exiling its people to Mesopotamia in the heart of their empire. Athens would have faced a similar fate had their hoplites not been victorious on Marathon's beach.

Artemisium was a brilliant strategic location. After the Persians finished the challenge of sailing south along the Magnesian coast, their naval route would face a fork at the northernmost point of Euboea. The Persians had three options there: go east around the island and bypass the Greeks, go west around the island and meet them in narrow channels or split their ships in some variety and do both. Going around the island was the most difficult route with the autumn storms, but the sheltered straits of Euboea would also guarantee a confrontation with the Greeks who could strategize accordingly. The Persians opted therefore to use the divided approach and send 200 ships east around the island and engage the Greeks in the straits between Thermopylae and Euboea, perhaps in an attempt to outflank the Greek army at Thermopylae. This contingent of ships was to outmanoeuvre the Greek navy by looping around the island of Euboea and attacking either from behind or, if necessary, cutting past the Greeks entirely to lend support at Thermopylae. Either way, it was a risky strategy. The Persians knew they had manpower and ships aplenty, but the one thing they could not waste was time: the winter was quickly approaching and Xerxes's core strategy was predicated on securing a foothold on the Peloponnesian Peninsula before the winter storms.

In the final days of August, the Persians encamped at Aphetae on the southern shore of Magnesia, only ten miles from Artemisium. It was a location chosen for its practicality but, in another symbolic coincidence, this Persian camp was also the location of the departure of one of mythology's greatest heroes, Jason. He and his Argonauts departed from Aphetae on their quest for the Golden Fleece. Between the Homeric link to Agamemnon's fleet leaving to selfishly defeat Troy and Jason's relentless pursuit of the Golden Fleece aboard the *Argo*, it is hard not to see parallels with Xerxes's ambition. This sense of mythos only compounded the theatricality of the Persian invasion, heightening the opportunity for heroes like Themistocles to add to their reputation

The initial confrontations between the Hellenic League and the Persians near Euboea were marked by disarray. Three Greek scouting ships were waylaid by Persian ships, prompting an initial retreat back to Chalcis in a panic that the Persians were ahead of schedule. The Persian arrival at Thermopylae a week later induced their return to Artemisium, where the allies intercepted fifteen Persian ships that had miscalculated their position. Immediately after their capture, a furious storm battered the Euboean coast for three days. It was this very storm that destroyed the 400 Persian ships. Factoring in the 200 ships sailing eastwards, the 15 captured triremes, and the 400 wrecked ships, the Persian navy numbered about 1200 when the Greeks attacked the next day. They still had an advantage over the Greeks' 271 ships, but it was not the huge numbers that the Spartans had faced at Thermopylae.

The Greek fleet had, meanwhile, beached their intact triremes at Artemisium, the rocky coasts of Euboea safeguarding them from the violent storm. Triremes were typically beached when not required for immediate use. This was primarily to rest their rowers, whose exhaustion directly impacted the effectiveness of the fleet. Triremes also needed to avoid becoming waterlogged, as this could slow them substantially. This was wise preparation; the Greeks needed every asset available considering the Persians' significant advantage in speed over their lighter triremes. The Ionians, Phoenicians, and Egyptians were especially famous for their alacrity on the seas, and their ships had not been destroyed in the storm. Trireme warfare relied on speed and agility in a constant competition to best combine pace, positioning and timing in order to ram an opposing ship.

In an attempt to garrison the strait first, the Greeks returned to Artemisium well before the Persians. Surveying the extent of the storm's destruction, the Greeks convinced themselves that the Persian fleet would be all but destroyed. Yet, as the horizon cleared, it became abundantly clear exactly how truly colossal the Persian navy was, and that a loss of 400 ships had been far from debilitating. Across the ten mile strait, the Greeks could see the Persian ships sailing in and out of Aphetae falling into formation. With each Persian ship exiting Aphetae, the allied Greek navy became more dismayed.

The Spartan admiral Eurybiades was beset by the severest anxiety. There was significant debate among the generals at Artemisium over the wisdom of a retreat. The straits of Artemisium certainly limited the flexibility of Persian strategy but, in contrast to the circumstances at Thermopylae, the bottleneck effect would not eliminate full participation of their forces in combat. The admiral of Corinth's navy, second in size to Athens, passionately threatened to order the Corinthian fleet to sail home to prepare for the inevitable battle of the Isthmus. Themistocles fought fervently to continue the original plan but there was enough dissent that the Euboeans panicked. Like the Athenians, the Euboeans realized that another retreat to Chalcis would devastate their island and hand them over to Xerxes. Motivated purely by survival, they approached the one man in the Greek admiralty they knew would deliver results at any cost: Themistocles.

The Euboeans delivered a sum of thirty silver talents to Themistocles. This was an astonishing amount of money for one transaction and it's clear what strings were attached. The Euboeans wanted the Greeks to fight at Artemisium and repel the Persians as much as they possibly could. It was worth emptying the coffers for a glimmer of hope. The fact that they opted to deliver the entire amount to one man, instead of allocating it among multiple admirals, affirms Themistocles's reputation. He cultivated his image as pragmatically and unconventionally effective in order to engender situations like this – where he could transform policy and realize his vision for Athens.

The Euboeans gave Themistocles thirty talents but, in order to be of any value, Themistocles had to continue on the bribery circuit. Themistocles first approached Eurybiades and, without any mention of the money's origin, offered the Spartan five talents to remain at Artemisium and engage the Persians shortly. Eurybiades naturally believed this silver came from the Athenian treasury, surely having heard of the silver mine at Laurium. Themistocles did not bother to correct him and Eurybiades agreed.

With Eurybiades in line, Themistocles's next stop was the tent of the Corinthian commander Adimantus. Themistocles repeated his sales pitch but included an addendum: 'Nay, you of all men will not desert us; for I will give you a greater gift than the king of Medes would send you for deserting your allies.'[11] Themistocles paid him three talents of silver, never mentioning that it was less than Eurybiades's sum and far inferior to the twenty-two talent surplus. The Corinthian acquiesced and agreed to fight at Artemisium.

It is worth noting that Eurybiades, brimming with Spartan honour, would not have seen these payments as a bribe. Optimistically, Eurybiades might have interpreted this as clever statecraft and a demonstration of Athens' commitment to their shared military stratagem. But more likely, Eurybiades participated in the great Greek tradition of not asking too many financial questions. The historian Peter Green places great emphasis on the Greek perspective, 'economic naivety is a fundamental element of the Greek historical scene.'[12] For his part, Themistocles may not have called it bribery either. This strikes at the core of *arete* among the Greeks: it was the end result that mattered, not the means by which it was achieved. And since Themistocles had so far exhibited the most *arete* among the Hellenic navy, he was able to ascend into the role of admiral in all but title. This fact is made quite clear by Diodorus Siculus who highlights that Themistocles, at this point, 'by reason of his sagacity and skill as a general, enjoyed great favour not only with the Greeks throughout the fleet but also with Eurybiades himself, and all men looked to him and harkened to him eagerly'.[13]

One more obstacle stood in the way of the Greek stand at Artemisium. A Greek captain named Architeles, a man scarce of both funds and courage, was the final influential voice demanding an allied retreat back to the Isthmus of Corinth. Architeles lacked the status of Eurybiades and Adimantus but his greatest sin was that he was an Athenian. Themistocles decided to show the full extent of his artifice at the expense of this fellow Athenian, who should have known by now that a retaliation from Themistocles was inevitable. Themistocles took an unorthodox approach this time and fermented a mutiny among Architeles's crew, most likely informing them of Architeles's present lack of funds. The crew, hoping to impress the mighty Themistocles and earn a steady wage again, quickly besieged their captain. On Themistocles's order, the crew stole the man's dinner. Themistocles extended an olive branch and hand-delivered a lovely meal of bread and meat to Architeles, who quickly devoured it. As he finished his meat, Architeles must have been surprised to find a full talent of silver at the bottom of the bowl, concealed earlier by the generous portions. The crew, Themistocles explained, would certainly have a hard time understanding how the impoverished Architeles suddenly had enough money to pay his entire crew for a month. Themistocles then dropped the hammer: he would accuse Architeles of accepting Persian bribes and passing along the Greeks' battle plans unless Architeles remained at Artemisium and fought.[14]

Themistocles's bribery and blackmailing campaign ended the debate: the allied Greeks would fight at Artemisium. Themistocles kept the remaining twenty-one talents in his own keeping. Such an action, again, was by no means at odds with *arete* or the Greek notion of heroism. Homer's heroes constantly kept the great treasures for themselves, or were incensed when those treasures were withheld. The Athenians would place their value not in Themistocles's heavy-handed accounting but, instead, in his overall objective: the salvation of Greece. His personal enrichment was not only harmonious with Athenian virtue, it was, and (some say) remains, the best way for a politician to make an income in a democracy.

*   *   *

During the final preparations for the next morning's battle, a Persian man appeared among the Greek ships as if by magic. He was Scyllias, a prominent man renowned for his skills as a diver. He had made a fortune recovering supplies and money from shipwrecks and, given the incredibly poor luck of Persian navies, had not lacked in business recently. Eurybiades convened a war council where Scyllias delivered the bad news that 200 ships, in an advance guard, had been sent around the eastern side of Euboea. The Greeks met this news with consternation as the Persian plan to outflank both Artemisium and Thermopylae became abundantly clear. Scyllias also revealed the extent of the storm damage to the Persian fleet. The loss of 'only' 400 ships distressed the Greeks even further.

Themistocles capitalized on this fear among the Greeks and turned it into the impetus for the Hellenic League to strike first. They would soon be outflanked anyway, Themistocles argued, and there was no point in delaying the inevitable conflict. It would be better to attack now, while the Persians were unprepared and missing 200 ships. Themistocles also persuaded the war council to follow the unconventional tactic of delaying the offensive manoeuvre until late in the afternoon in order to gain one more Greek advantage.

Triremes always preferred to sail during the daylight. Night-time naval warfare was virtually unheard of for triremes, whose need for precision in ramming opponents depended on too many visual cues, not to mention the rowers' need to avoid exhaustion. Fighting at Artemisium would almost certainly not continue into the night if it began in the afternoon. By placing a deadline on the battle, the Greeks would force the Persians to act before proper preparation but also keep Greek tactics shrouded in mystery. The Greeks worked to make themselves unpredictable and to never allow the Persians to be complacent.

Themistocles couldn't avoid planning ahead, however. Scyllias apparently represented a growing contingent of Greeks fighting for Xerxes who were increasingly sympathizing with the Hellenic League's message of nationalist resistance. Themistocles took mental note of this useful information. After all, there were more Greeks fighting for Persia than for Greece. Any number of Greeks who could recover their patriotism would be profitable in the war effort and limit Persian success.

The twin battles of Thermopylae and Artemisium began, quite by chance, on the same day in early September 480 BCE. It is easy to get lost in the wonder of the event, and assume that the Athenians would be naval experts given their later success. But just as Thermopylae was the first true experiment of Spartan military superiority against non-Greeks, Artemisium became the first test of the Athenian trireme. It was the first chance for each soldier to examine their enemy in person. The Greeks and Persians had spent years preparing for this moment, and the chance to finally learn of the technology, strategy, and calibre of the opposition.

Further, Artemisium was the first opportunity for Themistocles himself to actually command Athenian ships in combat. His experience was so far limited to hoplite warfare, a rite of passage for all Greeks, but both he and the Athenian navy had not yet used their newly minted triremes in battle. It was the first major test of his Athenian-led thalassocracy and would be a watershed moment for Athens's naval vision. Their *thetes* had never rowed in combat, their commanders never forced to make split second strategic decisions in the heat of battle, their marines had never attempted to board another ship and their battering rams had yet to pierce an enemy ship. It would be Artemisium where the long-awaited battle reunion between the Persians and the Athenians, who had not met since Marathon, would take place. Each had become somewhat obsessed with the other in anticipation of meeting again, and Artemisium finally brought their passionate hate of the other to fruition.

* * *

The Greeks departed the Euboean shore in the late afternoon of September 8, 480 BCE and sailed their nearly 300 ships towards the Persian position at Aphetae. When the Persian admirals, led by two sons of Xerxes's half-brothers, saw the Greeks' foolhardy offensive they 'deemed them assuredly mad'[15] and were overjoyed at the prospect of an easy victory over a lesser force. The odd timing did not deter the mobilization of their ships and the rapid departure from Aphetae to meet the Greeks in the ten mile wide strait of Artemisium. If the Persians were sceptical of the afternoon assault, they presumably found the opportunity to swiftly destroy the Greek fleet to be worth the risk of making nightfall.

At the battle's onset, the Greek ships initiated a manoeuvre as peculiar as their 'peculiar freedom'.[16] As they approached the Persian position, a signal rang out and the Greeks 'drew the sterns of their ships together, their prows turned towards the foreigners'.[17] If Herodotus's depiction is accurate, it means that all 271 of the Greek ships formed a tight circle, or perhaps a crescent, with sterns in the centre and their bronze rams aimed at the enemy. This not only prepared them for a quick assault, but also minimized their surface area.

This radical formation certainly seems Themistoclean in origin, characterized by his hallmark unorthodoxy and risk. While the origin of the strategy is not clear from the primary sources, it is clear that Eurybiades departed from convention in order to mitigate the Persian advantage in number. On this count, it was highly effective. The spatial restrictions imposed on the Persian navy by the smaller size of the strait at Artemisium, and now also by the Greek formation, meant they could either surround the Greeks or range their own ships in several rows. The former would stretch their forces too thin, and the latter make them inflexible and crowded.

Forced to pick their poison, the Persians fanned out of Aphetae's harbour to encircle the Greek formation with a long, thin line of ships. This established two concentric circles, with a dense nucleus of Greek triremes at the centre, surrounded by a narrow Persian line stretched thin to cover the entire Greek circumference. Their spirits were still high in these final moments before the fighting. The King of Kings famously promised to lavishly reward the men who first drew Greek blood. Most Persians were anxious for the first opportunity to sink a Greek trireme and earn the ensuing riches and honours, and it would be all the more satisfying if that ship were Athenian.

It only took a split second for the fighting to begin. On a coordinated signal, the Greek triremes exploded out of their circle and executed a *diekplous* manoeuvre on the now-thinned Persian lines. The *diekplous* was the trademark manoeuvre of a trireme. Translated as 'sailing out through', the trireme burst forward with all 180 men rowing in a sprint aimed at slicing through the enemy's line. The triremes would not aim to ram their opposition quite yet, but instead disrupt and fluster their formation. The Persians were caught off guard by the sheer speed of the Greek ships. Popular opinion correctly held that the Persian navy was the fastest of its time. The Phoenician triremes, that were the backbone of Xerxes's armada, were especially agile and could change direction on the drop of a dime.

But as the Greek triremes charged out from their defensive position, the Persians were overrun as the Greeks moved with surprising alacrity. The Greek ships were heavier than the Persian ships, an ostensible disadvantage. But the nature of this manoeuvre weaponized the weight of Greek triremes and the short distance between the formations meant the Greeks reached the Persians quickly, yet did not need to reach as high a speed to deliver damage. The *thetes* must have rowed in what modern rowers call 'swing', the elusive state of perfect unison and teamwork. This remarkable acceleration over the short distance coupled with the heavy mass of the Greek ships in a perfect illustration of a physics equation to create force. The Greeks peppered the Persian line with punctures, cleaving through it before immediately turning about face.

With the Greek ships reversing on the backside of the Persians, trireme warfare began in earnest. The bronze rams of Greek triremes aimed directly at the most vulnerable part of a ship: the stern. As the trireme had evolved, captains had moved away from the typical strategy of ramming the centre of the hull. Instead of creating a single hole in the centre, by 480 BCE, triremes steered for the rear of an enemy ship to pierce it repeatedly as they moved forward. A perfectly executed ram would slice a series of holes or a long fracture and doom its crew to the waters. In this way, the greater weight of Greek triremes created far deeper and more frequent holes in the lighter Egyptian and Phoenician ships than vice versa.

If for some reason they could not aim for this manoeuvre, another option was to have one entire side of rowers pull their oars into the ship. The trireme then passed alongside the enemy ship at a distance close enough to shear off the oars of one entire side. This rendered the enemy dead in the water.

If the above manoeuvres were not possible, matters were settled by hand-to-hand combat. A trireme's deck seated a crew of up to a dozen marines who would be responsible for boarding and defending the ship. A handful of archers supported these marines during the dangerous boarding process. Both marine and archer were chiefly tasked with defending the rowers in order to keep the trireme safe and running at full capacity.

At Artemisium, however, the lightning-quick Greek advance left little time or space for an organized Persian response. The combination of cunning Greek defence and the narrow straits off Euboea limited the Persian reaction. It nullified their speed and manoeuvrability advantages, which they lacked the innovation to overcome. The Greek rams were busy all afternoon until the battle ended as darkness fell. Themistocles's deadline for the battle's end achieved its purpose as the Persians retreated back to Aphetae, having lost thirty ships. The Greek formation was so successful that, by the end of the century, the circle formation and the crescent formation were the standard defensive tactics.

The Greeks were jubilant and patriotic as they beached their ships at Artemisium. The Greek losses are not recorded but were clearly minimal. The Hellenic League would later award a prize of valour to one Lycomedes of Athens, himself sailing a ship built with Laurium silver, for sinking the first Persian ship. In a pleasing resonance with the Greek tales of old, Lycomedes was also the name of the man who killed the mythical hero Theseus – the symbolism of which was surely emphasized at the fireside festivities that evening.

There is no doubt the Greeks overachieved on the first day of Artemisium and won the day. One detail was more exciting for Themistocles than the victory; the Ionians, Persian-allied Greeks from the Ionian coast, had refused to fight in the day's battle. This discounted a hundred ships and certainly aided the Hellenic League's cause, but the motivation for their neutrality was an even greater boon. The Ionians had been 'sore distressed to see the Greeks surrounded, supposing that not one of them would return home; so powerless did the Greek seem to them to be.'[18] They had indeed scored one outright defection as one Ionian ship sailed home with the Greeks that evening to switch sides. It was Themistocles's observation that an increasing amount of Greeks under Xerxes were sympathizing with the Hellenic League, now to the point of outright treason by inaction. One turncoat diver was not enough to convince anyone, but a fleet of one hundred ships and their rowers was the start of a true insurrection. All was not well in the Persian camp, and the cracks in the facade of the world's largest military were growing. This became the bedrock on which Themistocles built his future statecraft as well as one of the enduring legacies of Artemisium.

* * *

The night after the first fighting was a tale of two camps. The Persian camp was humbled. They had expected an easy victory against a motley group of rebels. The size and scope of their military was supposed to be largely for show, threatening all other defiant states who would not submit to the King of Kings. That was clearly not the case off Artemisium. The Persians spent the night, and most of the next afternoon, licking their wounds and repairing their ships ahead of a new assault against the Greeks.

To make matters worse, Poseidon was not quite done toying with the Persian navy and that night another tempest ravaged the Euboean coast. Having somewhat learned their lesson, most of their ships were shielded by Aphetae's harbours. The advance guard of 200 ships sailing across the eastern coast of Euboea met a much different fate. All 200 triremes sank to the bottom of the Aegean Sea at a wickedly dangerous point named The Hollows. The citizens of Euboea spread news of this quickly and it reached Eurybiades and Themistocles within a few hours. They were overjoyed at the news, since part of their original strategy of meeting that advance guard at Chalcis had been frustrated by the same storm. Had those ships not sunk, the Persians would soon have had the Greeks surrounded. The gods once again appeared to work miracles in the Greeks', and especially the Athenians', favour.

The second day of the battle was not quite as action-packed. Fresh reinforcements of fifty-six triremes arrived from Athens, undeterred by the storm. Another afternoon attack repeated the formula of the previous day, although no circle formation was necessary this time. The Greek ships departed from Artemisium yet did not formally engage the full Persian force. Instead, they intercepted and sank a small squadron of Cilician ships. This diminished the Persian fleet further to somewhere around 600 ships – still formidable, but no longer overwhelming.

The third day was to be the climax of the battle. Despite the Persian admirals feeling, according to the description of one ancient source, 'ever more timorous before the conflicts which faced them,'[19] they settled on a strategy of leveraging their raw numbers. Their fear of the battle was far less than their fear of Xerxes's wrath should they fail. The Persians set out at noon, a time wisely chosen to avoid the calamity of evening fighting, to break through the pass at Artemisium regardless of the toll to its own fleet, leaving the Greek navy behind if need be. Their formation was directly inspired by the Greek dominance on the first day of fighting. They opted for a crescent formation, though it was designed for an offensive assault in response to the defensive arrangement of Greece. Herodotus tells us that the Persians sought to encircle the Greeks, and that the Greeks aggressively sailed at the Persians when they deduced the tactic.

The result was bloody. The dual advance brought waves of violence with it. After the initial advance, the allied Greeks quickly tried to block up the strait and deny the Persian advance to Attica. From noon until nightfall, the waters off Artemisium brimmed with the debris of ruined triremes and the drowned or arrow-ridden bodies of rowers who had unsuccessfully attempted to swim to land. It was the longest sea battle of the war. No specific number of ships lost is found in any ancient sources, but it is quite clear that the third day destroyed the most ships by far.

The flurry of good news began to wane as word from Thermopylae trickled in. The news of yet another Greek betrayal – by both Ephialtes and now also by the Thebans – and the outflanking of the Spartans was quickly followed by the news of the death of Leonidas and his 300. The pass at Thermopylae was lost and Xerxes now had an unchallenged path straight to Athens. The Greek admirals ordered a retreat first back to the beaches of Artemisium and then to Salamis. Salamis was to be a brief sanctuary to regroup and repair before another journey to the final battle's location at the Isthmus of Corinth. The Greeks withdrew from the straits of Artemisium and beached at the shores of Euboea for one final night; the Persians returned to Aphetae confident in their ability to sail unmolested along the western Euboean coast in the morning.

Apart from a successful delay of the Persian invader, there are two further implications for the Greek war effort from Artemisium. First, the Athenians distinguished themselves in battle and again an Athenian ship was awarded with the prize of valour. The Athenian navy was no longer a hollow marketing campaign by Themistocles; it was instead a gritty collection of veterans experienced in both combat and war. The Athenians had repelled the Persians as hoplites at Marathon and now as sailors at Artemisium. And while the entirety of the strategy may or may not have been Themistocles's, the ships that executed it surely were. His *kudos* – a good reputation earned by all the great heroes of Greece – surged substantially after his demonstrating his equal capability in war and politics.

Second, although the Greeks ordered a retreat, this was no surrender. The Battle of Artemisium was a stalemate which, considering the circumstances, might be interpreted as a moral victory. It was far more logistically successful than Thermopylae and they had wounded the Persian navy significantly, showing superior tactical skill in so doing.

There is good reason for the Theban poet Pindar's famous quote regarding Artemisium:

> Where Athenians' valiant sons set in radiance eternal
> Liberty's corner-stone.[20]

Furthermore, Thermopylae was a strategic loss but a spiritual windfall for the Greeks. For generations, the 300 Spartans' final stand was the pinnacle of *arete* and Greek supremacy. Their sacrifice was an infusion of passion, an emblem of the price of Greek freedom against the oppression of the barbarians. Thermopylae was not, however, a military victory. The Persians had passed through the Hot Gates just like they had sailed through the straits at Artemisium.

No boost to Greek morale could change the reality that the Persian military entered Athens just a week or so after Artemisium and Thermopylae. At the command of Xerxes, the city was immediately put to the torch. Athens, the home of unequalled cultural achievements and the birthplace of democracy, was destroyed. The elderly hoplites' quixotic stand at the Acropolis failed. The Temple of Athena was plundered. The Persians burned the city down, defaced its artwork, and defiled its temples. Xerxes marched to the Acropolis and, declaring himself lord of Athens, demanded that the medized Athenians make ritual sacrifice to him there rather than to Athena. The Athenian exiles, likely including Hippias the former tyrant, happily worshipped the King of Kings in the heart of Athens.[21]

And, since the island of Salamis is in within view of the city itself, the Athenians watched as their city burned. They could see the smoke and hear the screams of the faithful Athenians either defending the Acropolis or jumping off its cliffs to avoid giving the Persians the satisfaction of killing them. The Persian revenge on Athens was now complete. Athens had been destroyed. Only its people remained.

Despite his skill, Themistocles had not saved the city of Athens. He had thus far only delivered momentum, not victory. His contention that the 'wooden wall' was indeed the Athenian triremes at Divine Salamis would now be tested. And even if he won the battle at Salamis or at the Isthmus of Corinth, it would be to save a city of rubble and a homeless citizenship. Themistocles's *aristeia* was upon him. The coming days were to be the dramatic climax of his Homeric epic.

Chapter 6

Engineering Salamis:
The Final Stand of Greece

Men of Ionia, you do wrongly to fight against the land of your fathers and bring slavery upon Hellas. It were best of all that you should join yourselves to us; but if that be impossible for you, then do you even now withdraw yourselves from the war, and entreat the Carians to do the same as you. If neither of these things may be, and you are fast bound by such constraint that you cannot rebel, yet we pray you not to use your full strength in the day of battle; be mindful that you are our sons and that our quarrel with the foreigner was of your making in the beginning.[1]

These were the words the Persians found carved onto the rocks and hillsides of every fresh spring between Artemisium and Athens. Upon the Greek retreat from Artemisium, Themistocles ordered these words written at the public watering holes, all but mandatory re-supply points for any ships sailing along the western Euboean coast. He had a captive audience. Moreover, the words were written in Greek. Most sailors were illiterate, and even those educated in the Persian navy likely read other languages than Greek, but that was part of the design for Themistocles. He knew that the Persian rowers would ask incessantly as to the meaning of these billboards, guaranteeing that the Greeks in Xerxes's navy – most of whom were Ionian – would have to publicly read the message aloud to the crowds. Its length was also quite intentional, assuring that nobody missed the speech or its implications.

A new Themistoclean propaganda campaign had begun. He certainly knew his marketing strategies from years fighting tooth and nail for power in the nascent democracy of Athens. But after Artemisium, the landscape of the war was radically changed. The Ionian abstention and their small number of defectors to the Greek cause led Themistocles to diagnose the weaknesses forming in the Persian camp. There was also, of course, also the none-to-distant matter of the Ionian Revolt, when the Ionians had rebelled against the Persians a decade ago and allied with the Athenians in the events that instigated the Greco-Persian Wars. The final words of the above inscription made sure to remind the Persians that it was the Ionians who had first defied Darius the Great and dared to rebel. He pressed hard on that nerve. Herodotus's analysis of Themistocles's tactics is as incisive now as when it was first written:

> To my thinking Themistocles thus wrote with a double intent, that if the king knew nought of the writing it might make the Ionians to change sides and join with the Greeks, and that if the writing were maliciously reported to Xerxes he might thereby be led to mistrust the Ionians, and keep them out of the sea-fights.[2]

There was no wise option for the Ionians while they remained in Persian service. The Ionians could fervently affirm their fidelity to Xerxes, but their reputation could not overcome the lack of participation in the Battle of Artemisium. The Ionians now had a scarlet letter for their time in the Persian navy, and Themistocles exploited it. How did the Persians know that the Ionians would not rebel against them again, just like they had during the Ionian Revolt – but this time from behind enemy lines? The peculiar freedom of the Greeks was not limited to the mainland, and there was too much suspicious behaviour by Ionians to assume it was a coincidence. His aim for strife and discord in the Persian camp was successful, if not in military tactics then in information warfare to demoralize and manipulate the invaders. The Ionians lost their place as the foremost Greeks in Xerxes's navy, a position they never regained.

Themistocles would need every advantage possible at Salamis if he was to save the Athenians. On his journey back from Artemisium, he knew that Athens would be destroyed. After driving a wedge between the Persians and the Ionians, Themistocles next set his sights on ensuring that 'Divine' Salamis would replace the Isthmus of Corinth as the site of the Greek's final stand for their liberty.

The island of Salamis was cosily nestled only a few miles off the Attican coast, just a mile from the port at Piraeus. The island featured jutting peninsulas and pristine bays, with equal access to the Saronic Gulf on the

Bust of Themistocles. (*Rijksdienst voor het Cultureel Erfgoed, Wikimedia Commons CC0 1.0 Universal (CC0 1.0) Public domain dedication. Photography credit: Antonietti, J.P.A.*)

Bust of Themistocles. A Roman copy from the Hadrian Era modelled after a Greek original from ca. 400 BCE. (*Museo Pio-Clementino, Muses Hall, Wikimedia Commons CC0 1.0 Universal (CC0 1.0) Public domain dedication. Photography credit: Jastrow*)

A Roman-era bust of Themistocles in the 'Severe' style. The long-lost original from which this bust is copied is potentially the first sculpture of a European ever made. (*Museo Ostiense, Wikimedia Commons, Attribution 3.0 Unported (CC BY 3.0). Photography credit: Sailko*)

A replica of the Troezen Decree, the order by Themistocles to evacuate all men, women and children from Athens before the arrival of the Persian army. They would make their last stand at the Battle of Salamis just a few weeks later. (*Athens War Museum in Athens, Greece. Wikimedia Commons Attribution 2.0 Generic (CC BY 2.0). Photography credit: Dimitris Kamaras*)

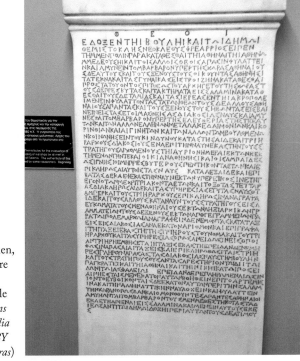

A fifth century BC trireme depicted in a dedication to Paralos, a sacred ship in Athens used in diplomatic missions during the Peloponnesian War. Although it dates later than Themistocles's construction of the Athenian fleet, it is one of the earliest representations of the Athenian trireme. (*Acropolis Museum in Athens, Greece. Wikimedia Commons. Copyright holder and photography credit: Ad Meskens*)

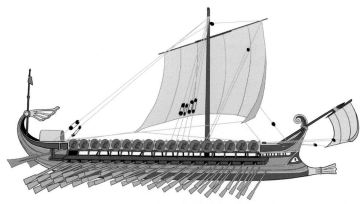

A diagram of a trireme in the style of the fifth century BC. Athenian triremes would often have no deck and an open galley for the rowers, a feature that allowed them to be lighter and faster than their opponents. (© *Jeffrey Smith*)

The reconstructed trireme 'Olympias', built to the exact specifications and measurements of the available archaeological record. Note the bronze battering ram on the very front of the ship, with which they attacked their opponents. (*Wikimedia Commons. Copyright holder and photography credit: Χρήστης Templar52*)

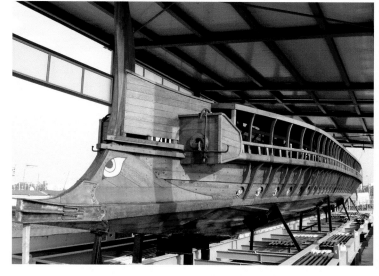

An illustration of the battering ram in action against an enemy trireme. In this image, the oars are being sliced off to immobilize the opponent who would then be stuck in the water. The battering ram aimed to create a long hole, or series of holes, in the opponent to maximize the damage. They would not typically ram at a right angle and aim to make a single smaller hole. (© *Jeffrey Smith*)

A detail from the tomb of Xerxes the Great. At the bottom, twenty-four soldiers are depicted in the dress and style of twenty-four different nations under Xerxes's rule, including the Persians, the Medes, the Elamites, the Babylonians, the Assyrians, the Egyptians, the Ionians, and the Lydians. All these nations and more participated in Xerxes's ill-fated invasion of Greece, turned away in large part due to the political and military brilliance of Themistocles. (*Wikimedia Commons & Flickr. Attribution 2.0 Generic (CC BY 2.0). Photography credit: A. Davey*)

The site of the Battle of Artemisium with the coast of Magnesia in the distance. (*Livius.org & Wikimedia Commons CC0 1.0 Universal (CC0 1.0). Public domain. Photography credit: Marco Prins*)

The Battle of Salamis trireme movements. The allied Greek and Athenian forces are in blue and the Persian forces are in red. (*The Department of History, United States Military Academy, Wikimedia Commons CC0 1.0 Universal (CC0 1.0). Public domain. Photography credit: Jona Lendering*)

'The Battle of Salamis' by Wilhelm von Kaulbach. This painting from 1868 depicts the spectacle at Salamis complete with Themistocles leading the Greeks to victory (right), Artemisia's valiant heroism (centre left), and even Xerxes's rage at the pending defeat (top left). (*Artist: Wilhelm von Kaulbach. Wikimedia Commons, public domain*)

The remains of the Themistoclean Wall near the Acropolis. Sensing a new threat from Sparta, Themistocles directed the construction of this wall out of the rubble of the destroyed Athens, which was burned by the Persians in 480 BCE. Just a few months later, the Spartans invaded Athens but were turned away by Themistocles's wall. (*Wikimedia Commons CC0 1.0 Universal (CC0 1.0) Public domain. Photography credit: Jebulun*)

The Themistoclean Wall on the north end of the Acropolis. This portion of the wall was built with columns from the 'Older Parthenon', the Temple of Athena that was destroyed when Persia burned Athens in 480 BCE. Themistocles led the Athenians in repurposing the rubble of that temple, and the rest of the city, to hastily build a wall to stop the Spartan threat just months later. (*Wikimedia Commons Attribution 2.0 Generic (CC BY 2.0). Photography credit: Seligmanwaite*)

The Theatre of Dionysus in Athens, where the Dionysia festival held its performances. *Phoenician Women, The Sack of Miletus* and *The Persians* would all have been performed here – although the stage and seating would have been simple wooden structures during the life of Themistocles. (*Wikimedia Commons & Flickr CC0 1.0 Universal (CC0 1.0), public domain. Photography credit: Gary Todd at WorldHistoryPics.com*)

Ostraka with the words 'Themistocles, Son of Neocles' written on them. These pottery sherds were all written by the same hand and were part of the unsuccessful attempt to ostracize Themistocles in 482 BCE. In that ostracism vote, Themistocles orchestrated the ostracism of his chief rival Aristides the Just. That these were all written in the same manner indicates potential voting manipulation by the political enemies of Themistocles as they would hand out these *Ostraka* – pre-labelled with Themistocles's name – to the illiterate voters entering the voting assembly. (*Ancient Agora Museum in Athens, Greece. Wikimedia Commons Attribution 2.0 Generic (CC BY 2.0). Photography credit: Sharon Mollerus*)

Ostraka with the words 'Themistocles, Son of Neocles' written on them. These pottery sherds were part of the total vote count that ostracized Themistocles from Athens in 471 BCE. (*Daily Life in Greek Antiquity Gallery, Museum of Cycladic Art in Athens, Greece. Wikimedia Commons & Flickr CC0 1.0 Universal (CC0 1.0). Public domain. Photography credit: Gary Todd at WorldHistoryPics.com*)

In this nineteenth century painting, 'Themistocles and King Admetus', Themistocles begs for mercy in the court of an old political enemy after being ostracized from Athens and hunted by both Athens and Sparta. It was a deeply humbling – and humiliating – moment for the saviour of Greece. (*Artist: Pierre Joseph Francois, 1832. Wikimedia Commons, public domain*)

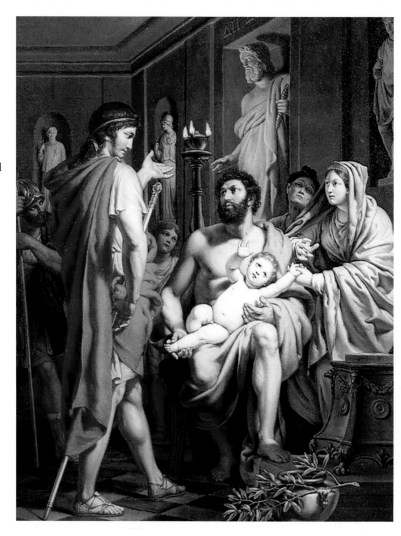

Coinage from Magnesia-on-the-Meander with 'Themistocles' written on the front surrounding an image of Apollo, and the letters 'MA' for Magnesia underneath an eagle. (*Gallica Digital Library, Wikimedia Commons CC0 1.0 Universal (CC0 1.0). Public domain. Photography credit: Bibliothèque nationale de France*)

A Roman-era coin depicting the statue of Themistocles he commissioned himself during his time in Magnesia-on-the-Meander. (*Public domain. Credit: R. Weill*)

Athenian side and the Megara Gulf on the Megaran side. In a single ship, one could circumnavigate the island quite easily. A whole fleet, though, would hit a series of chokepoints and thus jumble together. This was the crux of Themistocles's battleplan: to bottleneck the Persian navy and neutralize their numerical advantage. The Greeks would not win a direct battle, but they could survive a protracted series of smaller battles around the capes of Salamis if the Persian fleet was congested and disorganized.

The city of Salamis itself, now the home base for the Hellenic League's navy, was shielded by an especially long peninsula, Kynosoura, protruding eastwards towards Piraeus and Athens. From their defensive position here, the Hellenic navy was safe from the increasingly rough autumn waters and had access to an easy escape route to the north and west towards Megara. But most importantly, there was a blind corner around Kynosoura that the Persians would be required to pass through if they attacked the Greeks. A sizeable island, Psyttaleia, blocked a direct route from Athens' ports. Salamis was an exceptionally wise site for a defensive stand by the Greek navy.

And, in keeping with the mythos of Themistocles, Salamis was the ancestral home of Ajax the Greater from *The Iliad*, one of the greatest heroes of the Greeks in the Trojan War. For Themistocles, the reincarnated Odysseus, fighting in the footsteps of Ajax was an integral part of this world-changing moment – and its subsequent political impact.

Officially, however, Salamis was merely a temporary retreat selected by Eurybiades for the Greeks to regroup and aid the refugee Athenians before departing for Corinth. It was by no means an intended location for the battle; the Hellenic League explicitly rejected it after Themistocles proposed making Salamis the place where the Oracle of Delphi's prophecy would be fulfilled. In fact, the Hellenic League had not yet determined if they would engage in another naval battle with the invaders – the walls built across the Isthmus of Corinth were to be the great moment for the Spartan hoplites to save Greece. It was the Spartan *aristeia* that never materialized.

This did not stop the Hellenic League's war council from rejecting Themistocles's strategy. His passionate case was dismissed by the Peloponnesian admirals and Eurybiades himself, without much consideration. Ostensibly, it should have been easy to persuade the Greeks considering the momentum earned at Artemisium and Thermopylae. But the war council keenly observed that Themistocles's 'wooden wall' prophecy, despite its many cultural and morale contributions, had so far convinced only the Athenians, and all it had brought them so far was ruin. Salamis was going to be abandoned, and with it the Athenian people. The Peloponnesians decided to save their own city-states and forfeit all Greek land north of the Isthmus.

Moreover, many Athenians and Greeks had abandoned the Hellenic League after the burning of Athens. When they heard the screams from the Acropolis and smelt the smoke of their city, a significant number of ships set out from Salamis for parts unknown. One contingent of homeless Athenians wanted the refugees to sail to a new colony and re-establish Athens. Still others called for a fight at the Isthmus with the rest of the Greeks and abandon the idea of Salamis and the wooden wall. At the same time, and perhaps worst of all, the other members of the Hellenic League used this opportunity to exploit the divisions in intra-Greek politics. Athens, after all, no longer physically existed and so its leaders, they reasoned, should not have a say in determining the next steps for the Greeks. The situation was dire.

* * *

Themistocles's life, career, and vision of a free Greece and a hegemonic Athens was at greater risk than ever before. And so his singular ambition became to convince the Greeks to fight at Salamis, and not Corinth, no matter the personal cost. Themistocles's long-held belief was that the Athenian navy was the only chance the Greeks had to defeat the King of Kings, and that the moment they left Salamis they would be doomed. The reality was that Artemisium had been the one and only naval battle that the Persians had ever seen and, despite their staggering advantages, they had floundered. Nobody had yet to truly challenge Xerxes on the sea. To fight the Persians there was the best opportunity for Greek victory and survival, and that must be the essential strategy to win. If there was no other takeaway from Thermopylae, it was that that the Persian land force was simply too overwhelming. Artemisium gave the Greeks a glimmer of hope for victory – but it had to be through the trireme, not the *phalanx*.

However, the first night at Salamis saw an uncharacteristically sombre Themistocles. For once, he did not take the initiative in persuading Eurybiades and the war council to avoid sailing to the Isthmus. Instead, he was spurred by a visit from his old mentor from the earliest days of his political career, Mnesiphilus, who had taught Themistocles the intricacies of Athenian democracy, grooming him for politics while constantly skirting his own ostracism. Such survivalist instincts made him a perfect fit to entreat Themistocles at this moment, though this time it was the survival of all Athenians and not just himself.

The scant sources on Mnesiphilus paint a picture of a man who shows up at precisely the moment he is most needed. Considering his absence from the texts for the past decade, his journey to Themistocles's ship on the first night at Salamis was indeed fortutious. Herodotus indulges himself on this fateful encounter, chronicling a full conversation between the two men including direct quotes and explicit detail – something of a rarity in his discussion of Themistocles.

Mnesiphilus's ambition was to learn of the war council's plans. After Themistocles shared the discomforting news that the fleet was headed to the Isthmus of Corinth shortly, Mnesiphilus described the chilling reality of abandoning Salamis: 'your ships will have no country left wherefor to fight; for everyone will betake himself to his own city, and neither Eurybiades, nor any other man, will be able to hold them, but the armament will be scattered abroad; and Hellas will perish by unwisdom.'[3] Mnesiphilus demanded he go immediately to Eurybiades and halt the journey to Corinth, by any means necessary. It was a sobering moment for Themistocles, the great Athenian statesman, to hear his mentor's warning. The words stirred Themistocles so much that he didn't even bother to respond to Mnesiphilus. He left his tent and invited himself into Eurybiades's quarters forthwith. Mnesiphilus, meanwhile, vanishes into the historical ether. His two known contributions to the course of Athenian history were the mentorship of Themistocles, the greatest politician of his day, and this supplication to Themistocles that helped save the Greeks from conquest.

Themistocles burst into Eurybiades's quarters and, in so doing, forced a decisive meeting between the two most powerful free Greeks. Their dialogue, although short, is brimming with symbolism. The two men were the products of the two most influential Greek city-states, Athens and Sparta, and their partnership not only shows the desperation of the situation but also charts the path for the next century of Greek history. If Eurybiades remained firm in his desire to leave Salamis, Athens would perish. If Themistocles won out, then the 'wooden wall' would give Athens hope, if not all of Greece.

Their meeting, although painfully short in Herodotus's narrative, also recreated one of the defining scenes of Homeric Greek heroism. For much of Homer's *The Iliad*, Achilles, the greatest warrior in the world, refuses to fight in the Trojan War in a protest against his treatment by the king Agamemnon. In a desperate plea to get him to return to combat and turn the tide of the war, Agamemnon sends the cunning Odysseus to convince Achilles to fight again. Their dialogue is one of the emblematic examples of Homeric heroism. The scene pits his two main heroes – Achilles of *The Iliad* and Odysseus of *The Odyssey* – in a conflict that determines the course of not just the war but the future of all Greece. Each man epitomizes *arete* in a different capacity, Achilles with the physical excellence and battlefield-won glory and Odysseus with the cleverness and eloquence that earns results. Odysseus is unsuccessful in convincing Achilles, yet their encounter is deeply hospitable and the men, despite their radical differences, depart in friendship.

This is the prism through which the debate between Themistocles and Eurybiades should be viewed. Spartan honour and discipline are contrasted with Athenian rhetoric; the *arete* of effectiveness by traditional justice opposed to effectiveness by unrelenting pragmatism. Themistocles's methods, in many ways, grated against the Spartan emphasis on maintaining order no matter the cost. Challenging a commander, even in this respectful fashion, was inconceivable for the hoplites of Sparta.

Yet Eurybiades patiently welcomed Themistocles in the Greek tradition of hospitality for friends and travellers. In this case, Odysseus was successful in convincing Achilles to fight. Eurybiades laid aside his *hubris* and reconvened the war council in the dead of the night. It was an unprecedented and humble move, and it tells us much about the respect that Eurybiades now held for Themistocles.

*   *   *

The re-convened war council lacked the decorum of the private meeting. Eurybiades had agreed to bring the matter to the Hellenic League's admirals, but not to ensure its passing. Themistocles took the floor at the meeting and zealously argued for the case to stay at Salamis and fight the Persians with the entire strength of the Greek force. He would have been sure to leave no detail out: the more favourable ratio of ships when compared to the land forces, the relative success of Artemisium compared to Thermopylae, the religious prophecy of the 'wooden wall', the desperate desire for stateless Athenians to fight for their own survival, the foolishness of a land-based strategy at the Isthmus of Corinth, his propaganda campaign undermining the Ionians, the news of several defections from Persia and the cracks that must be forming in Xerxes's leadership, and the fact that Xerxes had still never truly won a naval battle against the Greeks.

Perhaps most of all, he opposed the idea that the Hellenic League should retreat back to the Isthmus and to their own separate city-states on the Peloponnesian Peninsula, saying that 'united they would be a match for the enemy, but declaring that if they separated they would be destroyed'.[4] We know his speech was exceptionally long because he was eventually interrupted by Adimantus, the very same admiral Themistocles had already bought off with silver to fight at Artemisium. Themistocles lacked the patience to realize his methods by bribery this time.

Adimantus interjected, saying, 'Themistocles, at the games those who start before the signal are beaten with rods.'[5] It was a reference to the Olympic Games and how those that begin the race before the bar fell are seen to be, at best, cheats and, at worst, lacking self-discipline. Adimantus's caustic remark was meant less for Themistocles and more for the other admirals, warning them that sailing to meet the Persian navy here would be a rash decision made by a man who had just lost his own city. Xerxes's navy would destroy them here.

Themistocles's reply was devoid of mercy for Adimantus's reputation: 'Those left behind win no crown.'[6] It was a short, effective rebuke that eliminated any counters from the war council. His time in the democracy of Athens had sharpened his rhetoric. No Corinthian admiral susceptible to bribery could outwit the man who had convinced Athens to ostracize Aristides the Just.

Themistocles turned now to Eurybiades. After such a display of Athenian political savvy, the Spartan admiral had now lost his previous respect for his Athenian counterpart. Eurybiades sought to retake control of the war council and dim the spotlight so brightly shining on Themistocles. The Spartan raised his staff as if to wallop Themistocles, when Themistocles gave a bitingly effective reply:

'Strike, but listen.'[7]

It was only four words in the Greek language, yet it's hard to convey how wisely chosen they were in context. His audience was overwhelming from the Peloponnesian Peninsula, where Spartan culture reigned supreme. The short, pithy rejoinder was the epitome of laconic speech. Named after the Spartan home region of Laconia, a laconic phrase was brief but highly effective. They prized a penetrating statement that avoided the loquaciousness of high societies like Persia or Athens. Laconic speech was taught in the *agoge* training camp to all Spartan citizens. Legendary examples include 'Come and get them,' which came from Leonidas to the Persians when the Persians demanded the 300 Spartans lay down their weapons, or the simple 'If' rebuttal to the envoys of the Macedonian conqueror Philip II who threatened the Spartans with ruin 'if we invade.'

Themistocles's ability to speak the language of the Spartans not only earned immediate honour from the admirals but also won them over enough for his audacious battle plan to earn consideration. It was also the next step in the unique relationship that was forming between Themistocles and the Spartans. Despite Themistocles representing the very best and the very worst of Athenian democracy, the Spartans began to see that he was not quite the mercurial agitator his reputation had foretold. His consummate pragmatism and ability to win over Eurybiades, and now many of the Peloponnesian admirals with thoughtful words, demonstrated his growth as a statesman and general.

Of course, it made more sense for the Spartans to connect with Aristides, given his admiration for their justice and his conception of Sparta as the ideal Greek state. Themistocles had even painted him as a *laconophile*, a Spartan lover, during their duel for ostracism. But Themistocles's surprising flexibility in assuming second-in-command and his performance in word and deed charmed the Spartans enough to see his utility as a politician. But it also placed a target on his back, as the Spartans realized the threat that he posed to Sparta. If one man could manipulate not just Athens but all Greece in the fashion Themistocles had done, he needed to be neutralized.

Although some admirals now considered Themistocles's case for a great battle at Salamis, they were not fully convinced. He followed up his impressive laconism with one last entreaty, this one more Athenian in style. His final, impassioned speech to the Greek war council was the culmination of a lifetime of climbing the greasy pole, using nothing but the grit and determination of an underdog, and was further saturated in the desperation of the Athenians who now watched their city burn at Persian hands. In recognition of their significance, his words are recorded at length by Herodotus:

> But if you do as I counsel you, you will thereby profit as I shall show; firstly, by engaging their many ships with our few in narrow seas, we shall win a great victory, if the war have its rightful issue; for it is for our advantage to fight in a strait as it is theirs to have wide sea-room. Secondly, we save Salamis, whither we have conveyed away our children and our women. Moreover, there is this, too, in my plan, and it is your chiefest desire: you will be defending the Peloponnese as well by abiding here as you would by fighting off the Isthmus, and you will not lead our enemies (if you be wise) to the Isthmus. And if that happen which I expect, you will never have the foreigners upon you at the Isthmus; they will advance no further than Attica, but depart in disorderly fashion; and we shall gain by the saving of Megara and Aegina and Salamis, where it is told us by an oracle that we shall have the upper hand of our enemies. Success comes oftenest to men when they make reasonable designs; but if they do not so, neither will heaven for its part side with human devices.[8]

Such eloquence might have immediately convinced the Athenian voting assembly, but the Corinthian admiral Adimantus apparently had not been swayed. Adimantus challenged Themistocles's very presence at the meeting, since the Hellenic League was an alliance of Greek city-states and Athens now conspicuously lacked its city. It was a tender spot, of course, and Themistocles lashed out at the Corinthian, with whom only days ago he had been cosy enough to bribe.

Themistocles had no more Odysseus-like rhetoric to offer. His final words were a threat, not a petition. He told Admiantus, Eurybiades and the council that Athens was far from a corpse – it was a thriving city superior to the rest of Greece – as long as they had their two hundred triremes. With Greece's largest naval force, the Athenians could still exert influence on both this alliance and the rest of the Aegean world. He then laid down the Athenian ultimatum:

> If you abide here [at Salamis], by so abiding you will be a right good man; but if you will not, you will overthrow Hellas; for all our strength for war is in our ships. Nay, be guided by me. But if you do not so, we then without more ado will take our households and voyage to Siris in Italy, which has been ours from old time, and the oracles tell that we must there plant a colony; and you, left without allies such as we are, will have cause to remember what I have said.[9]

The Athenians would take their fleet, the backbone of the Greek navy, and abandon the Hellenic League in pursuit of life at one of their colonies in Italy. With their departure, the allied Greek navy had no hope of survival. There is no reason to be sceptical of Themistocles's threat. Abandoning Salamis would, in Themistocles's judgement, entirely abandon the only hope of defeating the Persians. As if by way of poetic emphasis, an owl apparently flew onto Themistocles's ship as he finished this speech. Many Greeks interpreted this plainly: Athena had spoken and the Greeks needed to heed Themistocles's words.

At this juncture, the primary sources differ. Herodotus tells us that Themistocles's threat hastily convinced Eurybiades to fight at Salamis, more to ensure the Athenian triremes remained than anything. But Eurybiades changed his mind hours later upon hearing the outcry from the land army at the Isthmus, who now feared being outflanked by the Persian fleet. Plutarch, however, gives a dimmer outlook on the outcome of the Greek war council. In his account, Themistocles failed to persuade the Peloponnesian admirals and Eurybiades actually gave the command to sail for the Isthmus of Corinth in the morning.

The truth of the matter is that Themistocles was unconvinced that the Hellenic League would remain at Salamis in a meaningful way. Despite his impressive speech, he had failed like Odysseus had when trying to convince Achilles to fight. However, he had no intention of leaving the battlefield advantages of Salamis nor of risking the Athenian fleet in the open waters near the Isthmus of Corinth. His next steps were the most extreme and infamous of his life. He decided to bypass the Greeks and choreograph the war by contacting Xerxes himself.

*   *   *

A parallel war council occurred across the waters in what remained of Athens. The Persians made their camp in the old Athenian harbour of Phaleron, since Piraeus was risky given its proximity to the Greek camp on the eastern coast of Salamis. The Great King Xerxes had annexed Munichia, the citadel of Piraeus, where he intended to watch the looming battle from a majestic throne. In a symbolic turn, most of this setup was made possible by Themistocles. Piraeus was the harbour constructed by Themistocles during his archonship for this specific moment: the naval defence of Athens. Munichia was, ironically, originally built by the tyrant Hippias who now accompanied Xerxes after failing to retake Athens at Marathon. But it was Themistocles who had fortified Munichia to make it the great citadel defending Athens' navy. And, of course, Athens had been emptied by Themistocles weeks earlier in preparation for a naval battle like Salamis.

Xerxes called together his generals, admirals, and advisors to formulate a final tactic to eliminate the Greek navy in advance of their march on Corinth. Xerxes had earlier surveyed the fleet personally, asking questions of his commanders and gathering their strategic input. This was a theme for the Persian king during the war, he was constantly evaluating his admirals, generals, advisors, ships, and tactics. The environment was like a pressure cooker, to say the least, as the military was rewarded or punished based on his perception of their success. It was quite common for the captain of a particular trireme to be beheaded after a perceived failure the King of Kings noticed while he watched the battle from his throne. It was just as common to have a captain promoted and lavished with prizes if he impressed the king with valour and success.

The war council would have been arranged by rank. The most favoured admirals, the Phoenician kings of Sidon and Tyre, sat to the immediate right of the king while the other commanders were seated in descending order. The king's general of the land force was Mardonius, famed for his failures en route to and at Marathon, and was near the front as were many members of Xerxes's royal family. He had brought along several of his half-brothers, wives and cousins and installed them in leadership positions, especially across the naval fleet.

Feelings amongst the council pressurized further when Xerxes interrogated his admirals on whether the fleet should attack the nearby Greeks or hold off until the presumed battle at Corinth. Xerxes, however, was too sacred to participate in such mundane matters and, while he sat silently, his lieutenant Mardonius led the questioning of his commanders. This was a clever approach for Xerxes, who could not only claim a plausible lack of culpability by scapegoating a general if things went wrong, but also give himself a further chance to evaluate his admirals at a time when they needed to capitalize on the momentum of a destroyed Athens after the relative failure of Artemisium.

Mardonius and the commanders almost unilaterally agreed that the advantage in Persian numbers meant that a direct assault of the Greek forces was the best option for an expedited end to the Greek naval resistance. The land forces would then overwhelm the Greeks at the Isthmus, an even more palatable location for the Persians than Thermopylae where they had already won. This was a sensible strategy, though perhaps rushed. The massive Persian fleet needed a harbouring for the winter that the shallow, sandy port of Phaleron would not provide. The Peloponnese offered the Argolic Gulf and other harbours with plenty of space for the Persians, and the admirals may have wished to make haste to arrive there before the autumn windstorms began to wreak havoc on their armada.

It was only the Carian queen Artemisia, the navy's only female admiral, who had both the courage and discernment to push back against the most powerful man on the planet:

> If you make no haste to fight at sea, but keep your ships here and abide near the land, or even go forward into the Peloponnese, then, my master, you will easily gain that end wherefor you have come. For the Greeks are not able to hold out against you for a long time, but you will scatter them, and they will flee each to his city; they have no food in this island, as I am informed, nor, if you lead your army

into the Peloponnese, is it likely that those of them who have come from thence will abide unmoved; they will have no mind to fight sea-battles for Athens. But if you make haste to fight at once on sea, I fear lest your fleet take some hurt and thereby harm your army likewise.[10]

The Ionian and Carian admirals thought Artemisia mad for going against the grain and were concerned that this would be her downfall, an event many Persian commanders evidently hoped for. After all, many considered her to only be there as an insult to the Greeks, showing that they would be conquered by a woman. But Xerxes rejoiced to hear her contrarian position, moving to promote her in status, sensing her military prowess as much as her courage to speak. Artemisia indeed had military prowess in discerning the probable Greek plan; Xerxes, however, was too enticed by the prospect of ridding himself of the thorn that was the Athenians.

He justified the decision to attack the Greeks with the most important thing in the Persian empire, himself. The lack of success at Artemisium, he concluded, was clearly his own absence. With the Persian king seated on high at the citadel at Munichia, he would motivate his navy to sure-fire victory – and critically evaluate his own fleet to see which ships were deeply loyal and which, like the Ionians, might underperform. Xerxes would judge accordingly. Plans were made for the Persians to attack the following day, and a contingent of Persian triremes sailed out from Phaleron that evening to covertly block off any escape routes.

* * *

Shortly after the Persian war council concluded, a man reached the shores of Piraeus in a small boat, demanding to speak with the Persian admirals. Most astonishingly, he claimed to come from the admiral of the Greek navy – without the knowledge of the rest of the Greeks.

His name was Sicinnus and he was an elderly man who spoke fluent Persian, most likely meaning he was from the Ionian coast and was an ethnic Greek raised under Persian rule. Sicinnus had been taken as a prisoner of war some time ago and found his way to Athens, where he served in the home of an influential Athenian politician named Themistocles.

Themistocles sent Sicinnus promptly after the failure to convince the Peloponnesian admirals and Eurybiades. Despite his status as a slave, Sicinnus was a deeply trusted advisor to Themistocles and had even been entrusted with the role of *paidagōgos*, the highly paid teacher of aristocratic youth. Themistocles trusted Sicinnus with his children and with his own life. He had certainly sought Sicinnus out on Salamis among the Athenian refugees for this primary purpose, though his Persian appearance and language skills were certainly an asset. There was nobody else that Themistocles could count on to deliver a message of treason.

Sicinnus quickly secured a meeting with the Persian commanders and unveiled the mysterious message:

> I am sent by the admiral of the Athenians without the knowledge of the other Greeks (he being a friend to the king's cause and desiring that you rather than the Greeks should have the mastery) to tell you that the Greeks have lost heart and are planning flight, and that now is the hour for you to achieve an incomparable feat of arms, if you suffer them not to escape. For there is no union in their counsels, nor will they withstand you any more, and you will see them battling against each other, your friends against your foes.[11]

Another ancient historian's version of the same message makes sure to include specific instructions to exploit the Athenian retreat, saying 'while they are in confusion and separated from their infantry…set upon them and destroy their naval power.'[12] Given the Persian position on the Athenian side, the Greek camp on Salamis allowed only one escape route to the north, circling the island and exiting into the Megaran Gulf. That would provide a direct route to the Isthmus of Corinth, where the Persians already knew of the battle fortifications.

Themistocles had sent the authentic Greek battle plan to the Persian king through his personal slave, and even provided helpful advice on assaulting his own ships. He was counting on the Persian tradition of rewarding traitors from the opposing side, following the recent model of Ephialtes at Thermopylae. Themistocles was ostensibly looking to join the ranks of medized Greek leaders now advising the invasion, such as Hippias, former tyrant of Athens, and Demaratus, former king of Sparta.

Xerxes was overjoyed at the news and at once ordered two hundred ships to follow Themistocles's instructions and barricade the far side of Salamis. The Persians decided to attack the next evening and capture the Greeks in their pincers mid-escape. This guaranteed a naval battle at Salamis by closing off the Greek retreat to the Isthmus – the exact strategy that Themistocles had demanded of the Greek admirals.

The question must be asked, then: was Themistocles actually serious here? Was this a genuine attempt to join the Persian ranks after realizing the hopelessness of the Greek cause? Was Themistocles so frustrated with the Hellenic League's eagerness to sacrifice Athens and hide behind their walls at the Isthmus? And would Themistocles really abandon his decade-long mission to prepare Athens and Greece for the inevitable Persian invasion?

It is impossible to discern his true intent from the text, but it is most telling that this ploy guaranteed triumph for Themistocles no matter the outcome of the battle. If the Greeks were to heed his plan and fight at the straits of Salamis, then Themistocles would have divided the Persian forces and tricked them into a foolish strategy where they would be caught off guard. It maximized the Greek – and Athenian – odds of success.

But if the Greeks actually were to retreat to the Isthmus, then Themistocles would have now endeared himself to the King of Kings and set himself up for a governorship or administrative role in the new Persian-ruled Athens. He would also contribute a massive fleet to the Persian navy, securing influence in the Persian war council and have the ear of Xerxes himself.

So was Themistocles a conniving traitor or a cunning patriot? The answer is probably that he was simply a survivalist. Regardless of his newly flexible patriotism, one truth is clear: Themistocles single-handedly engineered a battle between the greatest empire in the world and the Greeks. It would be fought on Themistocles's personal terms with his personal strategies. He manipulated the terms of the battle to fit his own vision. It was his own version of the Trojan Horse, and just like Odysseus's cunning ruse, this manoeuvre would determine the outcome of the entire war – and make its heroes cultural icons of Greece.

* * *

The endless night continued with one more conclave for Themistocles while he awaited the return of Sicinnus. The man who arrived at his tent in the dead of the night was none other than his perennial rival, Aristides the Just. The two men had not personally spoken since the latter's ostracism a few years earlier.

It was quite impressive that Aristides had even managed to reach Themistocles. The admirals had sent Aristides on a mission of the highest significance, to recover religious icons from Aegina before the Persian fleet could destroy them like they had the statues of the Athenian Acropolis. The Hellenic League recognized that a man of Aristides's unique reputation sailing into camp with recovered icons would be an encouraging omen. However, despite the quick success in recovering the idols, Aristides faced the challenge of sailing past the Persian fleet that was now barricading Salamis after Xerxes's recent commands. Aristides's single ship managed to slip past the Persian patrols, but he was the first Greek to lay eyes on this new Persian formation.

Instead of reporting the news of the Persian movements to Eurybiades the high admiral, Aristides went straight to Themistocles. This alone is an intriguing development as Aristides would normally have committed himself to following the proper command structure, especially when his revered Spartans were at the top. But, perhaps illustrating the distress of the Athenians in this moment and knowing the plans to retreat to the Isthmus, Aristides shared the report with Themistocles alone.

Although each man had deep quarrels with the other, their reunion was magnanimous. Any grudges were laid aside for the greater task, that of surviving the next day. Themistocles even showed a rare air of humility, telling his lifelong opponent, 'I should not have wished, O Aristides, to find thee superior to me here; but I shall try to emulate thy fair beginning, and to surpass thee in my actions.'[13]

Moving then into the pressing business, Aristides informed Themistocles that the Persians had surrounded Salamis and that the Greeks were trapped. Themistocles was delighted at the news that his subterfuge with Xerxes had succeeded, and although he still had the option of joining the Persian ranks if the Greeks failed the next day, he proceeded to tell Aristides about his plot with Sicinnus. And he asked Aristides to help him continue the scheme.

Themistocles knew that the impeccable *kudos* of Aristides made him a man who the other Greeks would listen to – a reputation that Themistocles no longer enjoyed with the Hellenic League's admirals. Themistocles implored Aristides to put his *kudos* to work and, after sharing the news of the Persian barrier surrounding them, vote to stand and fight at Salamis.

The reconciled Aristides and Themistocles proved an effective partnership, as Aristides's campaign among the admirals was effective enough to reconvene – again – the war council. Many admirals finally committed to Themistocles's plan, but it took one more Persian defector to tip the scales. A trireme from Tenea, no doubt part of the Persian patrol blockading the straits, entered the Greek camp. The ship's captain was executing the same manoeuvre as Themistocles, sharing battle plans with the enemy. The captain informed Eurybiades and the Greek commanders that the Persians had indeed closed off any escape and that there was no way to avoid naval combat.

The historian Diodorus Siculus also adds that the Greeks received one final turncoat, a Samian man sent by the Ionian admirals with a detailed copy of the Persian strategy.[14] By this point, the Persian tactics were old news but the real development was that the Ionians had discovered their Greek patriotism. Themistocles's information warfare after Artemisium had the intended effect for at least some Ionians, who now were actively undermining the Persian cause. Whether that would translate into an intentional underperformance in battle was still debatable, but Themistocles was jubilant that his deception had worked on so many fronts, and decided to bring this news to the Peloponnesian admirals.

Eurybiades called for one final vote – this time the true decision. Themistocles entered the meeting once more with a call to fight at Salamis and not waste the bottlenecking advantage of the narrow straits. This was to be the 'wooden wall'. But when Themistocles demanded the vote, Aristides remained silent.

A Corinthian admiral, fed up with the litany of meetings and indecisions, leapt on the opportunity. If Themistocles now claimed that Aristides and several more admirals were aligned with his view on the battle plans, why would Aristides not stand up and support him publicly? Aristides replied, in his trademark style, that his silence was 'not out of any good-will to the man, but because he approved of his plan'.[15]

The war council was moved by Aristides the Just's wisdom and voted, at very long last, to confront the Persians in the narrows of Salamis. They would attack the next day at a strategic time. With dawn approaching, Themistocles went to survey the straits and interrogate local fisherman and Salamis residents for any piece of data he could uncover. No doubt he also spoke at length with Sicinnus and the Tenian deserters for more information on the precise Persian formations and movements. Sleep never came.

Eurybiades and the rest of the fleet prepared for war forthwith. The thousands of *thetes* awoke, well rested from several days of not rowing, and climbed into their triremes. The marines loaded onboard, their spears sharpened and polished. Archers stocked their quivers, itching to get a good shot at Persian marines. The Greek triremes pushed off from shore, lighter and less waterlogged from their beaching but still heavier than the Persian ships. That weight would be needed at Salamis if their rams were to get enough momentum to pierce the Persian hulls. But most of all, the future of Greece rested on their oars. If the wooden wall was truly to be successful, it would be decided on this September day.

As dawn finally broke, an earthquake shook the ground. It was as if the gods themselves declared that Divine Salamis would indeed see the promised battle and allow them to 'gather the harvest' in the fall. The Oracle of Delphi's words would now be put to the test:

> Then far-seeing Zeus grants this to the prayers of Athena;
> Safe shall the wooden wall continue for thee and thy children...
> Yet shall a day arrive when ye shall meet him in battle.
> Holy Salamis, thou shalt destroy the offspring of women,
> When men scatter the seed, or when they gather the harvest.[16]

Themistocles's wooden wall was finally being built.

Chapter 7

The *Aristeia* at Salamis

The three Persian princes were bound and marched to the makeshift stone altar. The altar had been hastily built alongside the admiral's trireme, overseen by the priest Euphrantides. The fire crackled gently until the young men came closer. The flames shot up, almost as if it was calling out for them. Off to the side, a man sneezed violently – a traditional omen from the gods due to its involuntary nature. Euphrantides took these signs as a divine harbinger. The seer passed a knife to Themistocles and instructed him to sacrifice the Persian princes to Dionysus, called Dionysus the Devourer when the god of wine demanded human sacrifice.

It must have been an incomprehensible ending for the nephews of Xerxes, who had known nothing but luxury and comfort their entire lives. Even though they held them in captivity, the Greeks marvelled at their exotic beauty and their gold-adorned attire.

The handsome youths had been captured from Psyttaleia, the island with a Persian garrison. Upon the launching of the Greek fleet in the morning, Aristides had led the invasion of the island of Psyttaleia in a series of small boats that could steal under the Persian watchmen. Xerxes had placed the soldiers at the island so that they could slaughter the shipwrecked Greeks swimming to shore and rescue any Persians in the same position. Aristides and the Athenian hoplites overwhelmed the forces and put the majority of them to the spear. He spared only these three young men, who were the sons of Sandaucé, the sister of Xerxes. They had no doubt been placed in charge of the Persian contingent on Psyttaleia as a nepotistic act, hoping to earn enough favour with their slaughter of the Greek camp to be given higher commands or governorships in the future.

The priest Euphrantides passed a knife to Themistocles. Despite his recent religious fervour over the wooden walls prophecy, Themistocles had no desire to sacrifice anyone. He was revolted, finding the entire situation

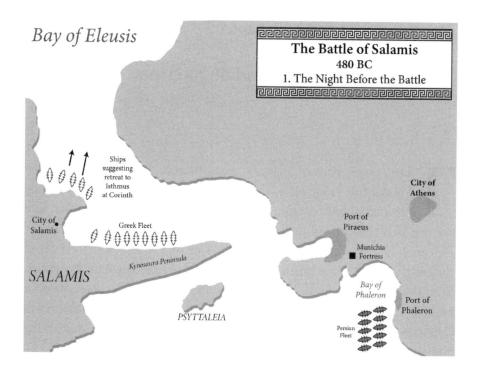

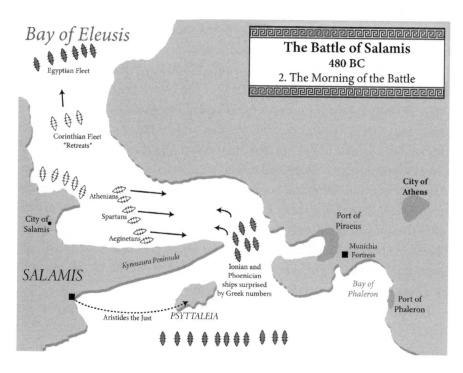

savage, and was gripped with fear. But despite his dread, he never once tried to stop it. Themistocles's knack for recognizing populist patterns was still razor sharp, and he knew that the anxious Greeks crowding the altar would be vitalized by the sacrifices. He knew that in perilous times like this, men 'looked for safety from unreasonable rather than from reasonable measures'.[1]

Themistocles grabbed the men, dragged them to the altar, and with a prayer of supplication he cut their throats with the sacred knife. He threw their bodies on the fiery altar, proclaiming that the gods would be pleased by this sacrifice and grant prosperity to the Greek ships on this very day. For him, it was a necessary sacrifice to save the Greeks.

It was not the first time that a Greek leader had made human sacrifices on a beach before sailing off to a fateful war. Agamemnon, leader of the Greek army off to invade Troy, had offended the goddess Artemis. Artemis frustrated the Greek fleet's departure until Agamemnon made the unthinkable sacrifice of his own daughter. Relentless of vision like our own hero Themistocles, Agamemnon killed her with his own hand at Aulis, near to where the Greeks had camped prior to Artemisium. Even the noble and heroic Odysseus had pressured Agamemnon to slay her. There is perhaps no clearer example of the chasm between the Homeric hero and the modern hero.

His religious duties fulfilled, Themistocles seized the moment for his greater interest, mobilizing the masses to achieve his vision. He gave the Greeks a pep talk for the ages, with the historian Herodotus saying that 'the tenor of his words was to array all the good in man's nature and estate against the evil.'[2] Over the past twenty-four hours, Themistocles had given nearly a dozen public speeches to war councils and admirals, but this was his first exhortation to those he connected with best, the non-elites.

One more symbolic moment added to the drama. As Themistocles's speech ended, a Greek ship sailed into view. It hailed from Aegina, and its captain, Aristides the Just, announced the successful rescue of the religious icons from the Sons of Aeacus. He and his men had fulfilled their sacred mission. Brimming with divine approval, the Greek bloodthirstiness manifested itself as the men rushed off to fight the Persians in their climatic last stand, willing to die for their liberty and for their commander, Themistocles. By this point, hardly anyone remembered that it was actually Eurybiades commanding this navy.

After all, nobody needed to tell the crowds that Aristides had arrived hours ago with the statues. Theatricality remained one of Themistocles's best tools.

* * *

The precise moment of the Greek assault was carefully selected by Themistocles. It was based on his research over the past few days when he had spoken with the locals of Salamis. His flair for connecting with the commoners meant that he benefited from the expertise of the local fishermen and sailors. It appears that Themistocles was especially interested in local weather patterns, in search of anything that could be weaponized against the invaders.

He found that weapon in a wave. Themistocles learned from the sailors that the waters during that long, council-filled night were showing the tell-tale signs of a morning wind. Described by Plutarch as 'the breeze fresh from the sea and a swell rolling through the strait,'[3] the historian Barry Strauss suggests this would have been an *aura*. The *aura* is a sea breeze that occasionally sweeps in northwards from the Saronic Gulf.[4] When it came during this period, it typically was in the mid-morning, and as a low, sustained wind it had a habit of inflicting pain on those ships with a lighter, taller centre of gravity.

The Persian fleet fitted that description perfectly. Phoenician ships, the backbone of the Persian navy, were especially tall with raised walls on their decks. These bulwarks were designed to protect the ship against heavy waves, but the prolonged wave of an *aura* exploited the bulwarks as the height of many Persian ships made them bottom-heavy. The shorter, heavier Greek ships were at far lesser risk – something that the fishermen of Salamis would have explained to Themistocles since they would also be in smaller ships when an *aura* rolled in. Plutarch describes the impact of the wave in depth:

> This breeze wrought no harm to the Hellenic ships, since they lay low in the water and were rather small; but for the Barbarian ships, with their towering sterns and lofty decks and sluggish movements

in getting under way, it was fatal, since it smote them and slewed them round broadside to the Hellenes, who set upon them sharply, keeping their eyes on Themistocles, because they thought he saw best what was to be done.[5]

Themistocles timed the Greek attack of the Persian ships to be slightly before the biggest impact of the *aura*. Every part of his plan was orientated against and limited the Persian advantages to create as even a playing field as possible. The straits of Salamis bottlenecked the greater numbers of Persian ships. The Greek assault was timed to disrupt the Persian ships shortly into the battle, mitigating their famous ability to move quickly and with great agility. And Themistocles already knew the Persian battle plan, since he had written it himself. The Greeks put all their hope in this moment.

*   *   *

While the Greeks were busy sacrificing his nephews to the gods, Xerxes ascended his throne at Munichia, the hill fortified by Themistocles a lifetime ago, to watch the battle unfold. He watched his ships intently, excited to award prizes of valour to the Persian ships that finally sank the Athenians for him. With the King of Kings watching, there was even more of an ardour for drawing first blood and many Persian captains were eager to earn recognition before the emperor.

The Greeks had pressed their main formation tightly to the northern coast of the Kynosoura peninsula, in order to shield their visibility from the Persians who were arranged in a crescent behind Psyttaleia. The Persians stacked their formations three lines deep, a width spanning from the Kynosoura peninsula all the way to the harbour of Piraeus. The battlefield demanded such a formation given its narrow width. In order to advance to the Greek position, the Persians had to blindly round the tip of the Kynosoura. The Persian sight lines were consequently poor at the battle's onset, another point of leverage arranged by Themistocles. The nexus of the battle would rage just north of the Kynosoura after the Persian fleet entered the narrowest parts of the straits.

In this main Greek formation, the Spartans, Aeginetans and Megarians took the southerly position, allowing them the first strike at the Persians who cornered the peninsula. When the Persians finally assembled their whole formation, they placed the Ionians directly opposite the Spartans. Themistocles's Ionian propaganda proved to have had limited success, as only a minority of the ships intentionally fought poorly. But this still amounted to perhaps a dozen ships, which makes no small difference.

The Athenians took the left part, to the north of the main formation, in order to oppose the Phoenicians in a duel of each side's most elite triremes. The numbers of these ships were more even than most other encounters in the war, with about a hundred more Phoenician ships, although they had to be layered back towards Piraeus given the small width of the straits.

Mardonius sent the Egyptian contingent to the north end of Salamis to cut off the Greek escape. Expecting this, Themistocles ordered the Corinthian ships to meet them there. With roughly 200 Egyptian ships and only 40 catalogued Corinthian ships, the numbers were dire.

In all, the Persian fleet at Salamis again numbered about 1200, minus the small amount of Ionian ships that were feigning combat. The Greeks, despite the reinforcement of fifty-six triremes after Artemisium and a handful of Persian defections, were somewhere shy of 400 total ships. Critically, only about a hundred Persian ships could fit in the straits at once. This meant that, while the Persians had waves of reinforcements available, the Greeks would never truly be outnumbered during the combat, and indeed they might even have more ships. This was the precise reason why Themistocles fought so hard to make the battle occur at Salamis.

The Greek navy sailed out from the city of Salamis a bit after dawn, aiming to draw the Persians out of their three-tiered formation and into the straits just as the *aura* struck. Herodotus's account says that a wave of *phobos* – unbridled fear in the midst of battle – overcame the Greeks upon seeing the Persians enter the straits. Many ships began to retreat and even beach their triremes, but one Athenian ship captained by a man named Aminias of Athens pushed through and drove his trireme towards the enemy. Sailing quickly past his fellow Athenians, the battering ram of Aminias's trireme collided with a Persian commander's ship, their hulls interlocking and not untangling. The Athenian marines scrambled over the breach and butchered every Persian aboard, publicly slaying the Persian admiral.

With Aminias's bravery, the *phobos* migrated from the Greeks to the Persians. The admiral had been slain right as the Persian formation was narrowing to enter the straits. It was a crucial moment in that all the other Persian ships were relying on specific instructions from this unfortunate admiral as to their next manoeuvre. Having lost this lead, every Persian ship captain immediately promoted himself to admiral and gave different orders. The Persian formation burst apart into a dozen smaller formations, each thinking the other ships were following their lead. The Greeks, who had kept their formation, charged.

The chaos spread malignantly across the Battle of Salamis. It was a lawless affair, far from the more polished choreography of Artemisium. A *thete* rowing for a nameless Athenian trireme captured the spectacle at Salamis in a unique medium. After his time rowing in combat, Aeschylus went on to become one of the most formative playwrights of the Athenian Golden Age. Less than a decade after Salamis, he recreated the battle. So as not to stoke any political tensions, Aeschylus takes the perspective of the Persians, hence the play's title of *The Persians*. Aeschylus animates the moment the Persians broke ranks:

> At first the encountering tide of Persians held;
> But caught in the narrows, crowded without sea-room,
> None could help other; nay, they fell aboard
> Their own ships, crashing in with beak of bronze,
> Till all their oars were smashed.[6]

While the Persians devoured themselves with a lack of discipline, the Greeks managed to maintain a semblance of order. The Athenians lead the main assault after the Persian line disintegrated, although the straits were too crowded for conventional trireme tactics. Any defensive formation, like the circle or crescent, was spatially impossible once the Persians entered the narrows. The earliest charges of the battle featured *diekplous*, the piercing charge through the enemy line and subsequent reversal to strike the enemy from behind, by the Athenians. Much like Artemisium, the Persians could not find enough of a runway to reach their high speeds. The Persian rams, while undoubtedly used, were less effective when they could not attain significant velocity given the lightness of their ships. The denser Greek ships brought the same blunt force they had at Artemisium, maximizing the damage without needing higher speeds.

Athenian and Aeginetan ships were especially successful in ramming during the initial advance. Coupled with the disorganization, this push likely caused the Persian front line to fold in on the two behind it. These Persian ships experienced the worst of the crush. As Diodorus Siculus recounts, 'when the men at the oars could no longer do their work, many Persian triremes, getting sidewise to the enemy, were time and again severely damaged by the beaks of the ships.'[7] The Greeks, though, relied also on reducing Persian rowing power by speeding past the sides of their triremes and shearing off half the oars. It made the victims sitting ducks.

Salamis eventually became so congested that it became something of a land battle, as marines boarded enemy ships to fight on foot. The Greek marines had seen little action at Artemisium, and so the heavy armour of their hoplites was in huge contrast to the wicker shields and light raiment of the Persian marines. This was another fortuitous move by Themistocles as, although the Egyptian marines were peerless in boarding enemy ships, Xerxes had already sent the Egyptians to the northern escape route. The straits were wider going around this northern channel of Salamis, and the Corinthian-Egyptian engagement there consequently focused more on the ramming, slicing, and shearing varieties of trireme manoeuvres.

At some point during the early stages of the action, the *aura* swept in. The Phoenician ships were most heavily hit by the sustained assault of the *aura*'s waves. Many of those Phoenicians who had not yet been pushed back by the Athenians were slowed or convulsed by the wind. Most importantly, the *aura* effectively trapped the Persian ships in the straits. Their bulwarks and high centres of gravity made the typically agile triremes unwieldy. The Phoenician fleet quickly lost their world-class advantages as they unsuccessfully struggled to adapt to the new sailing environment. Meanwhile, the heavy and slow Greek ships were unimpeded, their former weakness now transformed into a strength.

The battlefield conditions unfolded exactly as the fishermen of Salamis had predicted to Themistocles. Plutarch labels its impact as 'fatal'[8] to the Persian ships. The symbolism behind this humbling of the great Persian fleet at the hands of the lesser Greek ships is not lost on Plutarch's retelling.

Themistocles led the Greek rebels in spirit and in tactics, the de facto admiral over Eurybiades. His trireme, now the flagship, was the bellwether during the crucible of combat. The Greeks looked to him because, as

Plutarch describes, 'they thought he saw best what was to be done'[9] in the moment. It sealed his position as the powerbroker of Greece and Athens' position as Greece's hegemon.

Themistocles, meanwhile, earned himself a bounty among the Persian admirals. Perhaps because of his ever increasing *kudos*, one of the most influential Persian commanders stalked Themistocles's ship. Ariabignes was the half-brother of Xerxes and possibly the highest ranking commander after Mardonius. As a descendant of Cyrus the Great's best general and the son of Darius the Great himself, his Persian credentials were impeccable. His virtue and justice was deeply respected even by later Greek writers. Ariabignes captained the greatest ship in the Persian fleet with the entirety of the Ionians and Carians answering to him. He was, in short, far out of Themistocles's league in combat.

Ariabignes's trireme chased Themistocles's ship in a game of cat and mouse, pelting the Greek ship with arrows and javelins 'as though from a city wall'.[10] Themistocles was rescued by Aminias, the same Athenian who had been the first to attack. Aminias rammed Ariabignes's ship and boarded it alongside his marines. It took the spears of many hoplites, but Ariabignes was slain, his body dumped into the sea.[11]

Aminias turned his sights on another Persian admiral, the queen Artemisia. The choked Persian lines allowed little manoeuvring room for Artemisia's trireme to properly escape, and the bloodlust of Aminias was by this point renowned on the battlefield. Artemisia displayed a cunning akin to Themistocles and Odysseus when she paired survivalism and ambition by smashing into her own ally.

In the confusion and chaos of the battle, Artemisia had opted to remain directly in the sight lines of Xerxes's throne on Munichia. Knowing that Xerxes lacked the training or vision to digest the entirety of the battle, she opted to make a public scene of ramming a Persian vessel helmed by the king of Calyndus. The manoeuvre was brilliant. It had two implications for Artemisia, each better than the last.

Firstly, Aminias immediately stopped his pursuit of her ship, assuming her to be Greek, since she had just sunk a Persian trireme. Secondly, Xerxes showered the Carians with honours after the battle since he took special notice of her destruction of a kingly ship, right in front of his viewing throne. His attendants lacked either the discernment or desire to correct him, allowing him to assume that she had rammed a Greek king. It was a costly mistake for Aminias – there was a reward of 10,000 drachmae for the man who killed Artemisia. This Shakespearean case of mistaken identity earned Artemisia honours from both the Greeks and the Persians.

This is perhaps illustrative of the downsides of the constant evaluations by Xerxes. By this point in the battle, the Persian commanders strategized for personal gain and not actual victory. Herodotus pinpoints this weakness, describing that 'all were zealous, and feared Xerxes, each man thinking that the king's eye was on him.'[12] Once the front line of Persian ships began to retreat, the rear guard pushed forward vigorously, anxiously hoping to prove their courage in contrast to their allies' cowardice. Strategy was cast aside.

The limitations of the Persian meritocracy were now on full display. When marketing and image management triumph over military tactics, it is difficult to win.

*   *   *

The facade of the Persian navy began to crumble. With their triremes being pushed back, their front lines retreating, and the insurmountable gridlock of ships in the straits, the Persians turned on each other in frustration. First, a handful of Phoenician admirals, seeing their ships staved off by the Athenians, beached their ships and came to Xerxes's throne. They registered a complaint about the Ionians. They were treasonous cowards, the Phoenicians claimed, who had fallen for the propaganda of Themistocles and were sabotaging the Persian effort.

This was a fair claim, since many of the Ionians were visibly not fighting and the number of Ionians defecting to Greece had been growing every day. But despite their patriotic conflict, the Ionian situation was preferable to the Phoenician one. The Phoenicians were supposed to be the standard-bearers for the Persian armada. The Phoenicians, after all, had invented the trireme and were almost an exclusively naval state that funnelled all their money into expanding maritime trade and building ships. Despite all this, the upstart Athenians were crushing the Phoenician fleet, and doing it with rowers and ships that were less than five years old.

Thus far, the King of Kings was displeased with the Phoenician performance and had been instead impressed with several Ionian captains.[13] Xerxes had watched with a palpable rage as the Phoenician ships began to retreat. The discord sewn by Themistocles through those public messages to the Ionians was akin to Eris's golden apple at the wedding labelled 'To the fairest.' Of course, that message eventually started the Trojan War while this strife was more focused on ending a war.

With the Phoenician retreat, the bulk of the Persian forces followed. Aeschylus colourizes the Persian buckling with a poetic flair.

> But the Hellenes
> Rowed round and round, and with sure seamanship
> Struck where they chose. Many of ours capsized,
> Until the very sea was hid from sight
> Choked up with drifting wreckage and drowning men.
> The beaches and low rocks were stacked with corpses:
> The few barbarian vessels still afloat,
> Fouling each other fled in headlong rout.
> But they with broken oars and splintered spars
> Beat us like tunnies or a draught of fish,
> Yea, smote men's backs asunder; and all the while
> Shrieking and wailing hushed the ocean surge,
> Till night looked down and they were rapt away.
> But, truly, if I should discourse the length
> Of ten long days I could not sum our woes.
> There never yet 'twixt sunrise and sunset
> Perished so vast a multitude of men.[14]

By late afternoon, the Persians were in full retreat. Herodotus's measurement that the seas were the only place where Persia had yet to be truly challenged proved correct, as the Greeks had won the day. But there were still some heroic moments to be found as the Greeks hunted down the Persian stragglers. The ships of Aegina especially distinguished themselves, sinking dozens of Persian triremes that were fleeing the Athenians in the straits. This ambush was the result of teamwork between Athens and Aegina. It was an impressive development, seeing each side laying aside their hostility for heroism.

But the old rivalry between Athens and Aegina came once again to the forefront as daylight waned. They had ended their war at the Congress at Corinth a year earlier, yet the animosity had not receded. After all, Themistocles had used Aegina as the scapegoat in his efforts to convince the Athenians to build their fleet with Laurium's silver. Those wounds ran deep for the disaffected Aeginetans.

As Themistocles chased down one of the final Phoenician ships of the day, his ship was surpassed by an Aeginetan trireme captained by Polycritus, a distinguished admiral who had sank his share of Athenian ships in their prior battles. Polycritus got the better of Themistocles and gashed the Persian ship several times before the Athenians could successful ram it.[15] This was deeply personal for Polycritus, who had been imprisoned by the Athenians. Worse yet, Themistocles had accused the Aeginetans of being Persian sympathizers at the Congress at Corinth. For Themistocles, this accuastion was nothing more than a rhetorical tool, as he hoped to motivate the Congress by showing the immediacy of the Persian threat. But for Aegina, it was a national embarrassment that needed to be avenged.

To make such a display of superiority over Themistocles was calculated patriotism, and a rallying cry to the rest of Aegina. After sinking the Phoenicians, Polycritus hammered his point home with a taunt to Themistocles while sailing past his ship, 'See how friendly we are to the Persians!'[16] The words served as an omen for Athens' future relationship with the rest of Greece. Themistocles's heavy-handed diplomacy had alienated an important ally. Many smaller members of the Hellenic League heard the tale and sympathized with Aegina.

Remaining committed to his disapproval of Athenian triremes, Aristides the Just returned to his land assault on Psyttaleia. He took a special force of hoplites to fortify the island he had first invaded when he took the three Persian princes captive. He arranged his hoplites along the island's shore, just on the outskirts of the strait's fiercest fighting. They replaced the Persian garrison and targeted the survivors of the battle as they swam ashore. It appears Aristides's forces were bolstered by a contingent of archers from Crete, who Herodotus had named as neutral after the Congress at Corinth. But Ctesias, a Carian historian writing a generation later, recounts that Themistocles and Aristides partnered to convince the Cretans to join the Greeks at Salamis.[17]

Aristides's hoplites and archers massacred any Persian who managed to make it to dry land. The Greeks who had fallen into the waters were given safe passage, of course. There were many of them, as the Greeks did lose dozens of ships over the day, but the Greek refugees were also trained swimmers. The Persians, on the other hand, were not. The confederate nature of the Persian military meant that many of their rowers were not experienced swimmers and may not have even grown up near the sea. Many Persian rowers who survived the initial shipwreck in the straits did not survive the journey to nearby land.

Aristides had great success at Psyttaleia, especially when a detachment of Persian Immortals came ashore. They were put to the spear easily. This was a remarkable turnaround from the Immortals' victory over the 300 Spartans just weeks earlier. Aristides's success merited a statue on Psyttaleia that stood for centuries afterwards. In just a few short weeks, Aristides the Just had transformed himself from Athenian exile to Greek hero.

*   *   *

The Battle of Salamis ended with nightfall. The Persian retreat proved more disastrous than their assault. Between the *aura* and the rams of Aeginetan triremes, the withdrawal cost more Persian lives than the actual battle in the straits. The surviving Persian ships returned to the harbour at Phaleron, beaching their triremes and re-joining the land army.

The Persian navy was decimated. We do not have reliable numbers of lost ships for either side, but the Persians lost several hundred ships at a minimum. One ancient historian that was deeply sympathetic to the Persians – and deeply critical of Herodotus's Greco-centric account – numbers the Persian losses at 500 ships.[18] The Greeks lost only a few dozen. The Persian invasion plan, the culmination of a decade's work by two of the greatest monarchs of the powerful Achaemenid empire, was ruined. The lack of both numbers and advanced planning had put paid to an advance onto the Peloponnesian Peninsula. The Peloponnese, now the bread basket of Greek sovereignty, was safe from invasion for at least a year. In order to harbour their ships, the Persian fleet were forced to leave Athens before the treacherous winter storms.

The King of Kings' emotions now combined in a dangerous mix of vexation and rage. From his throne on Munichia, he judged that it was the Phoenicians most responsible for the failure. He had seen them flee the battle first, and had little tolerance of their accusations against the Ionians. Xerxes ordered those Phoenician admirals who had dared approach him and blame the Ionians to be killed. That was seemingly not enough blood, however, as he also ordered the execution of 'those Phoenicians who were chiefly responsible for beginning the flight, and threatened to visit upon the rest the punishment they deserved'.[19] Many Phoenician ships now fled, entirely to avoid (for the time being) a grisly fate. The Persian navy was thus reduced even further as they lost their best ships and captains.

Xerxes next turned his wrath on the Athenians. He demanded that his generals build a earthwork bridge across the strait of Salamis. But at this point, even the renowned theatrics of Persian conquest could not overcome the losses at Salamis. The Persians were simply not accustomed to losing, as Xerxes's foolhardy reaction illustrates. The plan would have been rejected in a democratic war council, but Xerxes had nothing of the sort.

Yet Xerxes had no intention of seeing the construction of the land bridge. His main focus now was on a hasty return to his pontoon bridge at the Hellespont. He feared that 'the Greeks (by Ionian counsel or their own devising) might sail to the Hellespont to break his bridges, and he might be cut off in Europe and in peril of his life.'[20] It is clear that Themistocles's mind games regarding the Ionians' true loyalty at work. The vast majority of Xerxes naval and land forces would accompany him, leaving Greece manned with a paltry Persian battalion that was sure to be quickly overrun.

It took his most experienced general to redirect the King of King's plans. In the sombre Persian council room, Mardonius entirely whitewashed the battles outcome. Playing into Xerxes's nationalism, Mardonius requested that the Great King of Persia not fully retreat:

Sire, be not grieved nor greatly distressed by reason of this that has befallen us…If you are resolved that you will lead your army away, even then I have another plan. Do not O king, make the Persians a laughing-stock to the Greeks; for if you have suffered harm, it is by no fault of the Persians, nor can you say that we have anywhere done less than brave men should; and if Phoenicians and Egyptians and Cyprians and Cilicians have so done, it is not the Persians who have any part in this disaster. Wherefore since the Persians are nowise to blame, be guided by me; if you are resolved that you will not remain, do you march away homewards with the greater part of your army; but it is for me to enslave and deliver Hellas to you, with three hundred thousand of your host whom I will choose.[21]

But this was all a publicity campaign orchestrated by Mardonius. He knew that his own standing was in jeopardy. Xerxes had already sent messengers back to the Persian capital with news of Athens' destruction, where it was met with jubilant parades. His subsequent update of Salamis's defeat was met with despondency and public displays of mourning. But the Persians were too wise and too proud to blame their own king, and so they blamed the second-in-command. Mardonius had, after all, been the most hawkish on Greece and had already failed in the previous invasion under Darius. He was an easy target.

His request to lead a homegrown contingent was a prudent move combining both self-preservation and clever military strategy. Mardonius would lead an army of true Persians, eliminating the bloated bureaucracy of the massive invasion force. His fighters would be a distilled version of Persia's best and brightest, those who had first won the empire.

But Mardonius had lost his influence, and Xerxes opted to consult with his new favourite advisor, Artemisia of Caria. Having not forgotten her disapproval of (and Mardonius's push) for the Battle of Salamis, Xerxes asked for her input before agreeing to the proposal to change his long-held invasion plans. Her answer was more Athenian than Persian. She said that Mardonis's plan was a golden opportunity, for if the Greeks were to win then the unfortunate general would take the blame entirely and deny the Greeks an indisputable claim to victory over the King of Kings. Although Xerxes's admiration of her skill led him to famously quip, 'My men have become women, and my women men,'[22] he was not yet ready to commit to the plan.

Mardonius was shortly aided in his proposition to continue the Greek invasion by Themistocles, of all people. Sicinnus, the servant of

Themistocles who had brokered the first correspondence between Persia's emperor and Athens' hegemon, reappeared at the Persian war council in the midst of their debate. Sicinnus came bearing another personal message for Xerxes the Great:

> Themistocles son of Neocles…who is the Athenian general, of all the allies the worthiest and wisest, has sent me to tell you this: Themistocles the Athenian has out of his desire to do you a service stayed the Greeks when they would pursue your ships and break the bridges of the Hellespont; and now he bids you go your way, none hindering you.[23]

But, as is so often the case with Themistocles, things were not as they appeared. Like his previous report to the Persians, there was nothing untrue in these words. Yet this was another machination by Themistocles to create a situation where he won, no matter the outcome.

After Salamis, Themistocles and the Greek navy had pursued the retreating Persian fleet as far as Andros, about six miles off the Euboean coast. When they saw that the Persians were in fact withdrawing and not attempting to fight by sea, Themistocles immediately demanded that the Hellenic League sail to the Hellespont, far across the Aegean Sea, and burn down the pontoon bridge. Xerxes would then be trapped in Greece, but more importantly the Persian supply chain would be irreparably damaged. The Persians would not be able to feed or equip their massive force.

However, slowly starving the Persian army was not enough for Themistocles. He wished to take the fight to Persian soil once Xerxes managed to return to the Ionian coast. He remarked that the Greeks should pursue 'till he come in his flight to his own country; and thereafter let it be that country and not ours that is at stake in the war'.[24] It was an incredibly bold proposal and ironically he convinced the Peloponnesian admirals straightaway. It seems he had finally won them over when he proved his acumen in orchestrating the Battle of Salamis. Nevertheless, they were the only voting bloc that Themistocles was able to convince.

The Athenians were especially incensed at the Persian retreat. Seeking retribution for their destroyed city, the Athenians assembled to give vent to their anti-Persian feelings. Most demanded that the Athenian fleet abandon the Hellenic League and chase after the Persian fleet. But Themistocles approached the Athenian assembly with a different idea:

> Wherefore I say to you, – as it is to a fortunate chance that we owe ourselves and Hellas, and have driven away so mighty a cloud of enemies, let us not pursue after men that flee. For it is not we that have won this victory, but the gods and the heroes, who deemed Asia and Europe too great a realm for one man to rule, and that a wicked man and an impious; one that dealt alike with temples and homes, and burnt and overthrew the images of the gods, – yea, that scourged the sea and threw fetters thereinto. But as it is well with us for the nonce, let us abide now in Hellas and take thought for ourselves and our households; let us build our houses again and be diligent in sowing, when we have driven the foreigner wholly away; and when the next spring comes let us set sail for the Hellespont and Ionia.[25]

It was a lovely speech, despite being mostly a deception. Themistocles knew he would be unable to convince the rest of the Greek commanders to follow through with the trip to the Hellespont. If Eurybiades and the Hellenic League conceded to Themistocles on another major policy decision, it would be a public proclamation of Athenian supremacy. The Spartans would never allow it. What's more, this was to be one of the final times that Themistocles spoke poorly either of Xerxes or the Persians.

Indeed, from this point onward, Themistocles's tone regarding the Persians would be unusually reverent for a nation that burned his home. Themistocles was already at work cultivating his relationship with the Persians, just in case his recent success was not to last. Herodotus notes that this was 'so that he might have a place of refuge if ever (as might chance) he should suffer aught at the hands of the Athenians'.[26] He was ultimately buying time so that he could contact Xerxes. Despite sinking their fleet the very day before, Themistocles's relationship with Persia was growing ever cosier.

As he expected, Themistocles was denied. Although the Athenians were 'ready to obey whatsoever he said,'[27] Greece was not. His proposal to sail to the Hellespont was roundly defeated and the Hellenic League opted to fortify the Greek peninsula and prepare for the inevitable land battle with the undefeated Persian army.

And so Themistocles turned to his most faithful tactic, that of subterfuge. Relying on his sterling reputation with Xerxes, which remained strong since he had provided the King of Kings with the battle plans of Salamis, Themistocles sent Sicinnus to mediate another deal. When Sicinnus revealed the half-truth that the Greeks would – eventually – sail to the Hellespont, Xerxes panicked. He made arrangements to retreat back to the pontoon bridge by land before the Greeks could sail there in the spring. Xerxes gave Mardonius a free hand in the choice of an army and then took the remainder back to Persian lands with him. For now, central and northern Greece remained under Persian rule, and Athens remained a smouldering pit. Their futures would be decided in the spring when Mardonius led his new army against the Hellenic League's hoplites.

This second cunning ploy with Sicinnus was a multi-layered win for Themistocles. As before Salamis, he maintained an open line of communication with Xerxes, just in case it would be necessary later on. Themistocles had ensured that the bulk of the Persians had departed Greece, their emperor along with them. He had not had to risk the Athenian fleet's journey across the Aegean, yet still secured the same result of a Persian departure. And most of all, he had amplified his reputation with the Persians. The King of Kings knew that, if ever it would become necessary, he could engage in dialogue with Themistocles for mutual benefit. It was a fact that Themistocles kept secret from all apart from Sicinnus. It would also determine his own future.

*   *   *

By the early spring of 479 BC, only Mardonius's battalion remained of the once-massive Persian military. Salamis had been an astonishing victory for the Greeks that utterly changed the course of the war. Heroes had been made in those bloody, cramped straits. Themistocles earned a reputation as one of the great saviours of the West, rebutting the Persian threat and ensuring the East would never successfully take over Europe. As one classical historian describes Themistocles's performance at Salamis, '[Xerxes] was defeated in consequence rather by the stratagem of Themistocles than by the arms of Greece.'[28]It was his *aristeia*, the moment when he grasped his own destiny and willed it into being through sheer determination and overflowing *arete*. To this day, it is the focal point of all writing about him.

But many more heroes were created at Salamis. The poet Aeschylus transformed his experiences rowing aboard an Athenian trireme into the most vivid and moving tragic literature of the ancient world. The young, ambitious Greek commander Cimon idolized Themistocles's excellence at Salamis and used it as the rubric for his future leadership of Athens decades later.

And most of all, Athens survived. Although their city was ruined and their population in exile, the Athenians were the ultimate victors of Salamis. Their triremes and strategies saved their own lives as much as their future. They increased their primacy among the Greeks tenfold, securing an independent Greece and an influential Athens.

They would, however, need to take their city back. The war was not yet over, as Mardonius and 300,000 of the world's best fighters still stood between the Greeks and true victory. Although Themistocles had engineered the expulsion of the Persian navy, their land forces were unswayed. If the warrior-philosopher Xenophon was correct in labelling Themistocles an 'amulet of saving virtue,'[29] then Themistocles would need to prove it by taking back Athens and rebuilding it. Otherwise, there would not be much to save.

Part III

The Hegemon of Athens and Greece

Chapter 8

A Defeated Persia, A Wounded Themistocles

He had single-handedly brought Greece to the brink of victory at Salamis, but he hardly participated in the rest of the war. 479 BC, the year after Salamis, was one of the most difficult of Themistocles's life. He was forced to distance himself from the politics of both Athens and Greece, completely vanishing from Herodotus's narrative shortly after Salamis and never reappearing despite two more large battles in the war. Leadership in the Hellenic League and in Athens was handed off to other men, the latter role falling to Xanthippus, who replaced Themistocles as admiral of the Athenian navy. Themistocles was thereby utterly denied the chance to experience the sweetness of celebrating the triumph of a Greek win in the Greco-Persian Wars.

The reasons for his decline are found in his actions after annihilating the Persian fleet at Salamis. The postscript of the Battle of Salamis was fully written by Themistocles's Athenians. In perhaps another propaganda campaign, the Athenians fervently denied the heroic claims of two other Greek city-states that helped defeat Xerxes. First, the Aeginetans claimed that they were the first to draw Persian blood in the straits. The ships of Aegina won prizes of valour and had ultimately been the best performers of the day, proportional to the smaller size of their fleet, regardless of whether they truly attacked first. But the Athenians would not tolerate any other city-state in their spotlight, especially after Polycritus's taunting of Themistocles. Herodotus notes the disparate accounts of the Aeginetan performance at Salamis; the Athenians recast the narrative to say that the Aeginetans were little more than auxiliary to the heroic deeds of the Athenian fleet, and shot down Aegina's claims to the contrary.

Next, the Athenians worked to underplay the Corinthians' role in the battle. The Corinthians claimed that they had stymied the Egyptians' attack from the north and protected the rear of the main Greek fleet. This was, after all, the formal battle plan devised by Themistocles, and the

Egyptians had not managed to outflank the Greeks. But the Athenian report was far less kind. They claimed that Adimantus, the Corinthian admiral who had repeatedly and publicly challenged Themistocles, was 'struck with terror and panic, and hoisting his sails fled away; and when the Corinthians saw their admiral's ship fleeing they were off and away likewise.'[1] Athenian heroism, of course, made up for the Corinthian cowardice. The Athenian account even included Athena herself chastising Adimantus for his failure to act with *arete*. It was an outlandish tale but, since the Athenians undoubtedly orchestrated the victory, it was a story that Themistocles was able to spread across Greece effectively.

The Athenian hubris bled over into policy decisions. After engineering the retreat of Xerxes and the bulk of his army, Themistocles set his sights on consolidating Athenian influence over Greece. The first step in this process was to subdue the Persian-allied territories closest to Attica and Athens, chiefly so that the Athenians could actually return home and begin to reconstruct Athens. With Mardonius's new force wintering in Thessaly in the winter of 480–479 BC, Themistocles sailed the Athenian fleet to Andros first.

Andros was among the most powerful Cycladic Islands off the coasts of Attica and Euboea, and they were also the most loyal to Persia. They joined the Persians shortly after Xerxes's victory at Thermopylae. Andros had sent ships to fight against the Greeks at Salamis, and Xerxes's fleet had stopped there the day after their loss, before the flight back to central and northern Greece. In the late fall of 480 BC, Themistocles, judging their Persian fidelity unacceptable, sailed into the harbour of Andros's capital. Eurybiades remained in formal command of the fleet but this was a thoroughly Athenian strategy to eliminate a local Persian outpost. Themistocles was making the leadership decisions for the Hellenic League now.

The settlements of Andros were on high plateaus with grand vistas of the Aegean Sea. From their acropolis, the oligarchs of Andros's capital, also named Andros, would have seen Themistocles and his armada of probably a hundred triremes entering the harbour. Although it would have looked small compared to the Persian fleet that had just departed, it was still more than enough to besiege and destroy their home.

The Athenians made camp on the beach below Andros's plateau. Themistocles dispatched messengers to the city with the Athenian terms.

Simply put, Themistocles demanded money. Such tribute was common in the ancient Mediterranean, although it was typically the more powerful empires like Persia, Assyria, or Babylon that demanded the payment. Athens was an upstart and held only a large navy, one without a home city anymore, over the people of Andros.

Themistocles had used rhetoric, religion, subterfuge, bribery, and blackmail to persuade others. But he had not yet used philosophy. Themistocles sent a message to the leaders of Andros that illustrated his vaunted rhetorical skills yet also foreshadowed the Athenian love of philosophy:

> Themistocles gave them to understand that the Athenians had come with two great gods to aid them ... Persuasion and Necessity.[2]

The threat appealed to two well-known deities of the Greeks, Peitho and Ananke. Peitho was 'Persuasion', the goddess of seduction and the soft word. An attendant and daughter of Aphrodite, Peitho was revered in Athens for her role in uniting the city under the rule of Theseus. She came to represent civic balance and harmony, with a special attachment to democratic participation. Her inclusion in Themistocles's speech is clearly a call to peace and goodwill, even if she is an Athenian deity who would benefit Athens primarily. But Peitho was also seen as the power that helped a marriage continue to work, typically by giving spouses their desires and avoiding conflict. And Themistocles's message also had the subtext that his call for harmony was contingent on the bridegroom – Athens – getting what it wanted. It was, in fact, a necessity.

'Necessity' referred to the goddess Ananke, the deification of compulsion and inevitability. She was a primordial deity who is present in the most ancient of Greek myths, including the creation myth of Hesiod, *Theogony*, where she is the daughter of Titans. She is deeply influential as an arbiter of the future of all things, including the fates of all people – gods and humans. As mother of the Fates, those seamstresses of human lives, she was also the only one who had sway over their cosmic machinations.

Given her position, Ananke has been a ubiquitous presence in philosophy from the days of Plato. Plato relied heavily on the idea of Necessity in the cosmogony found in his *Timaeus*, where he says Ananke founded the universe with Intellect,[3] with both heavily transformed by

Persuasion. Sigmund Freud, Victor Hugo, and even Philip K. Dick all draw heavily on Ananke. Ananke's significance is aptly summarized in the words of the ancient poet Simonides, 'Not even the gods fight against Necessity.'[4]

Yet it was Themistocles who first weaponized the philosophy of Persuasion and Necessity in his demand to conquer Andros. His message for the Androsians and the entirety of Greece was that the Athenians would now be the powers of both Persuasion and Necessity. Civil harmony and human destiny were both wrapped up in Athenian supremacy. Although Peitho might assuage the Androsian fears a bit, Ananke would make sure that they bent the knee.

Unexpectedly, Andros met Themistocles's demands with their own defiant eloquence. They may have hoped that the Persian fleet would return and protect them, or that the Athenians were perhaps unwilling to truly commit to another battle while the Persians still had a considerable military presence in Greece. Or, they may have simply preferred to die with honour than pay a tyrant. Their words for Themistocles were intriguingly fatalistic: 'we have two unserviceable gods who never quit our island but are ever fain to dwell there ... Poverty and Impotence; being possessed of these gods, we of Andros will give no money; for the power of Athens can never be stronger than our inability.'[5]

The Androsians resisted until the Athenian hoplites stormed their acropolis and agora. When Themistocles muscled his way into the Androsian palace, they submitted. It turned out that Persuasion and Necessity did prevail over Poverty and Impotence.

The siege of Andros was the first in a long line of bullying foreign policy exercised by the Athenians. In the following days, Themistocles arranged for similar tribute to be paid from two more powerful ex-Persian city-states, Carystus on Euboea and the wealthy Cycladic Island of Paros. Each are said to have given money because of their fear of what Themistocles himself would do: 'Themistocles was of all the generals the most esteemed; which so affrighted them that they sent money.'[6]

In what had now become his trademark move, Themistocles did not share the news that the Carystians and the Parians had sent money. He shared none of it with the other generals of the Hellenic League and kept it for himself, or perhaps (if one views his actions in a more generous light) for Athens' reconstruction. Shortly after departing Andros as victors, Themistocles's navy sailed to Carystus and, ignoring their tribute now that the money was in hand, besieged them as well. The Parians were spared, since they presumably gave a more impressive sum. This sparked a campaign to systematically regain Persian-allied Greek cities, something that continued in earnest after Mardonius's remaining army was dealt with.

It may seem merciless, but island-hopping for tribute had a rich tradition in Greece. The image of a king storming the beach to claim tribute and gold from a lesser power who was allied with the enemy was rooted firmly in the writing of Homer. In *The Iliad*, the opening scene concerns the aftermath of the Greek heroes, including Agamemnon, Ajax, Achilles and Odysseus, conquering the Trojan-aligned island of Chryses and taking money, women, and sacred relics. Despite the malfeasance of burning a temple of Apollo, the scene is presented as a heroic act and a turning point in the war. Intentionally or not, Themistocles drew on this imagery at Andros, Carystus, and Paros. The Mediterranean world was learning that Themistocles was grasping his destiny and shaping his *kudos* in the Homeric mould.

But more importantly, the siege of Andros and these other city-states became the model of Athenian foreign policy for the rest of the fifth century: demanding tribute, ships, or both from lesser powers or mercilessly taking it by force. These demands were usually cloaked in political villainization, of Persia or later of Sparta, and of course ultimately benefited Athens more than the Hellenic League. Like the Androsians, anyone who resisted would be destroyed. But in this instance, the siege of Andros benefited Themistocles, and not just the Athenians.

*   *   *

Such buccaneering diplomacy did not endear Themistocles to the rest of the Hellenic League. Themistocles continued to fly a bit too close to the sun when the Greeks went to award the customary prizes of valour during the winter of 480–479 BC. After they had confirmed Xerxes's return across the pontoon bridge to Asia, the Greeks voted to award these prizes to those individuals who showed the most heroism and *arete* at Salamis.

These awards were aptly named *aristeia* in Greek and were a kind of formal acknowledgement of a hero's rise and moment of glory. They are prevalent in Herodotus's narrative as a means of bestowing honour and political authority to its recipients. In a culture where one's *kudos* determined one's worth and one's future, this award was deeply significant.

Themistocles wanted such a prize, although perhaps more as a political tool than a personal honour. He hosted a feast at the Isthmus of Corinth later that year, after his sieges of former allies, aimed at persuading a majority of the Greek leaders to vote for him. He came up short. When the Hellenic League admirals cast their votes for the prize of valour, Aminias of Athens won first place resoundingly. He had sunk the first Persian ship and killed the first Persian admiral. It is difficult to argue against his selection. Similarly, Aegina won the prize of valour as a city-state for their role in the vice-like grip that crushed the bulk of the Persian triremes.

Yet if the Greeks had used ranked choice, Themistocles might have won. Aminias did indeed win a healthy plurality of first place votes, although most Greeks had voted for themselves or men of their own city-state out of self-interest. But Themistocles won nearly all of the second place votes. The rest of the Hellenic League did not want to reward Athens, especially after their malfeasance at Andros. Even the wave of post-Salamis Greek nationalism was not strong enough to prevent traditional Greek infighting.

Stripped of their awards, the Athenians were outraged and threatened retaliation. Rightly so, the Spartans were concerned that Athens was becoming too influential. While they could not possibly predict its meteoric rise, they knew that Themistocles and Athens might challenge Spartan command of the Hellenic League's navy. The newfound Athenian influence could not be directly confronted, though, until after Persia was dealt with in the spring when Mardonius's army would return to fight. The Spartans, 'fearful lest Themistocles should be displeased at the outcome and should devise some great evil against them,'[7] opted to orchestrate some Athenian-style guile of their own. After the formal prizes of valour were awarded, they awarded the two Greek naval admirals, Eurybiades of Sparta and Themistocles of Athens, with a special dispensation.

Eurybiades was given a standard prize of valour, but Themistocles was awarded a 'prize of wisdom and cleverness,'[8] the first of its kind ever given in Sparta. But it was not just for show. Sparta welcomed Themistocles into their city, lavishing him with honours, expensive gifts, a ceremonial crown of olives and public praise. In an exceedingly rare instance, Sparta rolled out the diplomatic red carpet, 'receiving him with honours such as had never been accorded to any foreign visitor'.[9] Eurybiades received the same fanfare, but this was nevertheless a serious honour for the normally laconic, reserved Spartans who communicated respect through stoicism. The Spartans even gave him a ceremonial 300 hoplite escort out of the city, an honour typically only reserved for one of their kings. Themistocles is the only outsider to have ever received this honour.[10]

For the notoriously xenophobic Spartans to treat any foreigner, not least an Athenian, with such honours is nothing short of remarkable. They were clearly deeply grateful to sidestep a Persian battle on their home peninsula. Their lavish gifts to Themistocles speak of the desperation of Sparta to avoid an unnecessary battle with Persians or, as was borne out later in the century, war with the Athenians. Yet this incident set the standard for Athenian-Spartan diplomacy in the new Greek political climate now that Persia was in flight. Their relationship became increasingly complicated and tense, with the Athenians systematically constructing a naval empire while Spartan supremacy in Greece was progressively threatened.

The Spartans were clearly wooing Themistocles both to placate Athens, in an attempt to keep their ships and rowers in the Hellenic League until the Persians were completely eradicated, and to bolster the perceived Spartan role at Salamis by elevating Themistocles and Eurybiades to equal stature. But they were also attempting to neutralize the emerging threat embodied in Themistocles. His antics with Xerxes were exactly why Sparta needed to court him – to keep him fighting for Greece but also remain more loyal to himself than to Athens. With the newfound power that was the Athenian navy, Sparta wanted to limit the imperial and political growth of Athens. Their shrewd manoeuvre was compounded by the well-known fact that Athenian democracy could not tolerate one man rising too far above the rest. The result was a cocktail of appeasement, division, and discord – and it was largely successful.

At the Olympic festival that year, the cult of personality that surrounded Themistocles was on full display. It is said that when he entered the stadium to watch an event, 'the audience neglected the contestants all day long to gaze on him, and pointed him out with admiring applause to visiting strangers, so that he too was delighted, and confessed to his friends that he was now reaping in full measure the harvest of his toils on behalf of Hellas.'[11] Nowhere in independent Greece was free from Themistocles's fame or influence.

*   *   *

The intriguing relationship between Themistocles's Athens and the Spartans developed a new layer after Themistocles's return to Athens. After hobnobbing with the Spartans, Themistocles was given a much colder Athenian welcome with decidedly less celebration. While Themistocles was being pinned with Spartan medals and prizes, the Athenians had continued to live in a destroyed city with defiled temples and ruined homes.

Most critically for Themistocles, serious cracks were forming in the bedrock of his political support. His Spartan excursion had given a foothold to his political rivals, who were emboldened by the aristocrats who now, more than ever, saw Themistocles as an existential threat to the very idea of aristocracy. They funded politicians whose task was to fan the flames of lower class discontent with their formerly beloved populist. One famous incident illustrates the escalating peril that Themistocles, champion of Salamis and the man who defeated Xerxes the Great, found himself in:

> When a man from the little island of Seriphus grew abusive and told [Themistocles] that he owed his fame not to himself but to the city from which he came, Themistocles replied that neither would he himself ever have made a name if he had been born in Seriphus nor the other if he had been an Athenian.[12]

Herodotus's version of this encounter is an even more biting look at the fickle nature of democracy:

> But when Themistocles returned to Athens from Lacedaemon, Timodemus of Aphidnae, who was one of Themistocles' enemies but a man in nowise notable, was crazed with envy and spoke bitterly to Themistocles of his visit to Lacedaemon, saying that the honours he

had from the Lacedaemonians were paid him for Athens' sake and not for his own. This he would continually be saying; till Themistocles replied, 'This is the truth of the matter – had I been of Belbina I had not been thus honoured by the Spartans; nor had you, sirrah, for all you are of Athens.' Such was the end of that business.[13]

Lost in this ever-increasing renown, Themistocles fell victim to hubris. His over-confidence, but more critically his interminable self-marketing, pushed him too far into the limelight. Despite his stature as the saviour of Athens, the city was still little more than rubble. Ownership of a world class navy and a homegrown hero had not given the Athenians a warm bed or secure walls overnight. Where the Greeks saw a saviour and political icon, many Athenians saw a self-serving opportunist and a potential tyrant.

The close proximity of Mardonius's remaining Persian soldiers, a large contingent of which was in Thebes, kept many Athenians – along with their cultural, social, and commercial activity – from fully returning home. Themistocles bore the brunt of their frustration. Stories of pushback by Athenians to his new station and Themistocles's subsequent disdain for having to justify himself are peppered throughout the winter and spring of 479 BC. Like the stories of the man from Seriphus or of Timodemus of Aphidnae, who each had told Themistocles that he was unworthy of the Spartan honours, many ancient historians also include anecdotes of the common man approaching Themistocles, disillusioned with their former populist champion. He was haemorrhaging support from his main constituency.

Themistocles's award ceremony at Sparta had been especially condemning, not because of a dislike of Sparta but because no democrat should willingly receive such praise and lavish attention. The Athenians were certainly grateful to Themistocles's for their lives and what remained of their city but could not tolerate his ambition. While they admired and respected him, they 'at the same time harboured suspicions of him, lest it should be with the purpose of preparing some sort of tyranny for himself'.[14]

Their patience having run thin, the Athenians voters acted quickly to strip Themistocles of authority in an effort to hammer down the nail that was sticking out. In the late winter or early spring of 479 BC, the voting assembly 'removed him from the generalship and bestowed the office upon Xanthippus the son of Ariphron'.[15] This meant that the grand Athenian navy, constructed by Themistocles after Laurium, harboured in the port he built at Piraeus, and led successfully by him at Artemisium and Salamis, now belonged to his old rival Xanthippus, whom he had personally exiled and later recalled. Themistocles, seeing the writing on the wall, relegated himself to political anonymity for the time being. The land forces were given to his arch-rival, Aristides the Just.

Both men would lead the Athenian military for the rest of the Persian Wars. Themistocles disappears from the ancient sources for the majority of 479 BC, only months after he rescued Athens, Greece, and the West. It was an astonishing about-face, although not the end of Themistocles in the historical narrative. It was however, the end of his presence in Herodotus's *The Histories*. He vanishes after his chastisement from Timodemus of Aphidnae, with barely a passing reference during the rest of the Persian Wars. It is clear that his demotion in 479 BC left an enduring impact, even as he would accomplish much more during Herodotus's lifetime. For many, the mythos of Themistocles had apparently peaked at Salamis. Much like Theseus after his conquest over the minotaur or Achilles after his victory over Hector, their stories moved on but their mythical status as heroes remained static.

* * *

Lost in the revival of intra-Greek conflict was the continued Persian occupation of most of Greece and its serious threat to the rest of it. Despite the victory at Salamis, Athens remained under direct threat since Mardonius had wintered his significant Persian force in both Thessaly and Boeotia, only a short journey from Athens. Exacerbating this threat was the Hellenic League's refusal to help protect Athens. Despite their recent accolades for Themistocles, the Spartans steadfastly remained in the Peloponnese behind their wall at the Isthmus of Corinth. No member of the Hellenic League would assist Athens if the Persians attacked. The Athenians were livid, expecting their naval victories to have changed the Peloponnesian generals' minds.

In response, the Athenian navy went on strike, refusing to join the Hellenic League's navy at the island of Delos. Athenian triremes harboured in Piraeus and set about bringing food and supplies to rebuild Athens. With the best navy in the Mediterranean out of commission, the Spartan king Leotychidas took more direct control and supplanted Eurybiades as admiral. While they added a few more Spartan ships, the Hellenic navy was paltry in comparison to its strength just weeks before. They settled into a stand-off with the now similarly small Persian navy harboured at Samos, not far away. Neither side had the confidence to attack the other, especially during treacherous winter winds.

Upon sensing the increasing Athenian-Spartan tension, Mardonius made a marked change in the Persian diplomatic strategy. Instead of continuing to antagonize Athens, he sent a delegation to Athens to convince them to join Persia. It may seem a desperate action given the recent Persian defeats, but the broader context was kinder to Mardonius. Even with the vast majority of the Persian soldiers back in Asia, the remaining fighters were not only the most elite forces, the most loyal, and the most ethnically Persian, but were still of greater number than the allied Greek city-states. And, of course, Athens – and especially their leader Themistocles – had already demonstrated an inclination to work with Persia, both before and after the Battle of Salamis. Themistocles's covert correspondences with Xerxes remained influential in the Persian war room.

Moreover, like the Spartans, the Persians wanted the Athenian naval fleet. Mardonius wanted Athens for a simple reason – 'to be easily master of the seas'[16] and match his enviable land strength led by the Immortals. The Athenian navy would make an admirable replacement for the now-departed Persian armada and, if Themistocles's congenial relationship with Xerxes and Athens' present tension with Sparta were any indication, it would be a straightforward transaction.

With that justification, Mardonius employed King Alexander I of Macedonia as his emissary. It was a wise choice. Despite being Persia's main recruiter in mainland Greece, Alexander had cultivated a strong relationship with Athens and the Hellenic League ever since his strategic kindness in revealing the defensive weaknesses of the Vale of Tempe. This had helped Themistocles and the Greeks avoid sure defeat and led to both the success of Artemisium and the moral victory of Thermopylae.

Alexander was sent with a generous offer: divine forgiveness for destroying the Persian fleet, an offer to return Attica and add any new Greek land of their choice, and funds to rebuild the destroyed city of Athens. It would have been an enticing proposal to many Greek city-states, but the Athenians, in general, were not willing to forgive the matter of their burned city. Especially after the victory at Salamis, the Athenian independent spirit was fervent and unbroken. They could taste the future expulsion of Persia and their dominance of their Greek neighbours.

The Athenians, however, also knew how to wisely navigate geopolitics. Why reject Mardonius's offer outright when they could manipulate it for profit? Athenian leaders, Themistocles apparently no longer among them, made a public display of the state reception of Alexander and the Persian delegation. Themistocles's influence on Athenian politics remained evident despite his recent demotion.

Their main goal was clear: to induce the Spartans and the rest of the Peloponnesians to finally travel north of the Isthmus of Corinth and defend the rest of Greece. So far nothing had caused the Hellenic League to budge on the issue as they waited for the inevitable Persian assault on their walls at the Isthmus. But as the Athenians publicly hosted Alexander, they made sure to demonstrate a willingness to work with the Persians.

Alexander was given the most lavish welcome the still-ruined city of Athens could afford. He knew the Athenians were chiefly aiming to motivate the Spartans, yet it did not sway his mission. The king of Macedonia pressured the Athenian voters to capitalize on their post-Salamis reputation with Xerxes, and to act while the Persians envied their naval fleet, since their city was unlikely to survive much longer. He told the Athenians plainly that 'if therefore you will not straightaway agree with them, when the conditions which they offer you, whereon they are ready to agree, are so great, I fear what may befall you; for of all the allies you dwell most in the very path of the war, and you alone will never escape destruction, your country being marked out for a battlefield.'[17]

The Athenians gave the public perception that they were considering the offer. Messengers with carefully crafted propaganda were sent south through the Peloponnese, whipping up a groundswell of frustration with Spartan leadership. News of new Persian envoys continuing the dialogue reached the Spartan ephors. Religious oracles touted a foreboding Spartan prophecy from before the war began: that Sparta could only be driven out of the Peloponnese by the combined force of Persians and Athenians. It was enough to rattle enough of the great Spartan fortitude.

It was this Athenian display of affection for the Persian emissaries that finally spurred the Hellenic League to send men past the Isthmus. Unfortunately, it was at first only Spartan ambassadors. The Athenians, disappointed at the refusal to send hoplites but encouraged by the progress, upped the ante by inviting more Persian negotiators. The Spartan envoys reached Athens shortly after one of Alexander's persuasive speeches.

Within one short speech, the Spartans agreed not only to march north of the Isthmus to confront the Persian army but also to feed the Athenian refugees who had now lost two harvests. The show of Greek camaraderie was unusually generous but most welcome for the Athenians. As a show of gratitude, the Athenians sent Alexander back to Mardonius with an eloquently arranged rejection:

> Now carry this answer back to Mardonius from the Athenians, that as long as the sun holds the course whereby he now goes, we will make no agreement with Xerxes; but we will fight against him without ceasing, trusting in the aid of the gods and the heroes whom he has set at nought and burnt their houses and their adornments.[18]

Perhaps no better illustration exists of Themistocles's original vision of an Athenian naval superpower than this bidding war between Mardonius and Sparta for Athenian loyalty. It was a snapshot of the future: a strong navy provided Athens, even after Themistocles was gone – as he was in this example. Even with the present demotion of Themistocles, the Athenians knew how to best manage this situation to strengthen their city-state.

With Sparta and the Peloponnesians now committed to leaving their peninsula and defending the rest of Greece, the time had come to end the war.

* * *

Mardonius's forces marched on Athens again in the early summer of 479 BC, prompting another full scale evacuation of Athenian citizens back to Salamis. With the Persians again occupying Athens, the

Hellenic League responded swiftly. After making another Marathon-like show of choosing a religious festival over helping the Athenians, the Spartan ephors sent five thousand Spartan hoplites, under cover of night, each attended by seven fighting slaves. With Leonidas now dead and his heir underaged, a fearsome and highly ambitious Spartan commander named Pausanias assumed regency and took command. The fact that the Spartans had finally marched past the Isthmus was such a surprise to the Athenians that Aristides the Just, on a diplomatic mission to Sparta to again request support, was told to shake off his sleepiness since Spartan hoplites were already in Arcadia. Perturbed at the news that he was now wasting precious time, Aristides chastised the Spartan ephors for 'deceiving their friends instead of their enemies'.[19] Nevertheless, all of Athens celebrated that the Persian invasion would now conclude, in one way or another.

By the summer, more Peloponnesian city-states had joined the Spartans, swelling their ranks to nearly 100,000. And most critically, the Athenians, with their home city in unending siege, mustered 8,000 Athenian hoplites. When the Athenian voting assembly elected the *strategos* for the looming battle, none other than Aristides the Just was given command, answering only to Pausanias the Spartan. Pausanias led the allied Greeks to Boeotia, with a climatic stand taking place at Plataea. A self-promoter in the vein of Themistocles, Pausanias was hellbent on taking grasp of his destiny in the approaching conflict.

Simultaneously, the Greek navy welcomed back the two hundred Athenian triremes. The Athenian fleet gave command to Xanthippus who, along with the Spartan king Leotychidas orchestrated a cat-and-mouse game with the remnant of the Persian fleet. The two forces eventually met at Mycale, near the Persian fleet harbouring at Samos, on the Ionian coast.

And so in late August of 479 BC, fighting once again resumed on two fronts. Much like Thermopylae and Artemisium, the Greeks and Persians met both on land and on the sea in concurrent battles. Unlike the first round, these actions were fought from positions of strength by the Greeks, to the extent that they actually initiated both. Long gone were the days of desperate, last-ditch tactical manoeuvres. On the same day, under the stifling summer heat, the Battle of Plataea and the Battle of Mycale resolved, at long last, the second Persian invasion of Greece.

At Plataea, the vaunted Persian cavalry and the legendary Spartan hoplites finally met in battle. Despite the Persian force doubling the Greeks in number, the Spartans dominated the day. Like Marathon, the *phalanx* formation and heavy armour of the Greek hoplites were too effective for the Persian cavalry. When Mardonius's skull was crushed with a rock by a Spartan hoplite, the Persians retreated. The Greeks lost only a few hundred men while the Persians lost up to 100,000. Pausanias won his much-desired *kudos* and quickly became a suitable heir to the role of iconic Spartan hero, last held by Leonidas. There would be no more land battles between Persians and Greeks on Greek soil ever again. The Persian invasion was successfully routed with a resounding victory at Plataea.

At Mycale, the naval battle never materialized. When the Persian admirals saw that the Athenian triremes had re-joined the Hellenic League fleet, the Persians beached their ships and fortified the base of Mt. Mycale. Even the legendary Phoenician triremes were left by the shore in a desperate retreat. Leotychidas, intent on earning his share of the glory Leonidas had won, ordered a land assault. Rowers became hoplites as the Greeks turned Mycale into a land battle. Both sides suffered heavy casualties, but the Persians had also utterly abandoned their ships, which the Greeks burned effortlessly. The entire Persian navy vanished in minutes. Most of the men, accomplished fighters and Persian loyalists each and every one of them, were killed in combat. Mycale and Plataea formally ended the Persian offensive. As if to put an exclamation mark on that fact, Herodotus ends his narration of the war here. Through sheer luck, cunning tactics and raw willpower, the Greeks had defended their homeland from the greatest fighting force ever assembled.

The Spartans, though, had taken note of the Athenian ascendancy – and of Themistocles's political demise and complete absence from the war's conclusion. Feeling threatened by Athenian power yet also emboldened by the loss of their sagacious leader, Sparta was preparing for conflict not only with Persia but with Athens. Yet it was only the demoted Themistocles who recognized that the new Athenian rival was Sparta, not Persia.

Chapter 9

Sparta Provoked

Although Mycale and Plataea were thoroughly Spartan victories, the Athenians again managed to win the marketing war. At Plataea, Aristides the Just distinguished himself with valour and clever strategies. His name became synonymous with the best Athens had to offer. His name became the gold standard among the Greeks, and he subsequently assumed leadership in Athenian diplomacy where he could best effect change.

Similarly, at Mycale, Xanthippus served with distinction and, like a true Athenian politician, turned the victory at Mycale into the first phase of a second Ionian Revolt. The Greek city-states near Mycale immediately allied with the Athenians and the Hellenic League to remove Persia from the Aegean world. Much like the first Ionian Revolt of 499 BC, it was the Athenians who helped spark the action – but, unlike the first round, this time the Persians were powerless to quell it. For his military and imperial accomplishments, Xanthippus was rewarded with archonship as the *eponymous archon* in 479–478 BC.

One more Athenian hero emerged at Mycale. The son of Miltiades, Cimon, led the burning of the Persian and Phoenician ships and established himself as the vanguard of the next generation of Athenian politicians. He had earned honours at Salamis as well, and, having learned from his father's political demise, was determined to glorify Athens.

Despite his fingerprints all over the diplomatic triangulation between Athens, Sparta, and Persia, Themistocles remained absent from these final two battles of the Persian Wars. He may have been commanding a regiment at Plataea underneath Aristides's generalship. However, he is not mentioned in any ancient source nor given any later credit for accomplishments there. It is more likely he remained in Athens and worked behind the scenes to set up his grand re-emergence into Athenian politics.

Just as suddenly as he vanishes from the ancient sources at the start of 479 BC, he reappears after the Hellenic League's victory over Mardonius and the remaining Persians. His resurrection opportunity came in the aftermath of Plataea and Mycale, when the Spartan king Leotychidas suggested abandoning the assistance of the Ionian Greeks in their rebellion against Persia. In the Spartan worldview, Greece had already been saved and assisting all of the far-flung Greek colonies was a fool's errand. He instead proposed forcing all Ionian and other Greeks in modern Turkey to emigrate from Asia to Europe, where the Hellenic League could better protect them.

Xanthippus and the Athenians had far too many colonial and trade interests in the Ionian world to tolerate such a proposal, and a sharp split in the Hellenic League formed. The Athenians were increasingly sceptical of Spartan motivations and viewed Leotychidas's suggestion as a ploy to cripple Athenian influence across the Aegean Sea. The Athenians took increased liberty to foster closer relationships with Ionian city-states as the Hellenic League's fleet island-hopped along the Ionian coast, freeing smaller cities from Xerxes's reign.

Themistocles, reading the tea leaves back in Athens, recognized the imminent new threat. He had dedicated his political life thus far to effectively preparing Athens and Greece for the onslaught from Persia. But now it was clear to him that, although the Persians were still a considerable presence and needed to be addressed, the new Athenian rival was Sparta. Redoubling his efforts to rise out of his demotion, Themistocles burst back into the Athenian political scene heralding the message that Athens must rebuild and fortify – not to prepare for the return of an old enemy, but for a Spartan insurgence. Themistocles brought with him the same focused and unrelenting fervour that had colourized his last two decades opposing Persia, but it was now directed at the Athenians' chief ally against the Persian invasion.

In the winter of 479–478 BC, the Greek navy harboured at Pagasae in Magnesia, a former Persian area of Thessaly. It was a large and safe harbour now that the Persians could not threaten their navy. Pagasae's name was linguistically descended from its mythological significance as the location where Jason's ship, the *Argo*, was constructed before his famous odyssey. Where Jason saw the opportunity to build the greatest ship in the world, Themistocles saw the opportunity to destroy Athens' current and potential competitors in Greece.

In a dramatic attempt to seize his lifelong vision of an Athenian-dominated Aegean, Themistocles decided to betray the Hellenic League and burn the entire Greek navy. It was a stunningly simple plan: have the Athenian triremes blockade their allies' ships in the harbour at Pagasae then set the rest of Greece's ships on fire. Athens would then have not just naval supremacy but would be the only Greek city-state with any triremes at all. Plutarch recounts the tale in his biography of Aristides the Just:

> Themistocles once declared to the people that he had devised a certain measure which could not be revealed to them, though it would be helpful and salutary for the city, and they ordered that Aristides alone should hear what it was and pass judgment on it. So Themistocles told Aristides that his purpose was to burn the naval station of the confederate Hellenes, for that in this way the Athenians would be greatest, and lords of all. Then Aristides came before the people and said of the deed which Themistocles purposed to do, that none other could be more advantageous, and none more unjust. On hearing this, the Athenians ordained that Themistocles cease from his purpose.[1]

In some ways, Themistocles can hardly be blamed for his attempted treachery. Had it been accomplished, Sparta and its allies would have certainly been crippled. The Peloponnesian War between Athens and Sparta, which would rage on for the rest of the fifth century, would have been avoided entirely. Athens would be the only city-state with ships in all of Greece. They would face no true rival, even from the Spartan hoplites whose allies would all be burned in Pagasae's harbour. It was a lightning-fast response to the budding Athenian-Spartan conflict and would end the next great war before it truly began.

Athens would have been the unchallenged hegemon of Greece with a vice-like grip on the economy and politics of the Aegean and, having repelled Persia, the entire eastern Mediterranean. Themistocles's grand vision for Athens would have been achieved by setting a few triremes ablaze.

But the justice of Aristides stymied Themistocles's vision and Themistocles, for once, showed restraint and did not carry out his plan anyway. Perhaps this was due to Themistocles's tenuous position in Athenian politics, given his recent return from political demotion. Aristides's actions certainly fit with his new diplomatic focus. He was increasingly representing Athens in foreign policy and wished to build partnerships with the allies of the Hellenic League. In his new role as the administrator, so to speak, of the Hellenic League, he didn't favour destroying navies as a diplomatic strategy.

Although his power grab didn't materialize, the move cemented Themistocles's triumphant return to Athenian politics by the fall of 479 BC. For the rest of the decade, Athens was unquestionably led by Themistocles. His populist credentials, his deft and unscrupulous navigation of democracy, his military vision and accomplishments, and his post-Salamis *kudos* made him the consummate Athenian. The rest of Greece knew that Themistocles was now vital to Athens, its naval empire, and its far-reaching diplomatic influence.

* * *

The Spartans hadn't yet received notice of the resurgence of Themistocles's influence. They were presently engaged with figuring out how to best stifle Athenian empire-building on the Ionian coast. After the Battle of Mycale, the Spartan king Leotychidas turned his attention to securing the mainland of Greece. After ensuring that the Persian pontoon bridge across the Hellespont was destroyed – which had happened naturally due to the storms some months earlier – the Spartan fleet had sailed back to Pagasae for the winter. Meanwhile, Xanthippus and the Athenian navy remained among the Ionian city-states, winning influence and new allies in trade and politics. Most critically, Xanthippus solidified Athenian pre-eminence by capturing Sestos, a port city in the Thracian Chersonese, and securing the chief Athenian import of wheat through the Hellespont. Coupled with Themistocles's navy, this resulted in Athens obtaining complete control of maritime trade in the Aegean.

This reconfigured the Hellenic League's leadership. As more and more Ionian city-states left Persian rule to join the allied Greeks, Athens gained an ever increasing amount of supporters. It was clear to Sparta that their generals would soon be excluded from influence. In order to challenge Athens' political and economic manoeuvres on the Ionian coast, the Spartans sent the commander Pausanias, the hero of Plataea, to liberate more Persian-ruled Greek city-states and ensure their fealty to Sparta. Taking charge of a fleet of eighty ships, including thirty triremes helmed by Aristides the Just (who would broker negotiations with the new Hellenic League members), he sailed to Cyprus and immediately drove out the Persian loyalists.

Pausanias then set off for the Hellespont, arriving in Byzantium at about the same time as Xanthippus's Athenian fleet. While Byzantium was not yet the fabled city of Constantinople or Istanbul, it was nevertheless a powerful city in a highly strategic location in the gateway to resource-rich Greek colonies scattered around the Black Sea. Control of Byzantium would realistically determine the outcome of this second Ionian Revolt and potentially be the foothold needed to remove Persia from the Greek world entirely. Further, if the Greeks took Byzantium, the Persians could not cross the Hellespont to invade Greece for a third time.

The Spartan-Athenian alliance quickly eliminated the Persian presence in Byzantium, a rapid reaffirmation of Spartan influence in the Hellenic League. Pausanias began to reshape Byzantium in the Spartan mould, setting himself above the rest of the Hellenic League and ruling as a monarch. But the Spartan ethos was disagreeable with the Ionians, who valued a more democratic, Athenian culture. The stoic and violent governance of Pausanias and the Spartans upset the Byzantines and the Ionians, who immediately appealed to Xanthippus and the Athenians for them to take control of the mission. Like any competent Athenian, Xanthippus happily acquiesced and cultivated more control. By this point, the majority of the Hellenic League outright rejected Sparta and favoured Athens as their leader.

When reports reached Sparta of Pausanias's unpopularity and despotic behaviour, he was recalled by the ephors, the five elected Spartans tasked with holding the two kings accountable. Forced to return to Sparta and face trial, Pausanias executed a move more akin to his Athenian foil, Themistocles. Upon the capture of Byzantium, the Spartans had imprisoned some Persian nobles with close connections to King Xerxes. When they were under Pausanias's care, they managed to pull off an astonishing prison escape with no trail of evidence. But the Ionians and

Byzantines knew that Pausanias had given the Persian nobles over to the care of Gongylus of Eretria, a commander with well-known Persian sympathies. As Diodorus Siculus describes:

> Ostensibly Gongylus was to keep these men for punishment, but actually he was to get them off safe to Xerxes; for Pausanias had secretly made a pact of friendship with the king and was about to marry the daughter of Xerxes, his purpose being to betray the Greeks. The man who was acting as negotiator in this affair was the general Artabazus, and he was quietly supplying Pausanias with large sums of money to be used in corrupting such Greeks as could serve their ends.[2]

Pausanias returned to Sparta and was acquitted of the charge of tyranny, but he soon returned to Byzantium and continued his courting of the Persians. It was soon revealed that Gongylus of Eretria, upon delivering the Persian aristocrats to Xerxes's court, had even carried a letter personally written by Pausanias to be delivered to the King of Kings. Like Themistocles's previous communications with Xerxes, the letter carried typical formalities and platitudes and made sure to let the king know that any future relationship might be mutually beneficial. But this letter also contained a much more direct betrayal than Themistocles had ever dared: 'to make Sparta and the rest of Hellas subject to you, [Xerxes]'[3] in exchange for wedding a Persian princess.

His plans exposed, Pausanias fully embraced the Persian lifestyle, publicly dressing and acting as a Persian and welcoming a stream of Persian commanders and aristocrats to Byzantium. His time in control of Byzantium was limited, since the Spartan ephors had recalled him home to Sparta to face more charges. It was more than enough, however, to pit the rest of the Hellenic League against Sparta. To the rest of the Greeks, Sparta – despite their reputation for *arete* and consummate Greek character – simply could not be trusted. They would invariably seize power. Aristides prosecuted the case diplomatically, winning over a dozen more Ionian Greek city-states to the Athenians, as he exploited Spartan vulnerability and seized control of the Hellenic League. Less than a year after defeating Persia together, Sparta and Athens were barrelling towards war.

* * *

While diplomacy imploded over in Byzantium, Themistocles was busy antagonizing the Spartans at home in Athens and preparing the city for what was, in his estimation, an inevitable siege by the Spartan hoplites. In an attempt to settle matters diplomatically, Themistocles hosted a Spartan envoy in Athens in early 478 BC. Ostensibly, the topic was a litany of preparations for a potential third invasion by the Persians. Such an invasion was not entirely out of the question and never would be, given the depth of Xerxes's purses and ambition, but it was a distant concern given the Hellenic League's success in removing Persian loyalists in Ionian Greece, Cyprus, and Byzantium.

The real subject of the meeting was much more immediate. The Athenians had begun to rebuild the walls around Athens, using the Persian threat as a scapegoat. The Spartans refused to believe the wall was for Persia. It was to keep the Spartans out. While the Spartans proposed making the Peloponnese the new naval headquarters of Greece, Themistocles plotted the best way to rebuild Athens and fortify it from a Spartan assault. Although Athens still functioned politically, little construction work had been undertaken since the Persian fires. As waves of Athenian refugees returned home to rebuild, talk had begun to surface about refortification of the walls of the city. Sparta could not abide it.

The diplomatic meeting pivoted to Sparta's disapproval of Athens' plans to resurrect their city of rubble. Drawing on traditionally direct Spartan diplomatic style, the emissaries outright stated their desire to bar most Greek cities from having walls, with Athens especially so. The Spartans claimed to act in response to the concerns of many Peloponnesian city-states, 'who were alarmed at the strength of her newly acquired navy and the valour which she had displayed in the war with the Medes'.[4] They offered a unique solution: if the Athenians abandoned their wall-building, then the Athenians could help the rest of the Peloponnesians tear down their own walls.

The topic of walls was historically a sticking point for the Spartans. They saw city walls as an admission of weakness. A truly strong city would be defended by its soldiers, not its walls. Their mythical founder Lycurgus inculcated this idea, famously stating: 'A city will be well fortified which is surrounded by brave men and not by bricks.'[5] He then founded the *agoge* and trained generations of fearsome Spartan hoplites to serve as the walls of Sparta. About a hundred years after Themistocles's salvation of Athens, the Spartan king Agesilaus II, when asked why Sparta never built fortifications, pointed to the Spartan hoplites and laconically replied 'These are the Spartans' walls'.[6]

Such anti-wall history makes the Spartan obsession with building walls at the Isthmus of Corinth during the second Persian invasion a curious case, but it is clear that the Spartans at least had a reputational ground for asking the Athenians to avoid building their own walls. Moreover, the threat of a third Persian invasion was still very real, and the Spartans did not wish to allow the Persians a fortified base in Athens such as they had in Thebes, especially since the Athenian flirtations with Mardonius prior to the Battle of Plataea. But to name it directly, it was a naked power grab. The Spartans were attempting to seize the Hellenic League, and Athens had almost no soldiers to defend themselves against a land assault.

It was in such dire situations as this that Themistocles thrived, and he put his talents at succeeding in a pressure cooker to use. After the formal request to cease wall construction, Themistocles advised the voting assembly to send the Spartan diplomats back to Sparta, ostensibly so that the Athenians could consider the proposal and shortly send their own ambassadors to Sparta to formalize an agreement. The Spartan emissaries returned home, encouraged that the Athenians would soon yield to Spartan leadership on this subject, despite the strained condition of the Hellenic League. The Athenian voting assembly promised to delay construction until after the next round of diplomatic talks.

Themistocles had no such intentions. He was already engineering a path for Athens to have strong city walls without losing any face to the sceptical Peloponnesians in the Hellenic League. Themistocles proposed that he lead a delegation to Sparta to continue negotiations henceforth, but he also gave detailed instructions on what the Athenians should do in his absence: begin construction on the northern walls of Athens immediately.

From the moment of his departure to Sparta, Themistocles ordered every man, woman and child in Athens to work on constructing a sturdy wall. He also commanded that the delegation accompanying him to Sparta not leave until the wall was at least functionally tall, a project which took several weeks. Athens had by now been twice destroyed by the Persians:

first by Xerxes before Salamis and then by Mardonius before Plataea. For the population of Athens to utterly abandon their own ruined homes and focus on the community goal of a wall illustrated not just their unflagging patriotism but also their renewed devotion to Themistocles. No image is more illustrative of Themistocles's ability to bend situations to his favour than convincing the refugee women and children of Athens to build a wall in their first moments home in their destroyed city. The depths of Themistocles's gift for populism were on full display.

Themistocles's new wall was built with the rubble of the old Athens. Shattered and defaced religious statues, the cracked cornerstones of once-beautiful temples and homes, and the crumbled remains of the colonnaded agora all served as the bricks for the northern wall of Athens. Nothing was spared. Historians later dubbed these pieces *Perserschutt*, German for 'Persian debris'. Most of the wall that Themistocles built in the weeks after the Persian Wars were made from this *Perserschutt*, colourizing both the desperation of the situation and the shrewdness of using any and all available building materials.

In fact, the ruins of the splendid Temple of Athena, which had once graced the Acropolis of Athens and overlooked the entire city as the predecessor to the Parthenon, were quickly transformed into the base of the northern wall near the Acropolis. Similarly, some of the most well preserved amphorae, column bases, and sculptures from antiquity were found built into the wall. A funerary statue of a sphinx was one of the most extraordinarily intact statues from the Archaic period in Athens, and would have not survived had it not been embedded into Themistocles's fortifications.

Thucydides reports its condition seventy-five years later, after waging a brutal war with the Spartans:

> [The wall] shows signs of the haste of its execution; the foundations are laid of stones of all kinds, and in some places not wrought or fitted, but placed just in the order in which they were brought by the different hands; and many columns, too, from tombs, and sculptured stones were put in with the rest.[7]

Although not an engineering marvel, it was fully functional and defensible, even by the meagre hoplite force that remained in Athens. The wall even expanded, quite ambitiously, to encircle the boundaries of the city proper. It was fittingly named the Themistoclean Wall, and it is still present to this day. A close examination tells the story of the destruction of a great city and the reconstruction of an even greater one.

Along with Munichia and the port at Piraeus, the wall would become one of the most enduring legacies he left in Athens. Themistocles ordered the city to have a main gate called the Dipylon. Though built hastily, the Dipylon was built with such excellence that it remained in use – with some significant additions centuries later – for nearly 800 years, until the third century AD.

Meanwhile, Themistocles himself travelled to Sparta at a tortoise's pace. He made sure to take his time visiting old friends and enjoying the hospitality of as many city-states as would accept him. The object was to buy as much time as possible in order to build the wall before the Spartans realized what was happening. When he arrived in Sparta, Themistocles leaned heavily into his warm relationship with their leaders. He gave no indication that he was already warning the Athenians of the growth of Spartan power, but instead gave every sign that the Spartan flattery earlier in the year had curried favour with him.

Most amusingly, Themistocles feigned ignorance at the location of his fellow Athenian diplomats. He remained in the Spartan guest house each day, refusing to meet with his Spartan colleagues until the Athenians arrived to begin formal talks. Thucydides describes Themistocles's award-winning acting: 'When any of the government asked him why he did not appear in the assembly, he would say that he was waiting for his colleagues, who had been detained in Athens by some engagement; however, that he expected their speedy arrival, and wondered that they were not yet there.'[8] His Athenian comrades, of course, would not arrive any time soon – on Themistocles's orders. Themistocles remained in Sparta for weeks, milking his *kudos* among the Spartan leaders until they finally caught on.

Rumours and whispers eventually trickled into Sparta of the Athenian wall construction, although the extent of the project was still unclear. Confronted with this revelation, Themistocles was unmoved. He told them 'that rumours are deceptive, and should not be trusted; they should send some reputable persons from Sparta to inspect, whose report might be trusted."[9] Themistocles's eloquence proved persuasive, and the Spartans astonishingly heeded his advice.

Yet another delegation of Spartan ambassadors travelled to Athens, this time on a fact-finding mission to inspect the walls. Themistocles was more than a few steps ahead of the normally perceptive Spartans. He had already sent word to Athens on the sly with instructions to delay the Spartan envoy as much as possible without actually arresting them. The Spartan ambassadors travelled as slowly to Athens as Themistocles had to Sparta as a result. And all the while, brick by brick, the Themistoclean Wall continued to be erected.

By this time, about a month after the entire ordeal had begun, the long-delayed Athenian delegation had finally reached Sparta to assist Themistocles and formally open negotiations. Counted among Themistocles's party was Aristides the Just, fresh from his negotiations among the Hellenic League and shining brightly with his prizes of valour from Plataea. As the former rivals and current Athenian war heroes greeted one another for the first time in months, Aristides shared his concern that the Spartan delegation was very near to Athens and sure to discover a nearly-completed defensive wall. If such word reached Sparta, and Aristides suspected it would quite soon, then Themistocles and Aristides would never leave.

Themistocles immediately organized an audience with the Spartans and finally confessed what was now a flat reality: that Athens had a wall. But he did not stop there. Themistocles launched into a sharp defence of Athens' ambitions and laid bare his vision for an ascendant Athens. After sharing his disapproval of Sparta's aggression, his speech relied heavily on a few harsh truths about the new Athenian superpower:

> That when the Athenians thought fit to abandon their city and to embark in their ships, they ventured on that perilous step without consulting them; and that on the other hand, wherever they had deliberated with the [Spartans], they had proved themselves to be in judgment second to none. That they now thought it fit that their city should have a wall, and that this would be more for the advantage of both the citizens of Athens and the Hellenic confederacy; for without equal military strength it was impossible to contribute equal or fair

counsel to the common interest. It followed, he observed, either that all the members of the confederacy should be without walls, or that the present step should be considered a right one.[10]

Cornelius Nepos adds an intriguing twist of Greek patriotism to Themistocles's speech:

> nor had [the Athenians], in acting thus, done what was useless to Greece; for their city stood as a bulwark against the barbarians, at which the king's fleets had already twice suffered shipwreck; and that the [Spartans] acted unreasonably and unjustly, in regarding rather what was conducive to their own dominion, than what would be of advantage to the whole of Greece. If, therefore, they wished to receive back the deputies whom they had sent to Athens, they must permit him to return; otherwise they would never receive them into their country again.[11]

His words won over the Spartans. Thucydides attributes this to the Spartan respect for Themistocles and Athens for their role in defeating the Persian invaders, even describing the Spartan feeling as 'very friendly towards Athens'.[12] Themistocles, Aristides, and the entire Athenian delegation returned to Athens not only without any conflict but in complete reconciliation with Sparta.

By the start of 478 BC, the wall was complete and fully defensible. Work could start on the city of Athens itself.

* * *

Themistocles was now fully committed to preparing the city for the Spartan threat. While he heralded the potential return of the Persians as the main motivation for the fortification and military projects in Athens after 479 BC, his main impetus was much closer to home. Themistocles was fully persuaded that the conflict with Sparta was set to eclipse the conflict with Persia. His lifelong passion to prepare Athens for war with Persia was amended to prepare them for war with Sparta. Just like his pursuits a decade earlier, most Athenians brushed off his views as conspiratorial and alarmist. And just like a decade earlier, Themistocles would be proven correct by history.

After the Themistoclean Wall was finished, his next project fused the newfound passion for preparing for war with Sparta with his old passion for Athenian naval supremacy. He returned to a policy that he had attempted, but failed, to realize during his archonship of Athens from 493 to 492 BC. That project was the full fortification of the port of Piraeus, the very harbour he had constructed during his archonship and the only port in Attica that could harbour the massive Athenian navy.

Fortifying the port of Piraeus was a necessary move both militarily and commercially. The destruction of the Acropolis under the Persians had illustrated the dire need in Athens for a true refuge, to where the citizens could flee and be protected when the city was threatened. The Acropolis and the prior walls of Athens had failed in that regard, and the semi-annual evacuation to Salamis was clearly unsustainable. A truly fortified Piraeus would not only protect the city from invasion, but bring a much-needed infusion of commerce and trade to the regenerating city. It would be the command centre for the fledgling Athenian empire, trading with every new loyal city-state that Xanthippus and Aristides were winning over. Themistocles's Athens-centric worldview surrounding the Piraeus project was aptly summarized by Thucydides, 'he was always advising the Athenians, if a day should come when they were hard pressed by land, to go down into Piraeus, and defy the world with their fleet.'[13]

But major political obstacles still lingered from his recent demotion. Themistocles had to engage in his trademark political cunning to pass the project's funding through the Athenian voting assembly, who controlled the purse strings on public projects. His fortification project had no hope without substantial redirection of existing funds. His budgeting strategy was a unique one: he announced at the assembly that he had a secret plan to revitalize Athenian commerce and bolster the state's security at the same time. However, the plan could not be shared publicly for fear of any Persian spies or Themistocles's own political rivals sinking the proposal simply because of Themistocles's name being attached. His proposal was to have the assembly vote for two men to hear out Themistocles's plan, evaluate its quality and feasibility, and then report back to the assembly their recommendations – all without sharing the plan itself.

It was a political manoeuvre reminiscent of his attempt to burn the entire Greek fleet at Pagasae, which Aristides had rejected in a similar format. But this time there was one key distinction: he opted not to vilify his fellow Greeks. Instead, the proposal's Persian fear-mongering masked the true reason for the fortification of Piraeus, Sparta. By this point, Themistocles was using the Persians similarly to how he used the Aegintans at Laurium, as the necessary scapegoats in public rhetoric yet not the true concern. Themistocles, balancing his humbling demotion a few months earlier and his drive to fully prepare Athens for their next existential threat, lacked no ammunition when pointing out the Persian threat to Athens. His talents for populist stratagems were perfectly suited for an Athens that was simultaneously rebuilding at home and expanding abroad.

The assembly agreed to Themistocles's proposal for a secretive evaluation of the project, but as a precaution elected the two men who best opposed him in politics and popularity. These two men were none other than his rivals-turned-allies Xanthippus and Aristides the Just. Their selection was a clever one by the Athenian assembly because, while each of them had prospered since their Themistocles-orchestrated returns from their Themistocles-orchestrated ostracisms, they were no friend to Themistocles. Each would do what they felt was best for Athens, and not surrender to any perceived debts or contentions with Themistocles. The historian Diodorus Siculus highlights the prudence of electing these two: 'not only because of their upright character, but also because they saw that these men were in active rivalry with Themistocles for glory and leadership and were therefore opposed to him'.[14]

Honour prevailed, and Xanthippus and Aristides kept their oaths and heard out Themistocles in private and without prejudice. They returned to the assembly announcing that Themistocles's plan was not only feasible but an important one for Athens to pursue. It is a vivid depiction of Aristides's personal honour and his newly reconciled partnership with Themistocles. Of course, it also revealed that no part of Athenian or Greek politics in the 470s BCE went untouched by Themistocles. Xanthippus and Aristides did not deny Themistocles's vision here, as Aristides had done for burning the Greek fleets at Pagasae.

Nevertheless, the voting assembly of Athens was highly sceptical of these three wealthy, influential men touting a 'secret plan' that still could not be shared. The accusations began to shower down on Themistocles, including the enormously serious charge of setting himself up as a tyrant – the mortal sin of Athenian politics. Themistocles acted quickly and offered to share his plan with the Council of 500 which proposes laws to be voted on. He would not budge, however, in making his plans for the port of Piraeus fully public – claiming that the interests of the state were too important to jeopardize.[15] The Council heard the plan and was enamoured with both the future it made for Athens and with the man who had proposed it. Diodorus Siculus glamourizes its impact, saying that 'every man departed from the Assembly in admiration of the high character of the man, being also elated in spirit and expectant of the outcome of the plan.'[16]

Themistocles had won over the Athenians for his harbour project but one more group needed to be convinced – the Spartans. Themistocles had just barely pulled off the erection of the city walls of Athens. There was no possibility that Sparta would tolerate a second wall-building project. Spartan hoplites were sure to march into Piraeus and destroy the wall before the foundation was even completed.

Diplomacy was the best solution. Themistocles knew that his welcome in Sparta was thoroughly worn thin by this point, and so he sent emissaries to the Spartans to convince them that Athens' new harbour at Piraeus would benefit all of Greece in their efforts against Persia, and not just the Athenians. The envoys heralded the ominous threat of a third Persian invasion, and how a renovated Piraeus was 'to the advantage of the common interests of Greece that it should possess a first-rate harbour in view of the expedition which was to be expected on the part of the Persians'.[17]

With the Spartans placated, new opportunities arose with the ability to design the walls, instead of the desperately rushed project that was the Themistoclean Wall. Themistocles orientated the fortification of Piraeus around a relatively radical concept – that it could be defended 'by a small garrison of invalids, and the rest be freed for service in the fleet'.[18] It was an ontological desertion of Athenian hoplites and the land army. All future policy, funding, and city planning was contingent on the Athenian fleet. The future of Athens was in its navy, just as its very survival had been.

Accordingly, the walls needed to be thick enough and tall enough to be defensible on their own. Themistocles took the design process upon himself, displaying a new skill for city planning:

It was by [Themistocles's] advice, too, that they built the walls of that thickness which can still be discerned round Piraeus, the stones being brought up by two wagons meeting each other. Between the walls thus formed there was neither rubble nor mortar, but great stones hewn square and fitted together, cramped to each other on the outside with iron and lead.[19]

It was only completed to about half of the height that he desired. Nevertheless, it was effective. The walls of Piraeus were never breached and the fortifications around the harbour invigorated the rebuilding of Athens. Ships from all over the Mediterranean poured into the city, allured both by the commercial opportunities and the political benefits that came from appeasing the Athenians. Themistocles's economic policies, passed shortly after the war by the voters of Athens, only stimulated the economic growth of Athens. He continued to lower taxes on skilled labourers, foreigners, artisans, artists, and merchants. Themistocles's vision of Athens as the cultural and political bellwether of Greece was rapidly being realized.

This is not to ignore his unceasing military preparations. He also convinced the Athenians to build twenty triremes a year in perpetuity in order to maintain their naval dominance, and with it their fledgling empire. Given the enormous cost of building just one trireme – most city-states could afford only a few dozen – this was no small feat, since the Athenians had yet to truly begin the reconstruction of Athens. Yet Themistocles convinced them to willingly and happily budget for not the rebuilding of homes, markets, and temples but walls, fortifications, harbours, and ships.

If Themistocles had his first choice, though, there would be one more construction project completed before attention was turned to finally rebuilding the city of Athens itself. Themistocles attempted to sell the voting assembly on a series of walls to fortify the seven miles between Piraeus and Athens. This would allow unfettered access to and from the city centre, meaning that there would be no possible way for the Spartans, Persians or whoever else to disrupt the Athenian political and economic machine. Themistocles again had the prescience that such a structure would singularly empower Athens to use their navy to control the war if Sparta ever attacked.

He was right, although he ran aground in this attempt to build yet another fortification around Athens. The voting assembly simply could not be convinced to build a wall for the third time, much less a wall that covered fourteen total miles. Later Greek politicians picked up on Themistocles's vision here and would use this unrealized policy from Themistocles as a campaign goal. Pericles would finish the project, dubbed the Long Walls, and shepherd the Athenians through the Peloponnesian War behind its fortifications. Had the Long Walls never existed, Athens would never have survived. Themistocles was proven correct once more.

* * *

Back in Sparta, Pausanias escaped imprisonment and was acquitted on all charges, although his reputation was now beyond redemption. His political career would improve slightly over the next decade, but would never recover his status as the hero of Plataea. Pausanias's departure opened up formal leadership of the Hellenic League to the challenging Athenians. His unpopularity caused the majority of non-Peloponnesian city-states to roundly reject Sparta as candidates for directing the league. The flashpoint occurred when Xanthippus refused to recognize the new Spartan commander sent to Byzantium to replace Pausanias.

Themistocles did his part to coalesce support in the Hellenic League around Athens and those allied with her political interests. When the Spartans proposed that the allied Greeks formally exclude Hellenic League membership from all city-states who had not fought for the allies in the Persian Wars, Themistocles sensed an opening. His fear was that Sparta was eliminating any potential rival not named Athens, thereby diplomatically neutralizing powerful Greek states like Thessaly, Argos, and Thebes and stacking votes in their favour against the swelling Athenian loyalists. Such a policy excluded not only the powerful states, but many of the small city-states who had reluctantly medized when they saw the massive size of Xerxes's army. These city-states were tiny in population, but numbered a great deal in total number of cities.

Themistocles realized that, since the Hellenic League allowed each city-state a vote, he could curry the favour of these small city-states that had been subsumed by the Persian tidal wave. Themistocles addressed the Hellenic League's assembly, to the consternation of the Spartans, and persuaded the representatives to empower all Greek city-states equally. His rhetoric was laced with the little-man populism that had carried his career in Athenian democracy. He pointed to the small number of Greek city-states that had defeated Xerxes's invasion as a symbol of what the underdog can accomplish.

His message was that it had been all of Greece – not just Athens and Sparta – that had defeated the invaders. It was a classic populist manoeuvre, pitting the people against the elite. He convinced them 'by showing that only thirty-one cities had taken part in the war, and that the most of these were altogether small; it would be intolerable, then, if the rest of Hellas should be excluded and the convention be at the mercy of the two or three largest cities.'[20] Themistocles's words resonated with the forgotten Greek city-states, so small in number that many of their names are not given in the text. The Spartan policy was rejected and the Athenians used their new loyal voters to exclude Sparta from the future of the allied Greeks.

The Spartans withdrew completely from the war against the Persian city-states, focusing instead on purely Greek matters and quelling slave rebellions back at home. It was the fulfilment of their earlier proposal to abandon the Ionians, or at least make them migrate to the Greek mainland. More importantly, though, their withdrawal ceded control of the entire Aegean Sea to the Athenians.

The end result was the complete dissolution of the Hellenic League. Despite uniting to save Greece, Sparta and Athens would never work together again. In place of the Hellenic League, two new entities arose. First, a loose confederacy of Peloponnesian and Spartan-allied city-states formed and took the name the Peloponnesian League. This alliance had already existed for about a century in an informal capacity, forged as a reciprocal military arrangement to protect Sparta and its allies in the south of the peninsula against a slave revolt at home and from the threat of Argos to the north. It was the generals and admirals of the Peloponnesian League who had spent the Persian invasion obsessing over building the wall at the Isthmus of Corinth to protect their homeland.

But now, its new opposition to Athens reconfigured its mission. While Sparta dominated the Peloponnesian League, many influential cities like

Corinth, Megara, and Pylos were given relative freedom and a heightened role, while traditional Spartan vassals like Tegea and the small city-states of the central Peloponnese were restricted in their participation. Curiously, the Spartan ephors and kings allowed each member of the league a vote, but recused themselves, instead allowing the Spartan voting assembly to vote on all policies. It was one of the few quasi-democratic features of Spartan government, and even its allies benefited. Nevertheless, the Peloponnesian League was no democracy. Sparta instead set the agenda and called upon the Peloponnesian League's hoplites as needed although, as compensation, they never demanded tribute or taxes from the league's allies. The alliance was predicated purely on military preparedness and political posturing. It was a mutual defence agreement in anticipation of war.

The Peloponnesian League now formally united the Peloponnesian Peninsula and, more critically, consolidated the city-states increasingly concerned about the growth of Athenian influence. The anti-Athenian sentiment was steadily increasing at the same rate as Athenian imperial power. Athens took notice. In order to strategize the best path against this rising power of the Peloponnesian League, the Athenian-allied remnants of the Hellenic League gathered at tiny island of Delos in the centre of the Aegean Sea.

Delos was a sacred island, the mythological birthplace of Apollo and Artemis. Very little other than a small marketplace, a harbour, and the temple complex crowded the landscape. There was, however, a large meeting area – an *ekklesia* – that served as the meeting area for the old Hellenic League, now without Sparta or its allies. At the *ekklesia*, the member cities voted to reorganize the Hellenic League and take it in a new direction that aggressively pursued Persia and eliminated their presence in the Greek and Aegean world. This new alliance would seek out any Persian-aligned city-states and forcibly submit them, carry away their valuables, demand tribute, and then share the spoils of war evenly among the league. Most importantly, the alliance prepared for war and any future enemies or invaders, including Sparta and the Peloponnesian League.

This new league was christened the Delian League, named after the holy island Delos that would serve as their headquarters in the strategically-located centre of the Aegean Sea. The Delian League's hegemon was Athens, who heavy-handedly pushed its allies and bent the league, its policies and its treasury to their interests. The Delian League functionally became a new Athenian Empire. The city-states of the league contributed taxes, ships and men in order for the privilege of being led by Athens and Themistocles. In just five short years after finding the silver of Laurium, Athens was already approaching the endgame that Themistocles had designed and laboured towards for his entire career.

*   *   *

The trio of Greek heroes from the Persian Wars, Themistocles, Xanthippus, and Aristides, all took the core leadership roles in both Athens and, by extension, the Delian League. Themistocles took the public reigns of political leadership and orchestrated the passing and vetoing of the laws through the voting assembly, with seats both formal and informal on all the legislative and judicial councils. His grip on Athenian democracy was never tighter.

For his consummately honourable treatment of Athenian colonies and allies, Aristides the Just was voted the lead administrator for the Delian League. He took his talents for diplomacy and advanced Athenian interests abroad while the Delian League aggressively recruited or subdued new city-states across the Aegean and Black Seas. He was given authority over the ever-increasing treasury of the Delian League and redistributed this wealth to its members, collected taxes from all the cities and oversaw preparations for the potential third Persian invasion. Few men were more influential across Greece.

Xanthippus continued to serve as *eponymous archon* and lived the rest of his days in luxury in Athens, working for aristocratic interests with the Alcmaeonids. Although he fades from the ancient sources after his archonship, his young son, Pericles, was the beneficiary of his father's high status, and was trained in the arts, rhetoric, and humanities in order to be an aristocratic politician in the Alcmaeonid tradition. Pericles would go on to lead the Athens that his father helped Themistocles create.

For the rest of the century, the Delian League would, directly and indirectly, conflict with the Peloponnesian League. The political tension between Athens and Sparta drove this, but long-simmering ethnic tensions added more fuel. The Delian League and its allies happened to be overwhelming Ionian and Attic, two groups of Eastern Greeks that were in opposition to the Dorian, Western Greeks of the Peloponnesian League. Linguistic and cultural differences made the political wedge all the more effective in dividing Greece and readying it for civil war. The hard-won unity after defeating the Persian invaders had lasted less than a year.

Themistocles settled into his unofficial throne over his grand creation, the Athenian *thalassocracy*, a naval-based empire. It was not a comfortable throne. Themistocles had severed any affection the Spartans once had for him and his actions, both individually and on behalf of Athens, increasingly became the impetus for Spartan involvement in Athenian affairs. After he had outwitted Sparta to build the Themistoclean Wall, he 'became obnoxious to the [Spartans], and they therefore tried to advance Cimon in public favour, making him the political rival of Themistocles'.[21]

Cimon, the son of Miltiades, had continued his rising-star campaign by adding new city-states across the Ionian coast to the Athenian cause. By virtue of his father's reputation, despite Miltiades's downfall, Cimon was destined for a strong political career characterized by a popular appeal and impressive rhetoric, much like Themistocles. But his distinguishing trait was a deep sympathy for Sparta. One need look no further than the fact that he named his son Lacedaemonius, after the Greek name for Sparta's territory of Lacedaemon. He was the perfect vessel for the cultivation of Spartan influence in Athens – especially as a new, pro-Spartan political rival for Athens-centric Themistocles. Sparta threw honours, money and titles at Cimon to recruit him. They found a reciprocal interest.

When war between Athens and Sparta finally broke out formally in 431 BCE, Thucydides famously points to 'the growth of the power of Athens and the alarm this caused in Sparta'[22] as the main factor. Many more factors would emerge after his departure from history, but it was Themistocles who had orchestrated this growth of Athenian power in the wake of Salamis. In 478 BCE, though, he was nearly the only Athenian who recognized the extent of the Spartan threat. For Athens, Sparta was the new Persia. And, just like with Persia, few Athenians gave his calls for alarm much credit. But this time around, Themistocles had consolidated power and influence in Athens, with the savviness and means to prepare Athens and its allies without sounding the alarm.

Supported by the massive influence of the Delian League and with the harbour at Piraeus as the new nexus of the Mediterranean, Athens grew to unparalleled political and cultural heights. It was the beginning of one of the most prosperous and successful civilizations in world history with unprecedented outputs in theatre, literature, philosophy, science, art, architecture, mathematics, and poetry. If Themistocles could survive both the Spartan threat and the constant perils of life at the top of Athenian democracy, then he would lead Athens through one of the greatest and most influential centuries in global history.

Chapter 10

A Reckoning in the Athenian Golden Age

In late 479 BCE, Themistocles had saved a city that didn't physically exist. Athens had a new wall to protect it from the Spartans but, apart from its people, there was not much of value inside to protect. The only sturdy structures were the Themistoclean Wall, Piraeus, and perhaps the fortress at Munichia – all construction projects of Themistocles. With his other great construction project, the Athenian navy, Themistocles was ready to catapult Athens into Mediterranean dominance through the Delian League and imperial projects. He had also fully weaponized the democratic system and curried enough favour with voters that his leash was impressively long. It was time for Themistocles to fulfil his childhood prophecy of 'taking in hand a city that was small and inglorious and making it glorious and great'.[1]

Although their city was still being rebuilt, Athenian fortunes had never been greater. Even the mythical days of Theseus paled in comparison to the golden age that Themistocles was preparing through the injection of culture, art, commerce and science. The 470s began what is generally referred to as the Athenian Golden Age, where Athens effectively created what we now understand as Western civilization.

In this period alone, Socrates, Plato and other philosophers transformed the life of the mind and pushed the boundaries of human knowledge. Construction and reconstruction projects like the Acropolis and the Temple of Olympian Zeus were beautifully designed and so expertly built that they still stand today. Sculptors like Phidias recreated the human body so ideally and precisely that the Romans made untold numbers of copies, many of which survive. Athenian pottery and ceramics were the gold standard of houseware in upper class households and they were shipped out across the Mediterranean world. Theatre productions became all the rage in Athens, with the works of Aeschylus, Sophocles, and Aristophanes setting the cultural and social trends both in Athens and abroad.

Democracy itself accompanied Athenian ships across the Aegean and democratic ideals spread to its Delian League allies. In short time, Athens became the nexus of influence both politically and culturally. The Athens that Themistocles built was the cosmopolitan centre of the world. Anything Athenian was inherently valuable and it wasn't worthwhile if it wasn't Athenian.

Themistocles was, meanwhile, at the apex of his leadership in Athens and no longer bothering to cloak his control of Athens. Nearly every council was populated by a handful of people loyal to Themistocles and unwilling to arouse his anger. Ancient writers give no shortage of anecdotes to illustrate his grip on Athens. In one such account, Themistocles was approached by Antiphatus, a scorned lover who, after despising Themistocles for years, wanted to flatter his way into a cushy government post. Themistocles relished the opportunity to gloat and answered, 'Hark you, lad... though late, yet both of us are wise at last.'[2] In another example, Themistocles's young son treated his mother insolently. Instead of rebuking his son, Themistocles said that 'this boy had more power than all the Grecians, for the Athenians governed Greece, he the Athenians, his wife him, and his son his wife.'[3]

Such prosperity provided Themistocles with a multitude of new opportunities that he was not willing to waste. Perhaps more pressingly, Themistocles was not receiving the entirety of the credit for the flourishing of Athens. Although Themistocles was not exclusively driven by ego, his image management was an essential part of his navigation of domestic and foreign politics. The wheeling-and-dealing style of leadership Themistocles had consistently demonstrated during the Persian Wars proved unsustainable in peacetime Athens, even if the Spartan threat continued to loom.

Themistocles was deeply concerned with projecting the proper image, especially in the wake of the founding of the Delian League in 478 BCE. While the Delian League was a profoundly successful endeavour for furthering Athens' reach, Aristides had boxed Themistocles out of substantive leadership in the league. Themistocles spent the decade intertwined with Athenian politics, but mostly uninvolved in the Delian League and its acquisitions. He was, in a sense, relegated to domestic Athens while Aristides focused on Athens' wider presence in Greece.

This made no small amount of sense, considering Themistocles had only recently been talked down from burning down the entirety of Greek triremes at Pagasae.

Plutarch describes how Themistocles focused on his role as Athens' hegemon, and the public perception of that role:

> And indeed he was by nature very fond of honour, if we may judge from his memorable sayings and doings. When, for example, the city had chosen him to be admiral, he would not perform any public or private business at its proper time, but would postpone the immediate duty to the day on which he was to set sail, in order that then, because he did many things all at once and had meetings with all sorts of men, he might be thought to be some great personage and very powerful.[4]

Athens was his own personal project for glory and honour and its citizens a part of his toolbox. His conception of his own role in Athens is aptly summarized by one account of a time when he and a friend saw the gold-adorned bodies of Persians, killed at the Battle of Salamis, wash up on the shores near Piraeus. His associate quickly removed the jewellery for personal gain, and when he inquired if Themistocles would partake in the free gold, Themistocles responded, 'Help thyself, thou art not Themistocles.'[5] This was a vivid image of the type of ruler Themistocles was over Athens during the 470s.

But to be successful at that, he had to overcome his own reputation. A little less than a century after Themistocles's death, the famous Athenian philosopher Plato wrote a dialogue in *Hippias Minor* debating the heroism of Achilles, the greatest hero of *The Iliad*, and Odysseus, the greatest hero of *The Odyssey*. Both Achilles and Odysseus were indispensably formative to the Greek world, and by questioning the veracity of their heroic status Plato was playing with fire. His dialogue posits that the common belief that 'Achilles is true and simple, and Odysseus wily and false,'[6] is ultimately a clever ruse of Achilles. Odysseus, the trickster and deceiver, could never outrun his reputation and thus was always viewed with scepticism by those who interacted with him.

Conversely, Achilles always played the honourable if ignorant warrior, one who nobody ever expected to be deceitful or to lie. That is why, when

Achilles does lie – in this case falsely attributing a quote – people always believe him. Achilles, ultimately, was the more deceitful hero since he falsely presented no sophistication and was able to outwit his peers when he decided to employ his guile. Odysseus, meanwhile, was doomed to and limited by his *kudos* of artifice and resourcefulness. Themistocles similarly struggled to rid himself of the characterization of him as a liar and cheat.

*   *   *

Themistocles needed to look to new methods to refine his surgical approach to subduing the Athenians to his leadership. His construction projects had fortified the city and his navy had financed its well-being but the fickle Athenian voting assembly would not let him run the city unchecked.

He turned to the arts to garner political support and capital. The Dionysia, the annual religious festival to Dionysus that featured a theatre competition for best-in-show tragedies and comedies was the perfect vehicle for Themistocles to recapture the public support. It was the grandest event in Athens and, as Athens grew exponentially by virtue of the Delian League and the flourishing harbour at Piraeus, all of the Aegean. Themistocles had not yet met a spotlight that he didn't want a part of, and the Dionysia's theatre was no different. Theatre productions in Greece typically had two types of topics: mythology and politics, and mobilizing theatre for political purposes was a time-honoured tradition.

It is hard to overstate the cultural impact of theatre in Classical Athens. Beginning about a hundred years prior to Themistocles, religious festivals began depicting the tragedies of Greek mythology as acts of worship and teaching parables. In places like Thebes and Athens, these plays grew in popularity to include tragedies, comedies, and satyr (raunchy tragicomedies comparable to burlesque) plays that critiqued Greek society and challenged it to know its rich history and grasp its destiny. Greek plays, especially those from Athens during the fifth century, became the standard of entertainment and high culture in the Mediterranean for the next dozen generations.

The vibrantly large and energetic chorus in each play only added to the religious experience. Dressed in lavish costumes and up to two dozen in number, the chorus was not just background music but was a main character, often a type of narrator, in the production. Comedies began with long, choreographed dances by the chorus with outlandish behaviour and songs, working the audience into fits of laughter. The chorus would move on to directly engage the audience, often commenting on the cultural topics of the day. Politicians, philosophers, and rival artists were especially at risk of the acerbic criticism in Greek comedies.

But it was tragedies, as the oldest form of Greek theatre, that held the highest regard and influence in Athenian society. Tragedy plays like *The Capture of Miletus*, *The Persians*, and *Seven Against Thebes* served as a type of news commentary for many Athenians, challenging and criticizing policy and culture. By the days of the Dionysia, theatre performances were open to the entire male citizenship, usually for a very low fee and eventually free of charge. Since it was only the male citizenship held voting rights, this essentially guaranteed that the voting assembly of Athens would be exposed to and influenced by the theatre productions of the year. Phrynichus had been the first to include historical content in theatre productions, and by the 470s it was an industry standard. Despite the nomenclature, topics of tragedy plays in the aftermath of the Persian Wars reflected the optimistic and enthusiastic Athenian spirit. Salamis and the defeat of Persia was an untapped well for art and theatre. It was the defining moment for Athens and was subsequently memorialized in all manners of culture.

Themistocles's first attempt at injecting his victory over Persia into the Athenian consciousness was less refined than traditional theatre performance. He arranged for an annual cockfighting tournament in the theatre. It was a spectacle with large crowds cheering on each fighter but the crowds were not motivated by gambling. Instead, the two fighting cocks represented Athens and Persia, and the fight for survival against any and all odds. The origin of this cockfighting came from the mythos of Themistocles, who at the Battle of Salamis is said to have proclaimed: 'These [Athenian soldiers] undertake this danger, neither for their Country, nor for their Country Gods, nor for the Monuments of their Ancestours, nor for Fame, Liberty, or Children ; but that they may not be worsted, or yield one to the other.'[7] Shortly after Salamis, the Athenian voting assembly enthusiastically instituted the annual cockfighting as part of the Dionysia festival by law.

Archons and other wealthy elites were charged with organizing and financing theatre productions outside the public funds. This was seen as a noble service to the city-state and was only allowed to those approved by a vote of the voting assembly. Although they were the political elite, those recognized with this status, named *choregos*, were also essentially producers. They managed the finances, arranged purchasing, oversaw set design and construction, scheduled rehearsals and worked on special effects. At the end of the production, a lavish party was hosted at the home of the *choregos* – a wonderful opportunity for networking and recruiting the movers and shakers of Athenian democracy. With such a vice-like grip on the production, the *choregos* were heavily involved in shaping the production's content. The winners of the competition at the Dionysia were granted a public monument in the heart of Athens, publicizing and memorializing their accolades.

The history of Athenian theatre is enmeshed with political and personal grudges. Perhaps the most famous example was Aristophanes, the most renowned comedic playwright of the closing decades of the fifth century. Aristophanes's dismissal of philosophy – and his personal hatred of Socrates – reshaped public opinion on the role of philosophy and education after his comedy *The Clouds* debuted in 423 BCE at the Dionysia. Even though it was not a successful play for Aristophanes, winning few awards and ranking near the bottom of his body of work, it nevertheless influenced public perception about Socrates as a troublemaker who corrupted the youth of Athens. Plato later blamed *The Clouds* and its persuasive message as one the main reasons for Socrates's trial and death a few years later. Socrates was convicted of impiety and corruption of Athenian youth – two of the main themes of *The Clouds*.

Themistocles himself had funded and organized a play during his archonship in 492 BCE, *The Capture of Miletus*, that was a not so subtle statement of support for the Ionians in the revolt against the Persians. At the time, Themistocles wanted the mould the Athenian zeitgeist in support of his preparations for the Persian invasion which would culminate in a few years later at Marathon. To do so, Themistocles partnered with the playwright Phrynichus, securing funding and sponsorship in exchange for overt political messaging. The play had sent the crowd into tears on opening night and resulted in a banishment and fine for Phrynichus, but the political impact was tangible as it was a rallying cry which prepared Athens against the Persian threat they would repel first at Marathon and then at Salamis.

In the 470s, Themistocles was offered another opportunity as *choregos*. He turned to Phrynichus once more to capitalize on the apex of Athenian patriotism in the wake of their victory in the Persian Wars. The resulting play, *Phoenician Women*, debuted at the Dionysia in 476 BCE. Also known as *Phoenissae*, in order to avoid confusion with a more famous play of the same name by Euripides nearly a century later, *Phoenician Women* is a quintessential Greek tragedy in structure and message. Like *The Capture of Miletus*, the play's plot begins with the proclamation of a tragedy; in this case, the play is narrated from the Phoenician perspective lamenting the Persian loss at Salamis. The chorus and women of Phoenicia spend the bulk of the play mourning over the great loss of their fleet and the ruination brought on Persia by the Greek hero, Themistocles.

The depiction of Themistocles was, of course, curated by Themistocles himself. He further intermingled policymaking and culture-making by dedicating a public monument to the victory at Salamis in 476 BCE, strategically aligned with the staging of *Phoenician Women*. The monument not only reminded the Athenians, and its voters, what Salamis had accomplished for Greece but also who accomplished it for Greece. Themistocles marked his victory with a monument in the heart of Athens, proudly inscribed with the words 'Themistocles the Phrearrhian was *Choregos*; Phrynichus was Poet; Adeimantus was *Archon*.'[8]

The thinking of Themistocles and his fellow *choregos* linked the ideas of individual reputation with the health of the state. The personal *kudos* of a politician, an Olympic athlete, or a famous playwright was entangled with all aspects of his city-state, from divine favour in war to athletic success at the Olympics. If Athens had a world-class sculptor, then it benefited the city-state's reputation just as much as it benefited as the individual. And Themistocles was, if nothing else, a patriot of Athens.

Put in this light, perhaps Themistocles was being nationalistic and even heroic with his antics at the Dionysia. Themistocles's reputation was soon wrapped up in his cultural contributions as much as his political and military accomplishments. The legacy continued long after his death, as the Roman historian Vitruvius even credits Themistocles with the construction of the grandest theatre in Athens, the Odeon, as part of his culture-making project in the 470s. While the Odeon more accurately dates to Pericles's reign in the 430s, the cultural link between Themistocles and the arts was prevalent enough for later historians to assume his involvement.

* * *

While Themistocles was busy with the theatre, the Delian League continued not only to add territory to Athens but also to colonize and antagonize Greeks. A binary worldview of Athens versus the world seeped into every decision made by the League. With Themistocles excluded from leadership, Cimon was appointed military commander, working alongside Aristides the Just's diplomatic leadership. Ostensibly, this was a position meant to be democratically influenced by the dues-paying members of the Delian League, but realistically this gave Cimon the keys to the Athenian empire.

This was problematic for Themistocles, given the strong support that Cimon enjoyed from both the aristocrats of Athens and the diplomats from Sparta. Cimon had been an excellent investment by the Spartans. After Themistocles had rebuffed their overtures when he covertly built his city walls, Cimon received the interest and funding from Spartan emissaries. Like his idol Aristides, Cimon better resembled the good Spartan than the good Athenian. Plutarch remarks that 'he lacked entirely the Attic cleverness and fluency of speech; that in his outward bearing there was much nobility and truthfulness; that the fashion of the man's spirit was rather Peloponnesian.'9 He drank and partied more like a Spartan than an Athenian, and matched Aristides in his personal sense of honour that men like Themistocles would label as Spartan. Cimon was a proud *laconophile*. This is perhaps explained by Cimon's origin story which began with a life among the upper class elites, but then dramatically swung down to the lower classes as he became poor and orphaned after his father died in prison shortly after Marathon. In seeking to regain his aristocratic status, he had acquired a taste for the finer things in life which he had re-earned through his military achievements. Both Spartan and Athenian power brokers took notice and Cimon had an open-door policy for both.

Since winning honours at Salamis, Cimon had spent the past half-decade winning territory for Athens and subduing other Greek city-states. The conquest of Eion, not far Xerxes's canal dug across Athos and a strategic location for ships sailing from the Hellespont to mainland Greece, was especially honourable and become a key Athenian territory enabling trade with Ionia and the Black Sea. Cimon was richly rewarded, including being given the chance to marry into the Alcmaeonid clan. He was subsequently the new favourite of the Athenian aristocrats and the next in a long line of Athenian statesmen entering the social class struggle between populists and aristocrats.

Themistocles was unwilling to let this next generation take hold just yet. For a brief moment, the two generational talents overlapped with Themistocles resuming his role as champion of the people and Cimon taking over for Aristides as the champion for the upper classes. Cimon was successful from the moment he entered Athenian politics. The Athenian voters gladly welcomed him 'since they were full to surfeit of Themistocles, to the highest honours and offices in the city, for [Cimon] was engaging and attractive to the common folk by reason of his gentleness and artlessness'.[10]

The two men had crossed paths before, with a young Themistocles targeting Cimon while the latter was still a young and privileged aristocrat, and the former was clawing his way up from the lower classes:

> [Themistocles] tried to rival Cimon in his banquets and booths and other brilliant appointments, so that he displeased the Hellenes. For Cimon was young and of a great house, and they thought they must allow him in such extravagances; but Themistocles had not yet become famous, and was thought to be seeking to elevate himself unduly without adequate means, and so was charged with ostentation.[11]

Yet just like Themistocles's rivalry with Aristides, they were able to lay their issues aside when their homeland was threatened. Cimon had been the first to spring into action when Themistocles ordered the first evacuation of Athens that had culminated in the Battle of Salamis. In matters of foreign policy, the two men often agreed; but in the arena that was Athenian democracy, they were constantly at odds.

* * *

Influenced by the string-pullers of Sparta, Cimon led a public campaign aimed at challenging Themistocles's heroic status in Athens. The enthusiastic welcome of Cimon into Athenian politics was strategically timed, since the voters were increasingly wary of Themistocles's ubiquitous power in Athens. Themistocles's propaganda with *Phoenician Women* had had limited success from an image management perspective – the voters had been able to recognize the heavy-handed political messaging despite the play's prizes at the Dionysia. He had perhaps pushed his image marketing campaign too far.

By now, Themistocles had well-earned a reputation for bribery and extortion, particularly after demanding tribute from Andros and the other islands that first came under the new Athenian empire. Even though it was quite accurate, it was not good for business. Spurred both by Themistocles's public actions and by his Spartan investors, Cimon assailed him for his penchant for bribery in front of the voting assembly, after which Themistocles could hardly enter a council meeting without his fellow peers wary of his murky financial practices. This political rivalry soon influenced the new crop of artistic and cultural productions.

The glory of the Athenian Golden Age had attracted Greece's most successful poet, Timocreon of Rhodes. Timocreon's influence as a lyric poet was formidable and his upbringing in Rhodes, a Persian territory in Greece until it was 'freed' by the Athenians in 478 BC, colourized his view of Athens and Themistocles. Prior to this, Timocreon had been ostracized from Rhodes for sympathizing with the Persians a bit too much – no small feat considering they were a Persian colony when he was ostracized. He had journeyed to Andros in the eventual hope that he could bribe the Athenians to help restore him to his homeland. Timocreon targeted Themistocles for help in this mission, the influential statesman who publicly courted such quid pro quos.

In that pursuit, Timocreon found himself on Andros when Themistocles sieged the island and demanded tribute. After the Androsians paid their tribute – in submission to the gods Persuasion and Compulsion invoked by Themistocles – Timocreon was able to earn an audience with Themistocles. They struck a deal for Themistocles to use his political influence to restore Timocreon to Rhodes. Themistocles, never one to turn away a bribe, took three talents of Timocreon's silver.

Money safe in hand, Themistocles's promise soon evaporated. He left Andros without Timocreon. The next year, Timocreon managed to catch up with Themistocles while Themistocles was fêting at the Isthmus of Corinth. In a transparent attempt to curry enough favour with the Peloponnesians to earn a prize of valour for his heroism at Salamis, Themistocles, hosted a series of banquets, and most certainly moved on from his dull dealings with the Rhodian poet. He had apparently accepted a separate fee from a different character whose presence supplanted Timocreon, and he departed the Isthmus with the poet's silver but without any concern for keeping his half of the arrangement.

In the Greek worldview, this was a deep violation of *xenia* – the concept of hospitality and generosity shown to guests or travellers. *Xenia* was one of the traditional pillars of virtue, with roots as far back as Homer, where *xenia* undergirds much of Odysseus's travels in *The Odyssey*. For Themistocles to treat a refugee with such disrespect, especially when he and all of the Athenians were refugees (since Athens had not yet been rebuilt following its destruction by Xerxes) was profoundly dishonourable.

Timocreon did not forgive or forget. He instead put his masterful lyrical skills to work villainizing Themistocles among his strongest supporters, the commoners. Timocreon penned a series of *scolia*, Greek drinking songs performed at feasts and banquets, that painted Themistocles as a crook. *Scolia* normally function as praise songs for the gods and the mythic heroes of Greek lore, extolling their *arete* and excellence. But Timocreon used them to reconfigure the image of Themistocles from Athenian hero to democracy's charlatan, who willingly gave up pursuing the Persians to exploit the Greeks – and Athenians – at Andros and then through the Delian League. Timocreon's incisive verses are recorded primarily by Plutarch:

> Come, if thou praisest Pausanias, or if Xanthippus,
> Or if Leotychidas, then I shall praise Aristides,
> The one best man of all
> Who came from sacred Athens; since Leto loathes Themistocles,
>
> The liar, traitor, cheat, who to gain his filthy pay,
> Timocreon, his friend, neglected to restore
> To his native Rhodian shore;
> Three silver talents took and departed (curses with him) on his way,[12]

Restoring some exiles unjustly, chasing some away, and slaying some,
Gorged with moneys; yet at the Isthmus he played ridiculous host
   with the stale meats set before his guests;
Who ate thereof and prayed Heaven 'no happy return of the day for
   Themistocles![13]

Timocreon's songs rapidly took the banquet scene by storm, and soon the *scolia* reached the lower classes. Timocreon's shrewd casting of himself as a refugee bound for Athens whom Themistocles exploited for personal gain struck a nerve with those Athenians who had recently returned from their own exile. Despite his reputation and stature in Athens, Themistocles had, at least in this case, cast aside his status as a Homeric-style hero the moment he denied Timocreon *xenia*. Worse yet, there was a subtle but clear implication that Themistocles had done so because he was too busy courting Persia. Timocreon and other politicians, namely Cimon (spurred on by his Spartan benefactors), had begun to spread rumours of Themistocles's links to Persian emissaries. Athenian aristocrats like the Alcmaeonids helped, making sure that Timocreon's songs were proudly sung at any Athenian banquet and that the lower classes heard it. The aristocratic and Spartan push against Themistocles was now in full force. By branding him as a Persian sympathizer, Timocreon finally accomplished what so many others could not yet do – successfully endanger Themistocles.

Themistocles was unable to manage his usual nimble response. He turned to a different accomplished poet, Simonides, to compose some rival *scolia* to recapture his reputation. Simonides was a clever choice considering Themistocles and he had a history together – Simonides had once asked Themistocles for an illegal favour that Themistocles had denied. And although one of Themistocles's earliest public political moves was to call Simonides ugly, he and Simonides got along quite well. Simonides was famed for military compositions and was in high demand for writing epitaphs for the greatest Greek heroes. Of course, the Greek victory in the Persian Wars had supplied him with a lifetime of material and Simonides had already composed poems celebrating the victories at Salamis, Artemisium and Plataea, and had also sung of the heroism of Pausanias and Leonidas.

It was a natural manoeuvre for Themistocles to demand that he be included among such heroes. Simonides was more than willing to duel Timocreon in a lyrical competition since the two poets already had a rich competitive history. Simonides was the chief rival of Timocreon at the Dionysia and had already publicly criticized Timocreon for his medism. Each poet considered himself to be the greatest lyricist in Greece and competed for work composing epitaphs for the greatest heroes. Their subject matter inherently overlapped, with each employing a similar style and playing to the same customer base. Both men even used the same fable as the basis for a poem, where a poor fisherman debates diving into freezing waters to catch an octopus that would feed his family but likely kill him in the process. Although these great minds thought alike, they despised the other.

Timocreon, though, appears to have been less successful in ingratiating himself into Greek politics. Simonides was a mainstay among the Greek nobility and famed for his incredible memory. He counted patrons among the rulers of Thessaly, Ceos, Athens and eventually Sicily. He was later given the deep honour of chronicling Olympic success, composing a hymn of victory for the Sicilian tyrant Leophon, one of the greatest Olympic athletes, who won a myriad of medals at the games. Timocreon, meanwhile, had a modestly successful set of patrons and, while he would later give in to his reputation as a medizer and serve in the court of the Persian king, his tenure there was largely unsuccessful. Timocreon was mostly known as a fighter and a glutton in Persia, composing boorish songs about athletes and drunkenly fighting Persians in court.

Their animosity continued into the next life. When Timocreon died, Simonides used his political connections to secure the job of writing the epitaph on Timocreon's memorial stone. Simonides did not waste the opportunity, writing:

> After a lifetime of much drunkenness, much gluttony, and much
> slander of men, here I, Timocreon of Rhodes, lie.[14]

Timocreon had planned well and struck back from beyond the grave, having composed an epigram late in life that gained popularity in response to the epitaph of Simonides, who was from the island of Ceos:

> From Ceos nonsense came to me against my desires,
> Against my desires nonsense came to me from Ceos.[15]

Yet at the height of their poetic rivalry, Timocreon's payback for the sleight by Themistocles was fierce. His drinking songs pummelled Themistocles and Simonides among the lower classes. Compounding matters, Simonides had at best an objectionable *kudos* among the bulk of the Athenian voters. Simonides's earliest Athenian patron was Hipparchus, the son of Pisistratus and the despised final tyrant of Athens before the emergence of democracy. He had been allied with Hipparchus until the latter was brutally assassinated on the eve of Athenian democracy, fleeing to cultural exile in Thessaly before returning to Athens to write the epigraph for the men slain at Marathon. Simply put, Simonides was perceived as too much of an elite and out of touch with the lower classes. Simonides was the archetype of 'the miser', one who hoards money and yet refuses to spend it. A few generations later, the famous playwright Aristophanes directly parodied Simonides's love of money, writing one character to say, 'though old and broken-down as he is, he would put to sea on a hurdle to gain a [coin].'[16]

This devotion to money may have been what spurred Themistocles to approach Simonides; the poet never turned down a money-grabbing opportunity and would happily sacrifice his artistic integrity for some coin and some status. His subsequent drinking songs, though, had far less of an impact than those of Timocreon. His elitist and money-loving *kudos* simply did not resonate with the people as much as Timocreon's work, and the situation was exacerbated by Cimon and the Athenian aristocracy's push for Timocreon's songs. The Spartan-backed Cimon may have even been a patron for two more Timocreon productions. The *Suda*, a tenth century Byzantine historical and grammatical encyclopaedia, even suggests that Timocreon wrote two plays lampooning Themistocles in one and Simonides in the next. In short, it was not one of Themistocles's best ideas to align himself with a miser like Simonides given his increasing unpopularity and reputation for accepting bribes. The end result only highlighted Themistocles's emerging reputation for corruption and fraudulent populism.

* * *

Soon, Themistocles was even targeted at the Dionysia. In 472 BC, four years after the debut of *Phoenician Women* and at the height of Themistocles's influence in Athens and abroad, a tragedy named *The Persians* debuted. The second instalment of a now-lost trilogy, *The Persians* was a retelling of the aftermath of Salamis from the perspective of Xerxes's family in the Persian capital. The tragic songs of the chorus lamenting the destruction of their ships, the passionate and heroic struggle of Xerxes's ambitious mother Atossa, and the vivid depiction of the ghost of Darius the Great chastising his son's foolish strategies captured the Athenians. It was the most influential play of its time.

This was in no small part due to its author, Aeschylus. Aeschylus was not the stereotypical playwright. He was a highly decorated and respected warrior, having been one of the very few Athenians to have fought at Marathon, Salamis and Plataea. He fought alongside his brother at Marathon, where his brother tragically fell underneath a wave of Persian arrows. He rowed a trireme at Salamis where he destroyed ship after ship under the leadership of his other brother Aminias, the greatest hero of the day after Themistocles. He joined Pausanias and Aristides the Just in breaking the Persians at Plataea and ending the threat of Persian invasion. In short, he was one of the few Athenians who could rival Themistocles, Aristides and Xanthippus in *kudos*.

Because of both its author and its moving content, *The Persians* was a phenomenon in Athens. Its message was of the resiliency of the Athenian city-state and that it was the people of Athenians, and not one man, who saved Greece. The message ignited a patriotic revival in Athens. Aeschylus's contrast between Persian monarchism and the Greek passion for independence is distilled to one revealing passage. When Atossa, the queen of Persia and mother of Xerxes, hears of the defeat at Salamis, she demands to know its leader. But there is no leader to name, since the Athenians govern themselves and submit to no man:

Queen: Who is the ruler of this people? Who
          Lord of their levies and their revenue?

Chorus. Subject they are not unto any man:
          They say 'slave' sorts not with 'Athenian.'[17]

The Athenians were inspired by the heroism not just of the mighty heroes of Salamis but the common men, women, and children who sacrificed everything for their liberty. This was epitomized in Aeschylus's vivid depiction of the start of the battle and the famous motivating words of a nameless Athenian commander:

> Seeing their judgment grievously at fault,
> Fear fell on the barbarians. Not for flight
> Did the Hellenes then chant that inspiring hymn,
> But resolutely goings into battle,
> Whereto the trumpet set all hearts on fire.
> The word was given, and, instantaneously,
> Oars smote the roaring waves in unison
> And churned the foam up. Soon their whole fleet appeared;
> The port division thrown out like a horn
> In precise order; then the main of them
> Put out against us. We could plainly hear
> The thunder of their shouting as they came.
>
> 'Forth, sons of Hellas! free your land, and free
> Your children and your wives, the native seats
> Of Gods your fathers worshipped and their graves.
> This is a bout that hazards all ye have.'[18]

The words inspired the Athenians to celebrate their city-state's victory at Salamis and their position at the top of the Greek world. The words of the commander echoed throughout Athens as a rallying cry for Athens to celebrate their community, and not to celebrate a single hero of Salamis when so many more sacrificed everything for the victory. Just like the prosperity of their city during this Golden Age, Salamis belonged not to one man, but to Athens at large.

His *choregos* was none other than Xanthippus's son Pericles. A member of the influential noble family the Alcmaeonids, Pericles was not even of voting age yet, but was already preparing for a distinguished political career. While Aeschylus and Pericles may not have intended to dissuade the people of Themistocles's contributions to the victory of Athens, it nevertheless had that effect. Some historians believe that *The Persians* was actually a pro-Themistocles text, with Pericles the son of Xanthippus making sure that, although he is not explicitly named in the play, that glory of Salamis is still attributed to Themistocles. This was especially important to combat the growing faction sympathetic to the aristocrats, led by Cimon, that targeted the populist Themistocles.

Such intentions led to the opposite effect. Themistocles had tried to hedge this off with *Phoenician Women*, but Phrynichus's work did not reach the Athenians on the same emotional level that the war hero Aeschylus was able to, despite covering the same subject matter. Unlike the other early Greek historical plays dealing with the Athenian's old foe like those by Phrynichus, *The Persians* humanized the aggressors, and did not present them as a mindless enemy but instead as three-dimensional characters who thought, felt, dreamt, and cried just like the Greeks. This made the propagandistic undertones of the play far less ham-fisted. Many Athenians were likely able to sniff out Themistocles's ulterior motives of *Phoenician Women*, but sat open-jawed during Aeschylus's powerful drama.

Themistocles was, for the first time since his very brief demotion in 479 BCE, having great difficulty navigating Athenian politics. His sense of his predicament was that the Athenians were jealous of his accomplishments and unable to handle his success, and that lack of empathy undergirded his responses. In a show of his frustration, he lashed out at the voting assembly by giving a lengthy summary of his contributions to the city-state and shouted to the 'malcontents: "Why are [you] vexed that the same men should often benefit you?"'[19] He pushed further in a separate tirade on the council floor of the voting assembly, comparing himself 'to a row of plane-trees, under which in a storm passengers run for shelter, but in fair weather they pluck the leaves off and abuse them'.[20] His cultural projects in playwriting, poetry and drinking songs were no longer simply an image management campaign. Themistocles was fighting for his life. His long-time support from the lower classes was beginning to crack and his brand of populism was less and less appealing to the Athenian masses. Ostracism soon became a clear and present danger for Themistocles.

* * *

Fighting against the fresh new wave of resistance to his power, Themistocles used his formidable influence to institute some major democratic reforms. While he had accomplished no shortage of construction and military projects, Themistocles had not yet focused his talents for reformation on the actual democratic process in Athens. A new partner emerged in Ephialtes, a *strategos* and populist himself. Ephialtes was a major reformer in Athens who pushed for more voting rights and less aristocratic privilege, and he would later inherit Themistocles's populist role in the *stasis* – that unceasing class struggle between the lower classes and the aristocracy. He was later succeeded by Pericles, who led Athens as a *strategos* during the rest of the Athenian Golden Age until the outbreak of the Peloponnesian War in the late 430s. But at some time in the late 470s or early 460s, Ephialtes focused his reformational ideas on the *areopagus*.

The *areopagus* was the council of former *archons* whose influence on Athenian politics varied widely by generation. At times, such as during the height of the Golden Age under Pericles, they were simply an advisory board and served as a jury during murder cases. But during the formational years of Athenian democracy, the *areopagus* was an aristocratic council of elders who unofficially shaped all manners of policy and had virtually no oversight. Cleisthenes had stripped the council of much of its powers in the earliest stages of democracy, but the *areopagus* clawed back influence piece by piece over the next fifty years.

In his *Constitution of Athens*, Aristotle recounts the heightened power of the *areopagus* in the aftermath of the Persian Wars and claims that they reigned supreme, emboldened no doubt by Themistocles's penchant for bribery, Cimon's influence in favour of the aristocrats and the Spartans and the monumental amounts of money raked in from the Delian League. Themistocles himself was a member of the *areopagus*, and so the council at large felt no serious threat from any Athenian before Ephialtes.

But it was the increasing threat of ostracism that spurred Themistocles into action. With the help of Ephialtes, he set about weakening the *areopagus* from the inside as a last-ditch populist effort to shore up support among the lower classes. Given his foresight, and the fact that he had not lessened the calls for alarm about rising Spartan enmity towards Athens, Themistocles likely was motivated also by a genuine hope to strengthen Athens for the coming conflict with Sparta. If the aristocrats of Athens were championed by Cimon, who was unquestionably influenced and funded by Sparta, then Athens had no viable future. And although self-preservation was a strong trait for Themistocles, he was still a true patriot of Athens. He knew that if the *areopagus* maintained its unbalanced power then men like Cimon could manipulate Athens to kowtow to Sparta. He sought to avoid this at all costs and, to him, saving Athens from its own democracy was every bit as essential to Athens' survival as victory at the Battle of Salamis.

Themistocles desire to remain in power, however, was his primary motivation to revamp Athenian democracy. Ephialtes and Themistocles first broke the support structures for many of the most powerful and aristocratic members of the *areopagus* by targeting them for demotion, and they 'ruined many of its members by bringing actions against them with reference to their administration'.[21] After knocking off several political rivals in the *areopagus*, Themistocles sought to constitutionally neuter his own council.

The goal was to distribute the *areopagus*'s legislative authority among less corruptible councils like the Council of Five Hundred, the voting assembly, and various law courts. Cleisthenes had designed those councils to be a system of checks and balances against the aristocrats who had dominated Athens until the late sixth century BCE, and so most of the council members were chosen by lot and from an intentional mixture of all social classes and tribes. Most critically, the law-making powers were originally localized in those councils, yet the *areopagus* had managed to bribe and blackmail their way into recapturing their position as main legislative power and hold the keys to the kingdom. But once Themistocles strong-armed the remaining members of the *areopagus* to vote away many of the law-making powers to the non-aristocratic councils, the long-venerated and the aristocrats lost a key cog in their political machine.

Deliberately tanking his own council was not quite the endgame, as Themistocles needed to accomplish a much more public victory to mobilize his defence against any potential vote for his ostracism. To accomplish such a feat, Themistocles engineered a spectacle worthy of the pageantry that was Athenian democracy:

> ... he warned Ephialtes that the Council intended to arrest him, while at the same time he informed the Areopagites that he would reveal to them certain persons who were conspiring to subvert the constitution. He then conducted the representatives delegated by the Council to the residence of Ephialtes, promising to show them

the conspirators who assembled there, and proceeded to converse with them in an earnest manner. Ephialtes, seeing this, was seized with alarm and took refuge in suppliant guise at the altar. Every one was astounded at the occurrence, and presently, when the Council of Five Hundred met, Ephialtes and Themistocles together proceeded to denounce the Areopagus to them. This they repeated in similar fashion in the [voting] Assembly, until they succeeded in depriving it of its power...In this way was the Council of Areopagus deprived of its guardianship of the state.[22]

Taking even his partner Ephialtes by surprise, Themistocles had given one last gasp in his Athenian political career, containing all of his trademark flair in service to both Athens and himself. His trickery here was not enough to stave off an ostracism vote. The populist manoeuvre could not overcome the increasing influence of Cimon and his Spartan-friendly policies. The voting assembly in Athens was much influenced by the cultural backlash against him and a desire to protect their city-state from corruption and Persian sympathizers. At Cimon's suggestion, the Athenians decided to solve their Themistocles problem.

In 471 BCE, the Athenian voting assembly decided to hold a vote for ostracism. In a symbolic move, the assembly used some of the very same powers Themistocles had just recently gifted them. Themistocles, saviour of Athens and the man who had ushered in its Golden Age, now faced exile from the city he had created.

Part IV

Themistocles Among the Dragons

Chapter 11

The Ostracism of the Saviour of Athens

The inscription in front of the Temple of Artemis read 'Aristoboulé, or Best Counsellor'.[1] It was innocuous enough in most circumstances and would be interpreted as referring to Artemis herself, the goddess of the hunt and of childbirth. But its location was too brazen to be denied. The Temple of Artemis was adjacent to Themistocles's own home, and it was Themistocles himself who had funded and overseen the temple. To the Athenians, it was an obvious statement: 'that it was he who had given the best counsel to the city and to the Hellenes'.[2] Like the heroes of the Homeric poems, Themistocles had a fatal flaw in his *hubris* of assuming he was above the gods. And like those heroes, he would pay for his actions.

It was one last stunning piece of evidence showing how out of touch Themistocles was with the Athenians. At Cimon's prodding, the voters returned to the roots of ostracism: safeguarding the city from those who threaten its democratic ideals. Themistocles gave too many signs that he was setting himself up as a king, perhaps for Persia or perhaps for himself. Either way, for many it was the final straw.

There had not been an ostracism in Athens since Xanthippus in 482 BCE – and it was clear that ostracizing him and Aristides the year before had been a mistake. While this might've soured the Athenians on the practice of ostracism in general, it more probably motivated them to consider Themistocles for ostracism this time since it was he who had orchestrated the exiles of Xanthippus and Aristides, men who had since their return served the city-state with distinction. Ostracism clearly waxed and waned in popularity and Themistocles had generated enough ire among the Athenians to resurrect the practice.

That the Athenians voted again to hold an ostracism for the first time in over a decade not only reveals the extent of their distaste for Themistocles but also his crucial role in shaping the Athenian state. Themistocles's involvement in the last three ostracisms is unparalleled in Athenian history. The ostracism of Themistocles was the most pivotal ostracism vote in Athenian democracy history, at least until Alcibiades figured out how to unravel the ostracism system – by pooling his supporters with his rivals supporters to vote out the candidate in third place – in 416 BCE, a full sixty-five years later.

In January or February of 471 BCE, the Athenian voting assembly passed the proposal to hold an ostracism vote. This began the two-month countdown of politicking and campaigning to determine precisely who would be ostracized. While such a vote was clearly a referendum on Themistocles, it nevertheless was subject to the Athenian constitution. At the end of the two months, a vote would again be held and if 6,000 *ostraka* (about twenty per cent of the voting body) were tallied in favour of any Athenian citizen then he was exiled from the city-state for a period of no less than ten years – unless, of course, they were recalled back in an emergency, as had happened to Aristides and Xanthippus.

The vote to hold an ostracism kicked the most important phase of the Spartan-endorsed campaign against Themistocles into high gear. It had begun a few months earlier as a consequence of the behaviour of Pausanias, that Spartan hero who had seen glory and shame in equal measure. Pausanias had managed to be recalled yet again to Sparta to face charges of medising, partially a result of his letter to Xerxes offering Sparta and Greece in return for marriage to a Persian princess. The Pausanias affair had gripped Sparta and its politics since the capture of Byzantium following the Battle of Mycale, and the Spartan ephors had failed to rein in his misadventures. Pausanias this time had been on the Ionian coast, after the failure of his tyrannical rule of Byzantium. After another set of letters were discovered proving that Pausanias was pursuing a relationship with the Persian king, he returned to Sparta to face trial. Yet again, he was acquitted of all charges. This time, however, he was clever enough to not leave Sparta.

The story of a hero from the Persian Wars turning on his city-state to pursue personal power and wealth with the Persians was too tantalizing for Cimon and the Spartans to utilize just once. While Pausanias faced his downfall in Sparta, Cimon used the two-month period leading up to Themistocles's ostracism vote to promote the notion that Themistocles was nothing more than an Athenian version of Pausanias.

It was rather easy for Cimon to paint Themistocles as a co-conspirator to Pausanias. Themistocles had shown sympathy and friendship to Pausanias during his trials for medism. The two had even engaged in a lengthy correspondence since the end of the war and Pausanias's rise to power, apparently becoming quite close: 'And again Pausanias inflicted on Themistocles, who was doing nothing wrong, the suspicion of treason by treating him as a friend, and by writing and sending messages to him continually.'[3] Cimon pressed on this nerve before the voting assembly, delivering daily lectures on the treachery of Themistocles and his affinity for Pausanias, Persia, and personal gain. The Spartans even formally participated in the prosecution of Themistocles and sent ambassadors to Athens, who demanded that the Athenians 'punish him as they had punished Pausanias'.[4] The Spartans arrived shortly after the final vote for ostracism, but their mission was strategically publicized.

Themistocles addressed the issue directly. In a speech to the voting assembly, Themistocles 'acknowledged that Pausanias had sent letters to him, urging him to share in the act of treason'.[5] But in his characteristic rhetorical style, Themistocles played this to his advantage. He argued that this was in fact evidence in his favour since Pausanias would never have gone to such lengths to try and convince him to support Persia if Themistocles had been so willing to collude. It was not as if Themistocles had not already had plenty of chances to medize, after all. This was a point he was sure to have shared with his audiences.

One more account of Themistocles confirms both his relationship with Pausanias and his reticence to actually participate in this particular variety of treason against Athens. Although his works are lost in the sands of time, the historian Ephorus of Cyme writes that Themistocles 'was acquainted with the treason of Pausanias and his negotiations with the King's lieutenants, but that he neither consented to it, nor hearkened to Pausanias's proffers of making him partaker of his hopes'.[6] The more even-keeled Thucydides apparently agreed and 'left the whole matter out of his story, as judging [Themistocles's sympathies and support for Pausanias] to be false'.[7]

Yet the Athenian voters did not see it the same way. For them, the Themistocles saga could only be seen through the prism of corruption and medism. Themistocles's counter strategy was harangued from the onset, but his defence was nevertheless wisely constructed and articulated. His *apologia*, or public defence, was predicated on the classic Greek practice that blackmail, bribery and corruption were perfectly acceptable as long as one never damaged the city-state itself. Themistocles did not bother denying his illicit financial habits and instead passionately argued that since he had never taken money against state interests, and only for himself, that he had never endangered Athens or its naval vision. There was truth to this; even when Themistocles had accepted a bribe of thirty talents from the Euboaeans, he had given eight away to the Athenian and Corinthian commanders and not actually sacrificed the Allied Greeks' position or strategy.

Themistocles's interactions with the Persians were a separate situation altogether. He deliberately left out his communications with Xerxes through his servant Sicinnus or his subsequent flirtations with Persia before Plataea. But the emboldened voters of Athens had seen the lure of Persian gold seduce too many Greeks, especially Themistocles's alleged friend Pausanias, to forget about Themistocles's well-reputed love of money. After Cimon's publicity campaign, too many of the Athenians saw Themistocles as another Hippias – that would-be tyrant of Athens who now served the Persians – and not as the modern version of Odysseus. The accolades won by his foresight in preparing for war with Persia had been supplanted by criticism of his comparable preparations for war with Sparta. The voting assembly had not been convinced by his clever wall-building campaign nor his fortifications to Piraeus.

The situation was in conflict with the stated objective for ostracism as a practice. As Plutarch described it, 'ostracism was not a penalty, but a way of pacifying and alleviating that jealousy which delights to humble the eminent, breathing out its malice into this disfranchisement.'[8] Of course, Themistocles himself had weaponized the practice to eliminate his political rivals in the previous decade. But now Cimon and his Spartans and aristocrats had managed to turn the tables on Themistocles and target him with his own weaponry. But at the core of his ostracism is the idea that his ascent to power threatened the essence of Athenian democracy. While the rise of an obscure man from a non-aristocratic family seems like a democratic fairy tale, Themistocles's story by 471 BCE was defined by his hoarding of money and power. He was by now known more as the miser of Athens than its architect and saviour. It was that *kudos* that the men of the voting assembly voted to ostracize. In Athenian democracy, no one man should have that much power – even if he had earned it and used it well. The city-state was always more important than the individual.

The combined forces of the Alcmaeonids and the other aristocrats, Cimon, Timocreon, the patriotic messages of *The Persians*, Timocreon's drinking songs, and Themistocles's own reputation for corruption were too much to overcome. For the first time in over a decade, the voting assembly gathered on a hill in the city-state's centre to vote on whether to ostracize another hero of Athens. Ironically, that same hill was situated well within the Themistoclean Wall. It was a vivid image of the extent to which Themistocles had become unpopular in the prosperous Athens he had created and saved.

* * *

The ostracism vote was overseen by the nine *archons* of Athens and the Council of 500. Votes were cast anonymously with the name of the accused written on an *ostrakon* potsherd, and the council members were tasked with ensuring that no citizen voted more than once. The votes would continue until one citizen's total reached 6,000 votes, and although any citizen could hypothetically be exiled in the day's vote, there was no doubt that the only name on the ballot was Themistocles.

Some of the *ostraka* from that day in March or April of 471 BC have survived. Their contents certainly animate Greek democracy and the deep emotional and vitriolic nature of ostracism. One simply states, 'Themistocles, son of Neocles, get out!'[9] Another sarcastically calls out Themistocles's reputation for corruption: 'This potsherd is for Themistocles, of the deme Phrearrhius, on account of his honour'[10] Another *ostrakon* reveals a somewhat illiterate citizen so dedicated to writing *Themistocles* that he failed three times. Leaving that *ostrakon* unfinished, he most likely relented and asked a colleague for assistance. And one Athenian voter did not bother to mince any words: 'Themistocles, son of Neocles, asshole!'[11]

Yet the final vote count may have been incomplete. At the bottom of a well near the voting hill, archaeologists found over 150 *ostraka*. These artifacts were scientifically dated to the early fifth century BCE, but the writing on each one left no doubt of its periodization. Over 140 of them were inscribed with a variant of the words 'Themistocles, son of Neocles'. These *ostraka* are among the strongest pieces of historical evidence for the practice of ostracism in general but also for Themistocles himself, who had precious little primary source material surviving until this discovery. Curiously, they did not count as votes in the final tally since the executive councilmen would typically destroy the official *ostraka* after counting them.

But the most intriguing aspect of these *ostraka* was the penmanship. Experts counted only fourteen different sets of handwriting among the 140 *ostraka*. How was it that only a handful of people had written these 140 votes for Themistocles? And why were they found at the bottom of a well, and not included among the actual vote tally for Themistocles?

The answer lies in the rarity of literacy in the ancient world. Even among the citizens of Athens in its Golden Age, very few were entirely literate. As such, a lucrative business model emerged wherein people would take payment to write down the name of a person on the *ostrakon*. Of course, this practice was soon abused as it became standard for political factions to set up camp outside the voting assembly and distribute *ostraka* for their targeted politician. This was almost certainly an invention of Themistocles himself, who had likely employed it in his ostracism duels against Xanthippus and Aristides. But this time around, it was his own name on the potsherds.

But the sheer number of surviving *ostraka* with his name on them suggests that Themistocles's political opponents were unable to distribute all of the pieces successfully. This may mean that Themistocles was still popular enough for a large portion of the voters to decline the chance to vote against him, meaning that the vote was quite close. It also may suggest that he was the victim of election interference. It is possible that these *ostraka* were never intended to be publicly distributed, but instead simply added to Themistocles's voting pile. Perhaps they were thrown in the well afterwards to dispose of the evidence, or perhaps they never made it into the final tally.

But at the end of the day, none of that mattered. The fickle tides of populism had at last turned against Themistocles. He was now the victim of his own political strategies. In 471 BCE, after fifty-three years of service and accomplishments, Themistocles was ostracized from Athens.

His father Neocles proved to have at least some of the foresight that Themistocles is so famous for. His prophecy that Themistocles, if he entered political life in Athens, would end up like the ruined trireme on the seashore proved to be true. Themistocles, now so, fled to Argos that very evening, without taking any of his personal possessions or even his family. He would never return to his beloved Athens.

*   *   *

The ripple effects of his ostracism were immediate and consequential. Shortly after his exile, Themistocles himself remarked to his successors in the Athenian navy that he was handing them the keys to an enormously successful empire that he – and not they – created:

> The Day after the feast contended with the Feast-day, saying that the Feast-day had much labour and toil, but she (the Day after the feast) afforded the fruition of the provision made for the Feast-day, with much leisure and quietness. The Feast-day answered after this wise: Thou speakest truth; but if I had not been, neither hadst thou been.[12]

Themistocles's former rival and current ally Aristides the Just had deliberately avoided the ostracism vote, in order to avoid a perceived conflict of interest and out of respect for his colleague. His behaviour during the ostracism of Themistocles was so impressive that Plutarch used it as evidence for his unwaning honour: 'Aristides remembered no evil; nay, though [the Alcmaeonids] and Cimon and many others denounced and persecuted [Themistocles], Aristides alone did and said no meanness, nor did he take any advantage of his enemy's misfortune, just as formerly he did not grudge him his prosperity.'[13] It was one of the last times that Aristides was mentioned in the ancient sources. Shortly before describing his death, Plutarch invokes Plato in his eulogy of Aristides and gives one last comparison to his long time competitor Themistocles:

> And Plato[14] maintains that of all those who had great names and reputations at Athens, this man alone was worthy of regard. Themistocles, he says, and Cimon, and Pericles, filled the city with porches and moneys and no end of nonsense; but Aristides squared his politics with virtue.[15]

Aristides's estate lacked the funds for even a basic burial after his death. Even though he oversaw the deepest pockets in Greece through the Delian League's treasury, he never skimmed a penny. His justice never abated.

Meanwhile, Timocreon and the cultural élite of Athens were filled with jubilee on the departure of Themistocles. Timocreon penned at least two more popular *scolia* to celebrate the ostracism of the man who, in his estimation, had plagued Athens and Greece. One simply thanked the gods for the justice they had shown in ridding Athens of its corruptor:

> O Muse, grant that this song
> Be famed throughout all Hellas,
> As it is meet and just.[16]

And a second put the icing on Timocreon's personal vendetta with Themistocles, which had long been affected by Timocreon's alleged pro-Persian sentiments. Timocreon drank a toast to the fact that Themistocles had been ostracized for medism of his own:

> Not Timocreon alone, then, made compacts with the Medes,
> But there are other wretches too; not I alone am brushless,
> There are other foxes too.[17]

The Spartan emissaries had finally arrived in Athens to demand the prosecution of Themistocles for colluding with Pausanias to hand Greece over to the Persians. Their support of Cimon and their public statecraft advertising his connections to Pausanias had succeeded in getting Themistocles ostracized, but upon arriving in Athens they had not yet expected Themistocles to have left the city-state. It seems that Themistocles's quick departure to Argos was yet another cunning manoeuvre, and his keen foresight had not quite diminished as much as was thought. By fleeing to Argos, Themistocles avoided being turned over to face a much more public trial in front of the entire alliance of Greeks. The Spartan ambassadors, upon learning of Themistocles's departure from the city, immediately 'asserted that [Themistocles's] trial, since his crimes affected all Greece, should not be held privately among the Athenians alone but rather before the General Congress of the Greeks which, according to custom, was to meet at that time'.[18]

Themistocles was now not only an exile from Athens, but also from the entirety of allied Greek city-states. His decision to flee to Argos, of all places, was wise. Argos was a neutral party during the Persian Wars, having steadfastly refused the Hellenic League and demonstrating subtle Persian support. Their main strategy, it seems, had been to wait out the Hellenic League's certain defeat and then welcome the Persians with open arms. But the Greek victory had thrown a wrench in such plans, and now Argos was in a state of turmoil in their own *stasis*. Populist factions had been increasingly popular in Argive politics, and the city-state was teetering on the edge of becoming a full-fledged democracy. Themistocles had travelled there to help tip the scales in democracy's favour. His ultimate goal was, as always, self-serving: he wished to transform Argos into a democracy and therefore make it a strong ally of Athens, which would endear him enough to the Athenians voting assembly that they would recall him from his exile. And if that failed, he might be able to set himself up as a tyrant of Argos.

It might have worked, but the Spartan campaign against him was not over. Their calls demanding Themistocles's trial before the Congress at Corinth had strengthened. His democratizing work in Argos only hardened the Spartans' hearts. If Argos became a democracy, that would strike directly at the Spartans' grip on the Peloponnesian Peninsula. A strong, Athenian-allied democracy in Argos was far too close for comfort. And Themistocles, who had now successfully implemented anti-Spartan policies in two rival city-states to Sparta, needed to be dealt with.

This prompted the Spartans envoys in Athens, who had demanded that Themistocles be tried before the Congress, to turn up the heat. Their ace in the hole was the revelation of the letters that Themistocles and Pausanias had exchanged. While Themistocles had never denied this relationship, he had also never revealed its true extent. One damning piece of evidence in the court of public opinion was a set of 'certain letters and documents regarding [his relationship with Pausanias]…which cast suspicion on Themistocles'.[19] Although now safely in Argos, the letters were apparently so damning that Themistocles felt the need to defend himself from afar and wrote a letter to the Athenian voters who had just exiled him, arguing that he had 'no natural bent nor even the desire to be ruled'[20] by any Athenian, Persian, Spartan, or ruler of any stripe.

Upon hearing of Themistocles's ostracism, Pausanias had sent a letter to Themistocles revisiting the potential of a Persian alliance. But by the time Themistocles would have written to decline the offer, Pausanias had been executed by the Spartan elders. Pausanias had returned to Sparta to face his trial and, upon hearing rumours that the elders were going to kill him, he fled to the Temple of Athena. The elders' troops surrounded the temple and starved him out. He died shortly after being carried out of the temple, his prosecutors not wishing to make it impure with his deceased body. With Pausanias now gone, nobody could accurately corroborate or deny the claims against Themistocles.

That is why the potential survival of some of the letters between Themistocles and Pausanias is so important. We have no concrete record of the letters presented as evidence of Themistocles's treason to the Athenian voters, but a collection of twenty-one letters purported to be written by Themistocles himself emerged a few hundred years after his death. Most historians date these letters to 100 AD, and thus they are more probably not a true primary source and are likely based on the character of Themistocles as cultivated in Plutarch's *Parallel Lives* and the histories of Herodotus and Thucydides. While their writers had access to sources unavailable today, they are not historically reliable. Nevertheless, they are a helpful data point in understanding the mythos of Themistocles that grew into legend during the Classical period.

The second of these letters is a purported correspondence between Themistocles and Pausanias shortly after Themistocles arrived in Argos as an exile:

I have been ostracized, O Pausanias, by the Athenians and I am now in Argos to avoid further suffering by the Athenians, which they believed was certain had I remained. I travelled immediately to Argos – it was impossible to delay anyway – and my departure relieved the Athenians of their fear. The Argives received me with more warmth than any other outcast would have received, as they wish to take advantage of the prosperity the Athenians once had under my leadership. They have asked me to take command of all Argos, yet they are making a mistake in not welcoming me as a mere exile as the Athenians intended. I find it uncomfortable to reject their plans for me given their enthusiasm, but it would be even worse to accept their offer and therefore justify the very reasons for which I was ostracized. It would be nearly admitting my own guilt if I – having been ostracized from Athens for conglomerating too much power – would then flee to Argos and do the very same by taking command here, even if under compulsion. But it would be completely futile for me, O Pausanias, to simply leave and find another city to make my dwelling in. If I am not careful then the unfortunate events in Athens might repeat themselves.[21]

True or not, the letter encapsulates Themistocles's lack of humility and the tenor of his relationship with the Persian-loving Pausanias. While Themistocles found Pausanias's unrelenting desire to medize akin to 'grasping after...strange and desperate objects',[22] he was nevertheless gradually becoming sympathetic to the allure of Persia's standing invitation to the élites of Greece.

Building on continued pushback against Themistocles after his ostracism, the Spartans next arranged for an influential associate of Cimon, Leobotes of the Alcmaeonid family, to come forward and accuse Themistocles of treason. The Spartans formally supported him, with their delegation claiming they had evidence of a direct agreement between Themistocles, Pausanias, and a Persian noblemen to seize Greece now that Themistocles was ostracized. This was no mere suggestion of a vaguely suspicious relationship with Pausanias; it was a direct indictment of Themistocles as a traitor who had coordinated all of his Athenian policymaking with the Persians. It was an entirely new development in the saga, and sheds light on the true reasons for Themistocles's ostracism. It illustrates that Themistocles was exiled for his political scheming and unlikability, but certainly not for suspicions of actual medism.

Upon hearing this new accusation and its 'proof' in the form of a respected Athenian aristocrat, the Athenians turned on Themistocles even more. Where they once saw a disgraced hero, they now saw an enemy of the state. The Athenians converted Themistocles's ostracism to the death penalty, and sent ambassadors to Argos to arrest him without delay. The Argives, not willing to risk the fury of the Athenian navy or the Delian League, agreed to extradite him immediately.

Themistocles had absolutely no intention of entertaining a meeting with the Congress. He knew that the Congress at Corinth was overwhelmingly slanted in favour of Sparta, as most of its members had refused to join the Delian League and bend the knee before the Athenian triremes. The Athenian-Spartan conflict would be on full display at that meeting, with each side seeking to make an example of Themistocles to fulfil their own political calculations. He knew that any trial he faced would be judged 'not on the basis of justice, but out of favour to the [Spartans], inferring this not only from its other actions but also from what it had done in making the awards for valour'.[23] Themistocles had simply been too successful in elevating Athens, and the formidable navy he had created now intimidated the majority of the Congress into siding with Sparta. Tragically, Themistocles had, in many ways, created the circumstances of his own demise.

He left Argos in the dead of the night, again without taking his family or possessions. He also left behind hoards of money secretly hidden away in Argos, preparations no doubt made before his ostracism from Athens. His next destination was decidedly far away from the Athenian-Spartan conflict that dominated Greek politics – yet it was also far away from the power centres of Greece. He travelled to Corcyra, an influential city-state on the island of Corfu off the north-western coast of Greece. Corcyra was certainly a few steps down from cosmopolitan Athens but was nevertheless considerably influential. They boasted of perhaps the third largest navy in Greece, an heirloom from their early days as a Corinthian colony. This navy had been scheduled to fight at the Battle of Salamis under Themistocles himself yet had arrived – perhaps strategically – too late for combat.

Themistocles, the man who shared so many qualities with Odysseus, was now on his own veritable odyssey – exiled from home and travelling the Greek world in search of home and heroism. Like Odysseus, Themistocles was incognito during his wanderings, unable to use his impressive *kudos* to wield power but instead relying on raw skill and effectiveness. And just like Odysseus, Themistocles would be successful at times and struggle at others; yet, unlike Odysseus, Themistocles would be denied his homecoming. Themistocles would never again return to Athens or participate in wider Greek politics.

When medieval cartographers drew maps, the distant and unknown peripheries were filled in with drawings of dragons to scare off explorers from risking life and limb. This became a symbol for the unknown, a life uncharted by experience or knowledge. Themistocles was now living among these dragons. His life was outside his beloved Athens, far from the political arena of Greece, and beyond the edges of the world he had known.

*   *   *

Themistocles's links to Corcyra went beyond their failure to help the Greeks at Salamis. He had once served as a mediator in negotiations between Corcyra and Corinth, in the interminable conflict between the colonizer and the colonized. The Corcyraeans were quite familiar with both the dexterous nature of Themistocles's political skills and his venal side. In the dispute, he had settled the matter by demanding the Corinthians pay a fee of twenty talents and hand over a long-contested colony to the Corcyraeans. It is easy to assume that Themistocles may have pocketed a portion of that sum.

The Corcyraeans had not relented in their struggle against Corinth, which would eventually culminate in the firestorm that set off the war between Athens and Sparta a few decades later. Themistocles was precisely the type of political figure they needed to strengthen their political fortunes – one who could improve their political standing and increase the odds of their survival against a stronger, wealthier opponent. It was exactly his element, as he had repeatedly demonstrated in Athens against Persian and then against Sparta. His political and military *arete* had made him little more than a high-end sellsword in his ostracism. It was hardly fulfilling for Themistocles.

The Corcyraeans soon agreed. They had apparently underestimated the Spartan thirst for revenge against Themistocles. Some Corcyraeans, looking to line their pockets with Spartan gold quickly revealed Themistocles's location to the Congress, where Themistocles was still wanted for trial. The Corcyraean oligarchs soon admitted it bluntly to Themistocles, stating that they 'could not venture to shelter him at the cost of offending Athens and [Sparta]'.[24] They arranged transportation for Themistocles back to the mainland of Greece and formally ended their partnership. *The Letters of Themistocles* captures the Corcyraean sentiment perfectly, stating 'but the Corcyraeans decided to be safe from danger rather than grateful'.[25]

Themistocles had now been run out of three Greek city-states within a few short months. His political skills were strong enough to find refuge, but divisive enough to prove counter-productive within a few months. Although he had once anticipated a quick return to Athens after his ostracism, as evidenced by his first correspondences from Argos, there was an ever-dwindling chance of him ever ascending to the positions of influence and power he had once known. And unlike in his earlier life, he could no longer benefit from being the underdog – his very name evoked too many reactions from the power players of Greece and the wider Mediterranean world.

A man of Themistocles's foresight clearly realized the danger of his situation. The apocryphal *The Letters of Themistocles* characterize the fear and anxiety that Themistocles felt at this time. Themistocles writes about his family back in Athens, who had remained in the city, since Themistocles had never planned on being exiled for long:

> I don't really believe that the Athenians, even if they despise me on account of my success or their present suffering, would seek to harm my wife and children either by themselves or through some other means. But since there is a chance of that, as slim as the suspicions I have may be, let us not risk their safety and plan for their escape out of Athens.[26]

He closes the letter pointing the letter's recipient to none other than Sicinnus, the servant who had saved Themistocles on more than one occasion already. Given Themistocles's family safely escaped Athens despite all the Greek world searching for him points to the fact that Sicinnus was yet again successful.

Themistocles's last great hope to remain in Greece was in Molossi. Although not geographically far from Corcyra at all, it was just across the channel to the mainland of northern Greece, Molossi was far from a major player in Greek politics. It had a storied history as legend told it was founded by Achilles's heroic son Neoptolemus, who helped conquer Troy after his father's death and established himself as worthy of his father's mantle. But Molossi was not quite the nerve centre for geopolitics that Themistocles had grown accustomed to. Themistocles was now stuck on the periphery of his great empire, a servant in the minor leagues to a king who didn't like him.

The Molossian king was Admetus, a monarch who had made the mistake of publicly opposing Themistocles's conglomeration of power for Athens and therefore deemed too unimportant to include in the Delian League. Admetus had further approached Themistocles for aid at the pinnacle of his power, yet Themistocles insultingly dismissed him. Admetus was likely not much more than an afterthought for Themistocles a decade ago, and yet was now the man on whom Themistocles relied to survive. Admetus had sworn revenge on Themistocles if he ever saw him again, but Themistocles never imagined seeing the forgettable backwoods king again. That Themistocles would turn to such a man reveals his desperation; as Plutarch describes it: 'But in the desperate fortune of that time Themistocles was more afraid of kindred and recent jealousy than of an anger that was of long standing and royal, and promptly cast himself upon the king's mercy.'[27]

Themistocles sidestepped Admetus's hatred of him by approaching the king through his one vulnerability, his family. Themistocles cleverly won over Admetus's queen, Cratesipolis, first as he correctly perceived that she was sympathetic to his situation. Cratesipolis was besmitten with Themistocles's charm and knew that he could enhance the Molossian kingdom if given the chance to advise King Admetus. But she also knew Admetus would order Themistocles killed on sight, and so used her own Odysseus-like creative problem-solving skills.

She informed Themistocles of a longstanding custom in that region of Greece to ask for mercy in an unusual manner – a man would prostrate himself by taking a child in arms and sit down in front of the hearth. It was a traditional act of *xenia*, and it would be the height of dishonour and inhospitality to those in need if the act were to be rejected. While *xenia* was prevalent in broader Greece, this particular act was unique to the region of Epirus where Molossi was located. To perform such an act signalled a newfound humility in Themistocles, one borne out of both necessity and a genuine attempt at empathy for Molossian culture. Cratesipolis's plan was to place her own son, Arybbas, in Themistocles's arms and for

Themistocles to cast themselves before the hearth in the royal throne room, just as Admetus entered. Although far more private, the scene had all the pomp, pageantry and strategic undercurrents of Athenian politics. Although it certainly lacked the funds of Themistocles's production of *Phoenician Women*.

Upon seeing the manufactured scene, Admetus could not refuse, on account both of his honour and his wife's affections. Admetus accepted Themistocles into his court and agreed to shelter him from Spartan and Athenian envoys, in exchange for political consultancy. Thucydides states Admetus's intentions more plainly, noting that Themistocles was by now 'far too low for his revenge; retaliation was only honourable between equals.'[28] Themistocles remained in Molossi, but only for a few months. The diplomatic pressure on Admetus was too intense to continue, and his diplomatic arrangements and trade with Spartan and Athenian allies – which is to say most of Greece – were in peril.

King Admetus soon offered Themistocles a sum of money to depart Molossi for parts unknown, further offering to delay the Spartan hoplites as to his direction. *The Letters of Themistocles* recounts Themistocles's awkward and tense stay in Molossi:

> I sat down at Admetus's hearth, as Cratesipolis instructed me to do, and held his little son Arybbas in one hand and a sword in the other. When Admetus saw me and the young boy, he immediately recognized me and – although he made plain his hatred for me – he pitied the child too much and was afraid of the sword in my hand. Admetus then told me to stand up and offered the hospitality due to travellers, but he refused to keep me safe in his house given his fear of the Athenians and, even more so, the Spartans. Nevertheless, he swore to send me to arrange my passage to safety and he kept his word.[29]

And so while his clever act of supplication worked to save his life, in the process Themistocles lost a part of his identity and his reputation. His *arete* extended even to these base acts that he surely considered below his station in life, but his self-preservation instincts were finely sharpened after the dangers he'd survived and thrived on in war and politics. Yet he was losing his grip as a Homeric hero, increasingly lacking the resources to grasp his own destiny and shape his future. His carefully cultivated *kudos*, which was the only thing providing food and shelter for him during this time period, was degraded every time he had to advise lesser rulers on lesser matters. The obscurity of his post was incompatible with a true Homeric and Greek hero. He needed to regain his glory, honour and *kudos*.

In the 460s BCE, there was only one option for a man of Themistocles's talents and ambition if Athens and Sparta were off the table. Themistocles set his sights on doing the very thing he was ostracized for: helping the Persians. Themistocles would travel to Persia in order to advise their king and governors on the Greeks and Athenians, in exchange for titles and riches. Themistocles embarked on a plan to join the enemy he had dedicated his life to fighting.

*   *   *

From Molossi, Themistocles's odyssey goes beyond the bounds of known history. Different ancient historians give divergent accounts of his next steps. Thucydides claims that Admetus arranged for Themistocles to be smuggled away to Macedon, where Themistocles had an amicable relationship with their king Alexander. Alexander had been Mardonius's chief envoy to negotiate a ceasefire between the battles of Salamis and Plataea and Themistocles had deep respect for the man. Alexander had also aided the Greeks at Tempe before the second Persian invasion, advising that the pass was indefensible and leading to the relative successes of Thermopylae and Artemisium. From Macedon, Themistocles disguised himself and stowed away on a merchant ship out of Pydna and bound for Persian territory on the Ionian coast.

Other ancient sources offer a few more layovers in Themistocles's odyssey before reaching Persia. Diodorus Siculus writes that Themistocles partnered with two local men to journey by night across the Greek mainland to a port on the Aegean Sea. After several precarious encounters with Spartan patrols, the trio managed to reach the port from whence Themistocles met a ship chartered by one of the few Athenian aristocrats still loyal to Themistocles.

Plutarch meanwhile briefly mentions that Themistocles journeyed all the way to the Greek colonies in Sicily to appeal to the heir of Gelon, tyrant of Syracuse. Gelon had been a main player at the original Congress at Corinth, the Hellenic League's contentious meeting that settled their defence strategy as the Persian forces were about to invade. Incidentally, that was the very conference where Themistocles had first made a name for himself in international politics. Gelon had been the talk of the Congress, offering the largest treasury and the most hoplites in exchange for their complete submission to him. The allied Greeks had barely had the time to reject the power grab before Gelon had to abruptly return to Sicily to face an invasion from the Carthaginians, leading to a parallel war in the wider Greek world, from Italy all the way to the Black Sea.

Gelon's successor Hiero had inherited a strong and prosperous tyranny and played his part in maintaining it, albeit without the flair of Gelon. But what Hiero lacked in force of personality, he made up for in cultural caché. Hiero aimed to raise Magna Graecia's standing in the Greek cultural world and was motivated especially to compete with the ongoing Athenian renaissance. This led him to entertain many members of the Greek cultural elite at his royal court, including the playwright Aeschylus and the poet Simonides. Other famous Greek poets and playwrights like Pindar, Bacchylides, and Epicharmus spent time there as well as some notable pre-Socratic philosophers such as Xenophanes. Hiero was the patron for many of their most famous works and they dedicated numerous lyrics and odes to the Sicilian tyrant.

With the great links to the Athenian Golden Age he had himself created, and especially with his close relationship with the poet Simonides with whom he had composed the drinking songs a few years prior, it is easy to see why Themistocles would have sought refuge in Sicily. It was, after all, where Themistocles had threatened to send the entire Athenian population after the evacuation of Athens before Salamis, had the Greeks not met his terms.

If the ancient Greek historian Stesimbrotus is to be believed, Themistocles had lost none of his swagger. Stesimbrotus records that Themistocles, the destitute exile who had been turned away even from the lesser Greek power, marched right into Hiero's throne room and 'demanded from Hiero the tyrant the hand of his daughter in marriage, promising as an incentive that he would make the Hellenes subject to his sway.'[30] Although it certainly seems in character for Themistocles, Plutarch roundly rejects the quality of Stesimbrotus's historical writing and points to Themistocles' marriage and family, who by now were taken care by his few Athenian friends, as evidence. Plutarch was never shy about criticizing those historians who disagreed with him on the sources.

But even if Themistocles had not insulted his host and quickly violated the *xenia* a guest must show to their host, there was already bad blood between Themistocles and Hiero. When Themistocles had ruled Athens, he had viewed the Sicilians as a threat – and rightly so given the raw strength and power remaining in Magna Graecia long after Gelon's death. In Themistocles' apparent mission to offend every ruler of the Mediterranean that he might later call on for aid, he had called out Hiero at the Olympic games. Hiero had set up a booth at the games selling patriotic decorations and fanfare to boost the visibility of Magna Graecia at the competition. Plutarch cites the historian Theophrastus, whose works now exist only in a few surviving quotes, and says that Themistocles delivered a speech to the entire Greek body at the Olympics urging them to 'tear down the booth of the tyrant and prevent his horses from competing'.[31]

Unsurprisingly, Themistocles lasted only a few weeks in Sicily. He soon set out for Persia. But Themistocles had one final adventure before making it to Persian soil. Travel across the Aegean Sea was harried by the Athenian naval fleet, and it was impossible to outrun their reach. The merchant ship carrying Themistocles was originally aiming to bypass all Athenian territory and land directly in Cyme. But the treacherous winds and storms of the Aegean Sea pushed his ship to the island of Naxos for emergency shelter.

For Themistocles, this was the worst-case scenario. Naxos was not a bustling harbour among the Cycladic Islands sure to have its share of Athenian ships, but it was presently in the midst of a rebellion against the Delian League. This was no surprise given the history of Naxos and their penchant for inserting their island in some of the greatest rebellions in Classical Greece. They had instigated the Ionian Revolt thirty years earlier, by fighting off Persian invaders and helping to march to the Persian regional capital of Sardis and burning it to the ground alongside the Athenians. Those events had helped begin the Persian Wars, and now Naxos was continuing the tradition by becoming the first Delian League member to push back against Athenian rule. The Athenians led the Delian League with an iron fist, especially after Cimon took command of Athens in the wake of Themistocles's departure. Despite Aristides the Just's honourable diplomatic vision for the league, Cimon's increasingly strict management of the Delian League's command had led to widespread oppression of dissidents. Greek territories like Melos and Mytilene would later experience genocide and mass deportation when they tried to unsuccessful throw off their Athenian hegemons.

Although he had been absent from Athens for at least a year, the Athenians still used the diplomatic strategy that Themistocles had perfected. Athens could not politically tolerate such a rebellion, or else the other Greek city-states under their thumb might be encouraged to revolt as well. Athens needed to make an example of Naxos. They had besieged the island of Naxos and placed an embargo on any and all outside ships. In essence, the Athenian triremes had encircled the island and made checkpoints for all ships going in or out. Their strategy was to starve out Naxos until a policy- or regime-change ended their hostility to Athens' ability to do as they please in the Delian League. It was the type of naval strategy that one could employ when you owned nearly all the military ships in the seas. And it was only possible for Athens thanks to Themistocles.

But that great Athenian statesman was far from the current state of Themistocles. Nevertheless, he would have known what stopping at Naxos would mean and could not risk mooring there no matter the cost to their merchant ship or its cargo and passengers. For one of the few times in his life, Themistocles was terrified.

The Letters of Themistocles offers one apocryphal tale that a man on Themistocles's ship recognized the Athenian politician, who had favourably adjudicated a case for him at Artemisium. Themistocles sensed the crew looking at him suspiciously, and so upon recognizing the opportunity jumped at the chance with his keen sense of manipulating relationships into a transaction. Themistocles replied, 'My present circumstances are not unfortunate, if I can work the situation to my advantage and get payment from you in return. I am thankful for you and wish you the best of luck – though only if you have the power to save and defend Themistocles.'[32]

His only hope was the ship's captain, but he was travelling incognito on the ship to avoid detection by the long reaches of Athens and Sparta. Disclosing his identity was a massive risk, as the ship's captain could simply decide to continue on to Naxos and turn Themistocles over to the Athenians themselves, who would be sure to reward him richly. While Themistocles currently lacked the funds to compete with what the Athenians could offer, he did still have his cunning talent for manipulation and foresight. He immediately revealed his true identity to the captain of the merchant ship and launched into the rhetoric that had won him influence in Athens. He convinced the captain to avoid landing in Naxos 'partly by entreaties, partly by threats'.[33] At one point, the captain was browbeaten by claims that Themistocles, if ever turned over to the Athenians, would testify that the ship's captain and his crew had taken Themistocles on board willingly after accepting a hefty bribe. This would have made them an accessory to his escape from Athenian forces and been a certain death sentence.

The ship's captain decided that the threatening storms and winds of the windswept Aegean Sea would be far less of a risk than what Themistocles would put him through if they harboured at Naxos. It was a wise idea; Athens shortly decimated the fleet at Naxos, confiscated all their triremes and military ships and increased their taxes to the Delian League in perpetuity. It was a distilled example of the Athenian foreign policy began by Themistocles at Andros, now fully realized with the Mediterranean Sea's dominant naval force that he had built. As his rundown merchant ship was battered by the sea towards Persian-controlled territory, Themistocles left all of that behind. After seeing Naxos from a distance, Themistocles would never lay eyes on a free Greece again. Themistocles, the man who had engineered the patriotic Greek victory over the barbarian kingdom of Darius and Xerxes, was now to pledge his allegiance to Persia.

Chapter 12

Themistocles of Persia

S hortly after his loss at the Battle of Waterloo in 1815, Napoleon sent a formal surrender letter to the British authorities that invokes none other than Themistocles of Athens:

Your Royal Highness A victim to the factions which distract my country, and to the enmity of the greatest powers of Europe, I have terminated my political career, and I come, like Themistocles, to throw myself on the hospitality of the British people. I put myself under the protection of their laws; which I claim from your Royal Highness, as the most powerful, the most constant, and the most generous of my enemies.[1]

Napoleon was not alone in his reference to Themistocles. The Enlightenment and subsequent Neo-Classicist movement led to a fascination with Themistocles – the exiled patriot forced to serve his former rival. It was a romantic and humanistic narrative that many artists and writers of the eighteenth and nineteenth centuries put into paintings, sculptures, operas, and books. The eighteenth century alone had over a dozen incarnations of a libretto for an opera entitled *Temistocle*, including one particularly successful version by J.C. Bach, the son of Johann Sebastian Bach. Wilhelm von Kaulbach captured the Battle of Salamis in a famous painting. Pierre Joseph Francois painted Themistocles begging for mercy on his journey to Persia. Quotes from Themistocles were engraved above a few French castle entrances. In short, Napoleon's invocation of Themistocles was far from obscure; it was trendy.

The desperate plea of an accomplished commander to find refuge in the arms of his former rival knows few comparisons in history. But Themistocles, mimicked by Napoleon two millennia later, was taking part in a great if dishonourable tradition of Greeks joining the Persian ranks.

Other Greek and Athenian leaders had provided a helpful rubric for Themistocles. Not only had Greek cities and states medized, such as Thebes, Thessaly, and Argos, but many individuals had proverbially crossed the Rubicon and joined the Persian empire. Themistocles had seen this time and again among those Greeks who were hungry either for power or for a restoration of status. The Persians famously rewarded famous individuals with titles, land and cities in Persian-controlled Greece. Demaratus, the exiled Spartan king, had advised the Persians in their invasion and, despite its failure, still held honours in the Persian military and a handful of cities. Gongylus, the middleman to Pausanias's failed treason, held similar rank and status.

As for medized Athenians, Hippias, the deposed tyrant of Athens who had been exiled from Athens before the advent of democracy's ostracism, was one of the most formative examples of success in exile. When Themistocles was an adolescent, Hippias, along with the very concept of tyranny, had been exiled from Athens and replaced with the democracy of Cleisthenes. Hippias subsequently travelled to Persia, offered his counsel and insider information, and helped the Persians attempt to conquer Greece. Although he was repelled alongside the Persians at Marathon, the Persians had likely agreed to install him as *satrap* governor over a new Persian territory. In short, Hippias was perilously close to ruling over all of Greece despite his ostracism from Athens.

Even though he fought against him at Marathon, the tale of Hippias was a blueprint for Themistocles. He saw what could become of an ostracized Athenian statesman among the Persians. The Persians would heartily reward those Greeks who could offer value to their empire, and the very idea of Themistocles the Persian was value in and of itself. No Greek with the *kudos* or stature of Themistocles had every medised. He would be a prized jewel for the Persian king to advertise. The propaganda that the Persians could use from his ostracism would go a long way in fracturing the Greek peace even more during the city-states' slow walk to civil war.

He had always worked to keep the door to Persia open for himself – even after he had defeated the Persian army at Salamis, he had sent emissaries to Xerxes to share Greek movements in order to earn favour as an insurance policy. Given the nature of Athenian democracy and their habit of ostracizing leaders, this was a wise move.

Yet after reaching Persian soil, it was far from an easy journey to the King of Kings' throne room. When his merchant ship landed in Cyme, an Ionian Greek city-state still loyal to Persia, he was met with fierce resistance on account of his reputation. Compounding the matter was the small fact that Themistocles's life had a bounty of 200 talents placed on it by the Persian king himself. This severely limited his options, incentivizing all those noblemen that Themistocles had counted on to make inroads with the Persian king to turn on him instead. Several Ionian Greeks were eager to hand over Themistocles as a tool to curry favour with the Persian king and governors.

Like Odysseus, the odyssey did not end the moment he landed on the soil of his destination. Aware of the price on his head, Themistocles fled to the north of Persian Greece to the region of Aeolis. There, he found refuge in the home of the wealthiest Aeolian, an aristocrat by the name of Nicogenes.[2] Again, like Odysseus, he was forced to rely on the *xenia* of others for his survival.

Nicogenes could not provide safety for long and Themistocles had no desire to remain in obscurity in Aeolis. His vision for his own destiny was, according to Plutarch, divinely appointed. One night after a dinner party at Nicogenes's home, the *paidagōgos* of his children entered a trance. These trances were common among the prophets and soothsayers of Greece, and the guests were enraptured with his words:

Night shall speak, and night instruct thee, night shall give thee victory.[3]

It was the promise that the gods would soon speak to Themistocles and give him guidance, bringing about an end to his odyssey. And that night, according to Plutarch, Themistocles had a dream. As he would later tell it, Themistocles was utterly convinced that the dream was a divine revelation and confirmation of his Persian mission. Plutarch described the dream as follows:

a serpent wound itself along over his body and crept up to his neck, then became an eagle as soon as it touched his face, enveloped him with its wings and lifted him on high and bore him a long distance, when there appeared as it were a golden herald's wand, on which it set him securely down, freed from helpless terror and distress.[4]

Plutarch offers no interpretation of the omen, assuming that its meaning was plain to the readers: that Themistocles will be saved from danger by the eagle that was the Persian King of Kings. Whether the inclusion of this dream in Plutarch's biography was a later justification for Themistocles's medism or an advertising campaign spearheaded by the Persians is unclear. To the Greek and Roman readers, however, it was a seal of approval for the heroic mythos of Themistocles.

His path to Persia now divinely appointed, Nicogenes was tasked with the job of connecting Themistocles with representatives of the Persian king to arrange his formal induction into the Persian court. This was no small feat considering the 200 talent bounty on Themistocles, and Nicogenes could not simply march into the Persian governor's palace to coordinate the meeting. They resolved to send a letter to the Persian king. Thucydides preserves that letter:

> 'I, Themistocles, am come to you, who did your house more harm than any of the Hellenes, when I was compelled to defend myself against your father's invasion – harm, however, far surpassed by the good that I did him during his retreat, which brought no danger for me but much for him. For the past, you are a good turn in my debt' (here he mentioned the warning sent to Xerxes from Salamis to retreat, as well as his finding the bridges unbroken, which, as he falsely pretended, was due to him) 'for the present, able to do you great service, I am here, pursued by the Hellenes for my friendship for you. However, I desire a year's grace, when I shall be able to declare in person the objects of my coming.'[5]

Themistocles was laying all his cards on the table. He cleverly included his previous links to Persia, now insurance policies he could cash in. He reminded the Great King of the letter written to his own father Xerxes at the Battle of Salamis, where Themistocles had cunningly tricked both the Persians and the Greeks to fight on his terms alone. He referenced his 'failure' to burn down the Hellespont pontoon bridge, thus allowing the

Persians safe retreat. And he further subtly relied on his post-ostracism reputation, no doubt leaning heavily into his relationship with Pausanias and his perceived sympathies for both the Persians and for his own tyranny of Athens.

His overtures to the King of Kings were successful. Themistocles received mutual interest from the king and, in a show of good faith, Themistocles was formally pardoned of his crimes against the Persian empire. The *Letters of Themistocles* offer a glimpse of the hope that Themistocles had upon news of Xerxes's intent to bring him into the Persian fold:

> I have already written a letter to Xerxes and received such a respectful and courteous reply that it left me astonished – if for no other reason than all my previous correspondences with him consisted of my deceiving him.[6]

Many historians, including Plutarch and Thucydides, pinpoint this Persian king not as Xerxes the Great but as his son Artaxerxes I. But Plutarch cautions that this cannot be known for certain, and even lists four other ancient historians that disagreed with him and identified this Persian king as Xerxes. But most sources indicate that Xerxes passed away around 465 BCE, and if Themistocles's ostracism was indeed in 471 BCE then it is entirely possible that it was Xerxes himself – the man who burned Athens and invaded Greece with the forces of three continents. No matter which king it was, they had no hesitation in accepting him. They offered Themistocles, the only man to engineer a defeat of Persia, status and power in the Persian empire. Themistocles's long odyssey was nearing its end, though with a new soil to call his home.

But the matter of actually reaching the Persian king was not simple. He had to travel from Ionian Greece to Susa, in modern day Iran, without being noticed and with a massive price on his head. Themistocles had to endure one more humiliation in his ostracism before counselling the King of Kings on the way to best lead Persia in the way he had aided Greece. The aristocrat Nicogenes, perhaps now desperate to get the troublesome Themistocles out of his home, took inspiration straight from Greek mythology when he offered Themistocles a direct passage to the *satrap* governor. Themistocles had to dress as a woman.

The Persians had a longstanding custom of strictly guarding their women, be they wife, slave or concubine. The practice was a result borne of both the Persian religion of Zoroastrianism and more traditional cultural conventions. Women were often confined to the palace or temple without outside contact. As such, it was not unusual for a covered wagon or chariot to contain a woman inside that the public was not allowed to see.

Themistocles became that woman. He stowed away, dressed as a woman, in a covered wagon bound for the palace of a loyal servant of Artaxerxes. To the outside world, the wagon carried a Greek woman who now belonged to a Persian aristocrat and should never be seen or heard by anyone except that lord. Themistocles spoke with nobody except a handful of servants inside the wagon, who communicated with the outside for him.

For the man who had engineered the Athenian empire and saved the Greek and Western world, this was the height of humiliation. Themistocles, hero of Greece, was reduced to a cross-dresser cowering in fear while he avoided the entire outside. Yet such an event was not without precedent among Greek heroes. Achilles, the greatest hero in all of Greek literature and the champion of the Trojan War, had himself gone through a similar experience.

Right before the great Trojan War, when Helen had been stolen by the Trojans and Agamemnon was recruiting a great Greek army to win her back, Achilles hid himself as a woman. The greatest warrior in all of Greece was concealed on the island of Skyros among priestesses, hoping to avoid the war. But Odysseus outwitted him, pretending to attack the priestesses until Achilles leapt to their defence, thus revealing who he was. All that said, the motif of a Greek hero in women's clothes only added to Themistocles's legacy as a Homeric hero.

* * *

The Persian courtier that the feminine Themistocles belonged to was a man named Artabanus the Chiliarch. The encounter between Artabanus and Themistocles was a fascinating meeting of two of the most ambitious and opportunistic powerbrokers of the ancient world. Artabanus was a *chiliarch*, a military title for the leader of the King's personal thousand man bodyguard. The title conferred far more than military power, though, as unofficially it was an advisory role with a say in all major matters in Persia. More critically, the *chiliarch* was the gatekeeper who controlled the flow of information and people to the King of Kings.

Artabanus, like Themistocles, came from a lesser family among Persia's aristocracy but had ascended the ranks of society through sheer willpower and grit. Nothing had been handed to him easily, even the throne itself. Artabanus had served as *chiliarch* to Xerxes in his later years, and Xerxes had placed consummate trust in his royal vizier. Yet Artabanus was not content with the second most powerful position – he wanted the throne. Multiple ancient sources point the finger to Artabanus for arranging the death of Xerxes the Great's son, the crown prince Darius. Darius had been groomed since birth to be the next Great King of Persia. He had the perfect mixture of royal blood as a descendant of Cyrus the Great on his mother's side and Darius the Great through Xerxes. Artabanus tried to covertly end that bloodline to allow himself to rule over a lesser son, Artaxerxes, as regent and later as a full-fledged king.

While Artabanus managed to avoid detection when he murdered Darius, Xerxes soon suspected foul play. Aristotle and other sources point the finger to Artabanus for the death of Xerxes the Great himself, a pre-emptive strike before Xerxes could act on his suspicions.[7] A later historian, Junianus Justinus, reverses that order of death but with similar details. The Persian-Greek historian Ctesias claims that Artabanus murdered Xerxes while Darius still lived, and then subsequently convinced Artaxerxes to murder the crown prince Darius, persuading him that Darius had been the one to kill Xerxes.[8] But the history is nonetheless clear that Xerxes died without a clear-cut heir to his formidable empire. Artabanus filled that void.

When Themistocles met with Artabanus the Chiliarch, it was after the death of both Xerxes and the crown prince Darius, and the king Artaxerxes himself was likely to be merely a puppet king. That would soon change. Regents typically only succeed when the king is too young to be under one's thumb, and the twenty-something Artaxerxes was hungry for his own glory and power. Perhaps suspecting Artabanus for the death of his kin, Artaxerxes killed him personally around the year 464 BCE, along with all of his sons.

Nevertheless, the meeting between Themistocles and Artabanus the Chiliarch certainly brought together two great figures driven by destiny and willpower. Upon meeting Themistocles, Artabanus delivered the deeply ironic news that, since the Persians honoured obedience to the king as the image of the god above all things, Themistocles needed to agree to complete submission to Artaxerxes in order to proceed. If Themistocles decided that he still held too closely to the Greek emphasis on liberty and equality, then he must write letters to the king instead, since the Persians would never allow their king to 'give ear to a man who has not paid him obeisance.'[9]

For Themistocles to agree to such a request would not be mere words. It would be a direct and total repudiation of the Athenian worldview that had propelled him to his greatest successes. The Athenians valued equality under the law, *isonomia*, and the individual liberty that drove them to choose certain death rather than submit to the Persian invasions. If Themistocles wanted to survive in Persia, he had to forsake his Athenian heritage and yield all of his previous proud Greek recalcitrance to authority.

Themistocles, nevertheless, acquiesced and forfeited the peculiar freedom that was Athenian liberty. His reply was nothing short of prostration:

> Nay, but I am come, Artabanus, to augment the King's fame and power, and I will not only myself observe your customs, since such is the pleasure of the god who exalts the Persians, but I will induce more men than do so now to pay obeisance to the King.[10]

Whether it was a strategic feint or an authentic renouncing of his Greek worldview is not clear, but Artabanus's intentions were a bit more transparent. His response was to ask for Themistocles's name, since such an entrance and eloquent reply were clearly the mark of a distinguished man and no mere Greek general. Artabanus the Chiliarch apparently gave every indication that he did not know Themistocles.

But if Artabanus was indeed the functional regent during his meeting with Themistocles, then his inquisitive nature was a ruse. The letter penned by Artaxerxes to Themistocles that pardoned his crimes against Persia would have been under the purview of Artabanus the Chiliarch, either a machination entirely directed by him or one selectively given to

Artaxerxes for approval. Either way, Artabanus was testing Themistocles: if Themistocles revealed his identity to a mere bodyguard, then he could never be trusted to truly work for Persia. Themistocles's life was still very much at risk.

The kingslayer Artabanus and the kingmaker Themistocles were about to enter the heat of their rhetorical duel. Themistocles's mettle never weakened. He refused to identify himself and channeled the Spartan rhetorical style in a simple response, 'This, Artabanus, no one may learn before the King.'[11]

*   *   *

At very long last, Themistocles and the King of Persia met face to face. When Artaxerxes's grandfather Darius had first heard of the Athenian resistance and the burning of his colonial capital Sardis in 499 BCE, he had commanded an attendant to announce at the start of every evening's dinner, three times in a row, 'Master, remember the Athenians.'[12] The Persian thirst for vengeance on Athens had not been quelled, but instead had grown in the years since. And it was Themistocles who had exacerbated the problem, most famously at Salamis but now more pressingly through the Delian League's use of the Athenian navy to liberate Persian colonies across the Mediterranean. It was only through Themistocles's vision and leadership that Athens could now challenge Persia, yet here he was in the King of Kings' throne room.

Themistocles's grip on the Persian language was not yet passable and so a royal interpreter translated the conversation for both parties. Considering his reputation for eloquence and persuasion, his opening speech did not disappoint. He certainly had enough time to prepare it in the short years since his ostracism from Athens. From holding Admetus's son at the hearth, fleeing Spartan patrols in the dead of the night, to the merchant ship nearly turning him over to the Athenians at Naxos, to disguising himself as a woman in Persian territory, Themistocles had looked to this very moment as his only hope of true liberty. The Spartans and Athenians would never allow him rest, but if he could win over the Persians then he might succeed in finding peace.

I who thus come to thee, O King, am Themistocles the Athenian, an exile, pursued by the Hellenes; and to me the Persians are indebted for many ills, but for more blessings, since I hindered the pursuit of the Hellenes, at a time when Hellas was brought into safety, and the salvation of my own home gave me an opportunity for showing some favour also to you. Now, therefore, I may look for any sequel to my present calamities, and I come prepared to receive the favour of one who benevolently offers reconciliation, or to deprecate the anger of one who cherishes the remembrance of injuries. But do thou take my foes to witness for the good I wrought the Persians, and now use my misfortunes for the display of thy virtue rather for the satisfaction of thine anger. For it is a suppliant of thine whom thou wilt save, but an enemy of the Hellenes whom thou wilt destroy.[13]

He followed these words with religious symbolism the likes of which he had avoided since his 'wooden wall' prophecies about Salamis. He spoke of the vision at Nicogenes's house, and how Artaxerxes must certainly be the eagle that brings true liberty and peace. He also displayed a familiarity with the Persian worldview, pointing to the dream as a compass pointing Themistocles to the world's two 'Great Kings,' Zeus and Artaxerxes.[14] It was not just a flattering comparison, but a rejection of Greek polytheism and an embracing of Persian monotheism. Themistocles was fully committed to his new Persian identity.

It was a masterpiece in rhetoric. This oration ranks high among Themistocles's most famous speeches, up alongside convincing the Spartans to fight at Artemisium or persuading the Athenians to build their navy with the Laurium silver. And like those, Themistocles exhibited *arete* when the moment allowed for no other option.

Artaxerxes was deeply impressed with Themistocles and surely realized the value he would bring both materially and politically to Persia as they wrestled with the constant wave of Delian League attacks across the Aegean. Yet Artaxerxes was also a seasoned politician, even if Artabanus pulled the strings, and he denied Themistocles any discernible response that day.

Themistocles left the king's audience utterly convinced of his failure. In fact, the next day when he arrived again at the royal court, the palace was abuzz with news that Themistocles of Athens was there. The palace guards insulted him brazenly. One royal advisor spoke plainly to Themistocles as he entered the presence of the king, saying, 'Thou subtle serpent of Hellas, the King's good genius hath brought thee hither.'[15] There were precious few reasons to be optimistic.

But not all was lost. On the contrary, Artaxerxes was elated that Themistocles wanted to medize. Artaxerxes was especially struck by the courage and boldness with which Themistocles spoke to the Great King of Persia; it was a stark contrast with the near-constant submission that was standard behaviour towards the king in Persian culture. Artaxerxes gushed to confidants about Themistocles and the opportunities that he would bring, congratulating himself and praying to the gods that more Greek leaders would be ostracized soon. But perhaps the most revealing affection that Artaxerxes had was recounted by Plutarch, who says Artaxerxes retired to his bedroom that evening, drunk on wine, and three times in the night could be heard joyously shouting,

I have Themistocles the Athenian!

*   *   *

On the morning that Themistocles returned to the throne room, he passed his final test by showing the deferential reverence required to greet the King of Kings. In return, Artaxerxes revealed his true affection. He offered Themistocles an unexpected reward: the 200 talent bounty on his head. After all, this medized Themistocles had been the one to do what Sparta, Athens nor Persia could do in delivering the Greek rebel Themistocles into Persian hands. Themistocles gladly accepted the money and, even more gladly, was relieved to be truly safe after years of exile.

Artaxerxes then gave Themistocles permission to speak openly and freely on the current state of Greece. This was not merely a chance to share political intrigue and gossip but was instead an opportunity to begin to grow the seeds of a third Persian invasion. The Persians never truly gave up their ambitions to conquer Greece, although at this point it was a matter of pride far more than an imperial calculation. Themistocles would have been clear on the overtures: if he could assist in delivering Greece to the Persians, then he would be restored to leadership in Athens or perhaps all of Greece. Themistocles could succeed where Hippias and Demaratus had failed.

But Themistocles dexterously avoided the temptation to jump straight into business. Long term survival in the Persian court depending on his utility and unveiling most of his advice so soon would limit that usefulness. Themistocles told King Artaxerxes that speaking so plainly at this point would not be truly helpful, since 'the speech of man was like embroidered tapestries, since like them this too had to be extended in order to display its patterns, but when it was rolled up it concealed and distorted them.'[16] It was a convincing sidestep to avoid overextending his position and to continue the mythos he had already cultivated even in the Persian courts.

Themistocles instead made an odd request to the king: more time. In a rare show of humility and patience, Themistocles asked for a full year to learn Persian culture, government, and language. Themistocles would stay near Susa and rub elbows with Persian powerbrokers, investing his future in the Achaemenid empire.

It was a masterful move. Artaxerxes happily accepted the opportunity to keep Themistocles around and learn more about his new chess piece in the game of thrones. Themistocles, meanwhile, took every advantage of the opportunity. He quickly became adept at speaking Persian and, under the guise of practising the language, arranged for regular meetings with Artaxerxes without a translator, or anyone else, present. This afforded Themistocles the latitude to influence Artaxerxes and sway his opinion, without any of his Persian hangers-ons or advisors. While Themistocles had no interest in truly manipulating him, Artaxerxes had little exposure to classical Greek rhetoric, especially to one of the raw skill and talent of Themistocles. Themistocles soon had the ear of Artaxerxes on a great wealth of issues. As crazy as it would have sounded two decades earlier, Themistocles was fast becoming genuine friends with the King of Kings.

The rest of the Persian court assumed these meetings between the king and Themistocles were exclusively tactical briefings on the state of affairs in Greece, and the first steps in the next invasion. But as Artaxerxes began to introduce more and more unique political and strategic ideas into the court, it was clear that Themistocles was ingratiating himself into all facets of the Persian government. Outsiders had simply never had this level of access and influence in the Persian court. And, despite their ancient reputation for treating conquered peoples well, the Persian noblemen began to despise Themistocles.

Leading this charge was Mandane, the sister of Darius the Great and the full sister of Xerxes. This meant she was the daughter of Atossa, the queen-mother of Xerxes and the sympathetic protagonist in Aeschylus's *The Persians*. Mandane's name held significant weight among the Persians; she was revered as a member of the old guard and, given her heritage, was viewed as the torch bearer for Persian traditionalists.

Unfortunately for Themistocles, Mandane had lost three sons at the Battle of Salamis. She was unwilling to offer forgiveness. This endeared her even more to the public and the rest of the courtiers of Persia, which compounded the issue. Her story reverberated with the most patriotic of the Persians, many of whom had little affection for the Greek mastermind of Salamis and his newfound influence in the palace.

Mandane used this perception to her benefit and made an overt and much publicized play to wreak vengeance on Themistocles, the man who killed her sons. Drawing from the theatrical playbook of her brother Xerxes, Mandane went to Artaxerxes's palace while he was holding court, dressed in accordance with Persian mourning customs, and passionately begged her nephew to arrest Themistocles and exact revenge on him for her sons and for the families of all those Persians who perished in the invasions of Greece.

Artaxerxes had no patience for his eccentric aunt's behaviour, her popularity aside, and dismissed her without any consideration. But she continued to press, convincing scores of noblemen that Themistocles was not only unwelcome in Persia but needed to be eliminated. Such a manoeuvre was a marked departure from Cyrus the Great's treatment of foreigners, and it clearly did not honour the Greek concept of *xenia* to its guests. It was nevertheless effective, and soon a 'mob rushed to the palace and with loud shouts demanded the person of Themistocles for punishment.'[17]

This time, the Great King Artaxerxes could not blindly defend his friend. Facing the pressure of masses, Artaxerxes proposed a unique solution. He offered to appease Mandane by revoking Themistocles's royal pardon and charging him with crimes against the Persian empire. It was perhaps at the behest of a trusted advisor like Artabanus the Chiliarch, or perhaps even the idea of Themistocles himself.

The preparations for such a monumental trial took time, especially since Themistocles was a novice in Persian law and language. It most likely took the majority, or the entirety, of his yearlong stay in the Persian capital. But, as Themistocles so often did in moments of extreme duress, he shone. Themistocles was able to not only learn enough about the Persian law code to defend himself persuasively, but also spent the year of the trial fostering a closer relationship with Artaxerxes and the requisite nobility, judges, and expatriates who could effectively shepherd his defence. He was fully acquitted, rather quietly to avoid any outrage, and allowed to live in luxury. Themistocles the Athenian was now, legally and culturally, a true Persian.

*　*　*

At the end of his year in the Persian palace, Themistocles was more influential and successful than perhaps any outsider, and certainly any Greek, had been in recent memory. Thucydides describes at length his standing among the Persians:

> Arrived at court at the end of the year, [Themistocles] attained to very high consideration there, such as no Hellene has ever possessed before or since; partly from his splendid antecedents, partly from the hopes which he held out of effecting for him the subjugation of Hellas, but principally by the proof which experience daily gave of his capacity.[18]

Indeed, for years to come, Themistocles would be the gold standard for how to medize. Later Persian kings invoked Themistocles's stature in Persia in their recruiting pitches to Greek statesmen and generals. His time in Persia was simply unprecedented for any Greek, and certainly any Athenian. He once again rewrote the narrative on how a Greek hero can take control of their own destiny, even when facing the great hardship of exile.

And he had quite the lifestyle to show for it. Themistocles participated in the royal hunts with Artaxerxes, a grand Near Eastern tradition reserved only for the most highly honoured guests. Most Persian aristocrats never came close to being considered to join a hunt. Parties, festivals, feasts, and parades were par for the course for Themistocles in Persia. The king allowed Themistocles to hear the lore of the Magi, secret knowledge never extended to the common man.[19] He lived a luxurious and somewhat hedonistic life, a far cry from the stresses of rebuilding Athens, plotting against invaders, forming democratic coalitions, and constantly outpacing your political rivals. He was as safe and secure as he had ever been.

Themistocles garnered so much capital with Artaxerxes that he was able to change the King of Kings's mind on state matters. Artaxerxes's reign was hampered by internal rebellions, limiting his focus on Greece and the potential third invasion. Themistocles therefore took the lead on many Greek matters, functioning as a shadow governor, at times, to shape policy. Themistocles advised the king to avoid another massive invasion, and instead to continue the strategy of piecemeal conquest and continue provoking the Greeks in their unceasing civil wars. This was especially true of the escalating conflict between Athens and Sparta.

His fellow Greek exile Demaratus, the former king of Sparta, had deeply offended Artaxerxes by asking to wear the formal crown of a monarch in a state parade. It was an amateurish error to infringe on the exclusive royalty of the Great King of Persia, and a move that illustrated Demaratus's clumsy statecraft even after decades in Persia. Artaxerxes, feeling no real gratefulness to the Spartan king who failed to reconquer Sparta, lashed out at the offence and was prepared to execute Demaratus. Only on Themistocles's intervention did the king relent. Themistocles was now so close that he could talk the king out of official government policy and judgements.

During his time at the palace, Themistocles made another curious friendship. He became very close with the queen-mother Amestris. Amestris was the widow of Xerxes, and the fact that Artaxerxes allowed Themistocles access to his mother, a woman of about the same age, was enormously revealing. His trust in Themistocles aside, their friendship is a fascinating historical case study. Themistocles was the sworn enemy of Amestris's late husband, singularly responsible for the deaths of her family members, and the source of great shame on the Persian throne. Moreover, Amestris is not well-regarded by the Greek historians. She was known for her cruelty, burying the sons of her rivals alive and mutilating the families of Xerxes's lovers.

On the other hand, Themistocles had dedicated his life to eradicating the Persian threat, lamenting the destruction of Athens at the hands of her husband, and constructing a great navy for the sole purpose of besting Persia. Themistocles and Amestris simply did not make sense as a pairing, and yet they became intimate friends. Yet perhaps they were not so different; Themistocles had, after all, sacrificed three humans before Salamis and was no stranger to eliminating political rivals.

*   *   *

After his acquittal, Artaxerxes had showered Themistocles with gifts. A beautiful and virtuous Persian noblewoman was given over to him as a wife, further legitimizing his Persian identity. Furnishings, gold, political connections and servants were the norm. His new wife came with more landed titles and slaves to support his growing family.

But the most important of his Persian rewards was governorship over three large cities in modern Turkey, the region of Greece controlled by Persia. These cities were Magnesia-on-the-Meander (not to be confused with the Magnesia in mainland Greece), Lampsacus and Myus. Lampsacus was a wealthy city on the Hellespont, not far from ancient Troy. Renowned for its wine, it had changed hands many times over, from Lydia to Persia to Athens. Lampsacus was ostensibly a member of the Delian League, but paid tribute to both Artaxerxes and Athens – a testament to their wealth. Themistocles pocketed their gold, after his own tribute to the King of Kings. Myus was a lesser city close to Miletus in central Ionia, the home of the Ionian Revolt that had instigated Athenian-Persian tensions.

Both cities were significant additions to Themistocles's status, but Magnesia-on-the-Meander was the crown jewel. Magnesia was a resplendent and influential city in Ionia near Ephesus, a traditional rival. Situated right on a bustling river connecting the coast with the inland, the Meander, Magnesia was a city of culture, history, and commerce and apparently brought in over fifty talents of silver a year just for its rulers. The legend told that the city itself was founded by members of Agamemnon's army after the sack of Troy, and the city was further lionized by the Oracle of Delphi who had declared it a city sacred to Artemis.

In the Persian hierarchy, it was one of the better cities to rule in Ionia. With his newfound favour with the king, Themistocles ruled over Magnesia with the wisdom and effectiveness that he had Athens, yet without the turmoil and insecurity of democracy. The Magnesians accepted him willingly and happily, and there are no known historical accounts of anything but prosperity for Magnesia during this time. His name became great in Persia, a rubric for what is possible for a Greek with the right mixture of virtue and effectiveness. The warrior-philosopher Xenophon used Themistocles as a standard for the true Greek hero. Xenophon wrote of one protege's potential that he could earn 'a name thrice famous in the city first, and next in Hellas, and lastly even among barbarians perhaps, like Themistocles'.[20]

The historian Diodorus Siculus captures the deep irony of Themistocles's prosperous years in Magnesia: '...on the one hand, [Themistocles] had been driven into exile by those who had profited most by the benefits he had bestowed and, on the other, had received benefits from those who had suffered the most grievously at his hands.'[21]

Themistocles had quite the war chest to fund his adventures in Magnesia, despite the tribulations of his exile. Themistocles had maintained close contacts with many Athenians, given his hope to one day return to power there, and had arranged for both his family and his fortune to arrive in Ionia with him. In addition to the 200 talents given to him for his own bounty, Themistocles had 100 talents of silver to begin life anew in Persia. It was a small fortune, and a far cry from the paltry three talents he had before entering political life.[22] It seems his reputation for bribery and blackmail had been lucrative.

Such finances afforded him comfort, and he used the opportunity to reunite with his family. By now, Themistocles had ten children by two wives, and his aristocratic friends in Athens had finally arranged for transportation for Themistocles's family to Persian territory. It was surely a heartfelt reunion, but the most significant addition for Themistocles was a ready-made political ally in his son Archeptolis. Now in his thirties, Archeptolis was a seasoned politician who had cut his teeth in Athens, like his father, yet had learned to deal with the hardship of an infamously divisive father.

Archeptolis had learned the management and leadership skills of his father but apparently also was alert to his father's winsomeness and stubbornness. He was now experienced enough to assist Themistocles in politics and in studying the Persian courts and noblemen. It helped that Archeptolis had kept his passions in the family; he married his half-sister Mnesiptolema. Themistocles, for perhaps the first time in his life, was a bit of a family man and groomed Archeptolis to carry on his legacy. It is fair to say that Archeptolis had a far better mentor than his father's mentor, the largely forgotten Athenian politician Mnesiphilus.

In a moment of joy, upon seeing a lavishly set table before him as he sat down for a family dinner party, Themistocles remarked on his past and present stations in life:

> My children, we should now have been undone, had we not been undone before.[23]

Despite Themistocles's prosperity in Persia, he never let down his guard. A lifetime in the midst of the political and military fight had prepared him well for the one true weakness of Persian governance, the in-fighting among bureaucrats. While the Persian practice of rewarding success and competence was laudable, the brutal underbelly of that reality was constant jockeying for influence and accolades at every rank below the king. This was prevalent in the Persian invasions, where different commanders sought to influence the king more than effectively execute military strategy. Artemisia embodied this when she rammed another Persian ship during the Battle of Salamis in order to impress Xerxes, for which she was greatly rewarded.

Themistocles had the pleasure of experiencing this Persian custom first-hand. Another local governor, Epixyes of Upper Phrygia, had grown envious of Themistocles's position in the empire. Perhaps Epixyes's motivation was raw jealousy of Themistocles's superior rank, or perhaps it was revenge for the Persian Wars influenced by the traditionalist Mandane. Either way, Epixyes risked his life and his fiefdom in Phrygia in an attempt to murder Themistocles.

Epixyes laid a trap in a town named Lion's Head, where Themistocles was to spend the night while travelling for state business. Epixyes had arranged for men from Pisidia, just south of his native Phrygia, to launch a surprise attack on Themistocles and his men, who were in no way expecting a military assault from allies in friendly territory. The assassination attempt was thwarted not by preparedness or even sabotage, but divine revelation.

The afternoon before arriving at Lion's Head, Themistocles was said to have a dream sent directly from a 'Mother of the Gods':

> O Themistocles, shun a head of lions, that thou mayest not encounter a lion.[24]

Themistocles took the meaning of the dream much as he had his previous, perhaps less authentic, prophetic visions in the preparations for Salamis. Themistocles rerouted his travels and avoided the trap laid by Epixyes. But his assassins did not give up quite so easily, and they tracked Themistocles to a tent not far from Lion's Head. But Themistocles had providentially arranged his tents in an unusual fashion. His personal tent's equipment had fallen in a river earlier and they had to hang up the tent curtains across the doorway of his servants' tent to dry, giving the impression to those outside that the servants' tent was his own. This confused the Pisidian assassins, whose situation was compounded by an extraordinarily dark night with no moonlight. The Pisidians not only entered the wrong tent to kill Themistocles, but found instead the tent of his armed bodyguards. The bodyguards made short work of the assassins. In so doing, Themistocles avoided what was the only recorded challenge to his rule in Magnesia, an otherwise peaceful and prosperous era for both the ruler and the city.

Themistocles was deeply struck by the dream, however. Its origin was apparently a goddess known locally in Ionia as Cybele, a deity popular with the commoners of Ionian Greece but not particularly favoured by the mainland Greeks. She was a kind of amalgamation of Rhea, the mother of the Olympian gods, and Gaia, the Mother Earth goddess, and found prominence in the Roman era as Magna Mater.

Cybele had made one more demand in the dream, after saving Themistocles's life. She required that Themistocles dedicate his daughter Mnesiptolema to the priesthood. As both his daughter and the wife of Themistocles's son and heir Archeptolis, Mnesiptolema was uniquely positioned to serve both the goddess and her new homeland Ionia. To serve as a priestess to Cybele, especially one personally appointed by the

Mother of the Gods herself, was a profound honour in the culture of Magnesia and Ionian Greece. This endeared Themistocles's family with many locals and gave his family the opportunities that his father Neocles had never been able to offer him. Themistocles constructed an opulent temple in Magnesia to honour Cybele, to the great joy of his citizens.

These were just the start of his construction projects in Magnesia. Although we do not have a complete record, his illustrious building projects in Athens certainly gave him the experience and ambition to follow suit in Magnesia. The city expanded its economic footprint under Themistocles's rule and certainly accompanied that with major buildings, including temples to their patron god Apollo, Greek markets, fortresses, and government buildings. However, apart from the temple to Cybele, we know of only one more specific project that Themistocles coordinated. It was a statue of himself, to match one he commissioned back in Athens, exalting his governorship and his accomplishments.

There is abundant evidence that this was a rehashing of Themistocles's tried and true strategy of image management. A significant amount of Magnesian coins bearing the name of Themistocles have been found dated to about 450 BCE, making them the oldest surviving primary source evidence for Themistocles and the only contemporary sources during his lifetime. About seven of these coins are known and illustrate the extent to which Themistocles reconfigured Magnesia in the Athenian image, even in its currency.

With a standard depiction of the god Apollo and the label of 'Magnesia', the coins would not catch the eye of modern museum-goers. But in the ancient world they were remarkably innovative. In the first place, Themistocles inscribed his own name on the coins, and in two versions even his own image. This was unheard of in the Persian world, whose governors and local rulers would never have offended the Great King of Persia by exalting themselves. Local administrators had been executed for far less. Demaratus of Sparta's aforementioned request to simply wear a crown in public had nearly made him the next victim. After intervening with Artaxerxes on Demaratus's behalf, Themistocles learned an important lesson; his own image on the coins was tempered by a 'type of bonnet'[25] and nothing resembling a crown.

Although this seems pedestrian on its face, Themistocles actually reshaped coinage. Coins were a recent invention, at least on a wide scale. They had first been minted by the Lydians in northern Asia Minor in the late seventh or early sixth century BCE. And just like Themistocles was the first to push the limits of democracy and pull its levels of power, he did the same with the emerging field of coinage. His main contribution was the practice of putting local rulers on coins, which was alien to both Persians and Greeks. Themistocles, in his unending quest to accumulate influence, made sure that his presence was known in every single financial transaction in Magnesia. It was an unprecedented move that both challenged the status quo in Persian-controlled territories and ensured that Themistocles's *kudos* was re-established despite being in a new land. And it became the uniform method of designing coins, a practice picked up by Alexander the Great a century later which continued into modern times.

Another, more subtle, calling card was found in the weight of the coins. Given the political division across the city-states of Greece and the Aegean, coin weight was standardized according to the main commercial hubs. From the sixth century, this meant that Aeginetan coins were the norm and easily used across the Mediterranean. But, with the rise of the Delian League, Athenian coins – which weighed about two grams less – were rapidly becoming the new standard. Themistocles made sure that the Magnesian coins he minted accorded to this Athenian weight, the Attic standard.

This was notable, as Magnesia was the first and only Persian state to adopt Athenian economic standards. While this may have posed problems for Themistocles, since it could easily be interpreted as an acknowledgement of Athenian economic supremacy, he weathered any criticism easily as the coinage in Magnesia multiplied in number but never wavered from the Athenian standard. Themistocles offered no explanation of his motive in doing so, but the careful historian might deduce that this was more than an homage to his homeland. Perhaps Themistocles was seeking out a clever way to send a message back to Athenian lands that he was prospering in Persia, either to recruit more Greek expatriates or to simply rub his post-ostracism success in their faces. Or, more probably, Themistocles knew the economic and commercial juggernaut that was emerging as a result of the

Athenian naval empire, and that Magnesia's quick entry into that trade network would lay a strong foundation for their own growth. Judging by Magnesia's continued prosperity into Roman times, this was yet another example of Themistocles's keen ability to see around corners and push his city-state up to maximum success, regardless of their level of participation.

But while he enjoyed his life in Magnesia, thoughts of Athens were never far from his mind. On a trip to the provincial capital Sardis, Themistocles happened upon a large statue of a maiden dubbed the Water-Carrier. Although it now resided in the temple to Cybele in Persian-controlled Greece, Themistocles knew the statue well. In fact, he had commissioned its creation. Early in his political career, he had served as the overseer of water in Athens. In that capacity, he had levied fines against those who had stolen public water. Those funds went to the construction of this statue, in yet another publicity stunt by Themistocles on his rise to the top.

The Persians had taken to the Water-Carrier and stole it away to their homeland after they burned Athens to the ground in 480 BC. In a spiteful move, they rehomed the statue in Sardis, the city that Athens had burned during the Ionian Revolt in the pre-cursor to the Athenian-Persian rivalry. The statue illustrated the deep hatred that Persia held for the Athenians and seeing it once more not only made Themistocles homesick but, more pressingly, made him more acutely aware of the ludicrous nature of his current position.

Themistocles endeavoured to return the statue to Athens, either out of his Athenian patriotism or his desire to show off his great fortunes in Persia to the city that had ostracized him. Themistocles wrote to the governor of Lydia, the Persian region that Sardis was in, and requested permission for the statue to be returned.

It was the action of a man who had become a bit too comfortable in his exile. Themistocles did not anticipate the offence taken by the Lydian governor, who penned an indignant reply and threatened to escalate the issue to the King of Kings himself. It was a bit of an empty threat, considering Themistocles's close relationship with the king, but it was still an awkward situation best to be avoided. To assuage the governor, Themistocles employed a tactic straight from his Athenian playbook. He bribed the concubines of the governor to divert his attention and change his mind on the matter. In short order, it was successful and Themistocles, spooked by the ordeal, spent the rest of his years in Magnesia avoiding any overt connections to his Athenian heritage.

Despite the glamour and glitz of his life in Persia, some sources paint Themistocles as fundamentally dissatisfied with his life outside Greece. The *Letters of Themistocles* cuts to the core of this sentiment as Themistocles concludes an account of his high status in Persia with the lines, 'I do not particularly enjoy the liberty and wealth I once again possess, but I do find that I have sufficient assets to make my exile acceptable if not productive – after all, I am far wealthier than you and all my other friends. But as Greeks, how could we possibly be happy with such excess? Therefore, I believe the current circumstances are a painful necessity and not good fortune.'[26]

Themistocles's forlorn Athenian patriotism would soon collide with his Persian patronage. King Artaxerxes, at very long last, grew tired of Themistocles's recommended strategy of waiting out the Athenian-Sparta infighting that was ripping Greece apart. The Athenians and the Delian League had been too successful in prying away Persian city-states and, as the Athenians turned their sights beyond Greece and into Egypt and the Levantine coast, Artaxerxes decided to act.

In 459 BCE, Themistocles was ordered to send Magnesian military support against the Delian League's forces in Egypt. To refuse would mean defying the King of Kings after his great mercies to the exile, a certain death sentence. He faced the most difficult decision of his life: choosing between spilling Athenian blood or his own blood. And, as always, he refused the available options and opted to forge an entirely new path.

Conclusion: The Legacy of Themistocles

Themistocles at all events, when Simonides or some one offered to teach him the art of memory, replied that he would prefer the art of forgetting; 'for I remember,' said he, 'even things I don't wish to remember, but I cannot forget things I wish to forget.'[1]

If Themistocles could indeed forget any part of his life, he would surely have hoped for it to be the command by Artaxerxes to go to war against his own countrymen.

The third Persian invasion of Greece never truly materialized during Themistocles's lifetime. Nevertheless, the Persians and Greeks did fight sporadically over the next few decades. In the so-called Wars of the Delian League, the Greeks and Persians met every few years over one colony's rebellion or another city-state's medising. But for the Persians, the goal was primarily to stem the growth of imperial Athens and its Delian League, and not to conquer land – the internal conflicts of the empire prohibited thoughts of engaging with an Athens who was now even stronger than they had been under Themistocles.

Cimon had aggressively and effectively led Athens and the Delian League during their systematic expansion across the Aegean. Themistocles's diplomatic model of threatening lesser states, as evidenced by his siege of Andros, had been highly successful and now extended to supporting revolts against Persian rule. Much of Thrace, modern-day Turkey and Cyprus was now either formally part of the Delian League or openly considering challenging their Persian governance. The Egyptians, with their long and proud history, were particularly prone to rebelling against Persian rule, having done so several times, including shortly before and after the second Persian invasion of Greece.

By 460 BCE, the Egyptians partnered with the Delian League to oust their Persian governor and eliminate any Persian garrisons who remained. That same year at the Battle of Pampremis, in the Nile's Delta, the

Athenians and Egyptians joined forces and routed a major Persian army that had been personally sent by Artaxerxes. Herodotus reported seeing the skulls of the Persian army in the sands of the battlefield decades later. By the following year, the remnant of that army had seized and fortified the Egyptian capital of Memphis. They held Memphis and its vast wealth and population while the Athenians sieged the city. But the Athenian strategy in sieges was to encircle the city and cut off the supply chain with their navy. This tactic was enormously successful on the islands and peninsulas of Greece, but less so along the banks of the Nile River which throttled their own supply chains and limited their offensive manoeuvres. The result was a stalemate for the next six years.

In a cruel twist of fate, this Athenian army was not led by Cimon. He had himself been ostracized from Athens a year earlier when he had led an Athenian battalion to Sparta to assist the Spartans in putting down a slave rebellion. Always sympathetic to the Spartans, Cimon had seen this as a powerful political move aimed to smooth Athenian-Spartan tensions. The Athenian voting assembly instead saw it as aiding the enemy, a matter made worse by the Spartans cleverly refusing Cimon's assistance and sending the hoplites back to Athens. Cimon was exiled shortly thereafter, turning Athenian political control over to his rival, Ephialtes. Although Cimon would eventually return to Athens a decade later, his days of any serious political influence were over.

Artaxerxes demanded that his best generals organize and train an army of up to 300,000 men to break the siege and redeliver Egypt to Persia. That army gathered in Cilicia over the next year, and it included Cilicians, Cypriots, Phoenicians and, of course, Magnesians. Themistocles was ordered to personally lead soldiers and triremes in this army, which Artaxerxes likely considered a precursor to Themistocles's role in a planned third invasion of Greece. As Plutarch phrases it, Artaxerxes the Great commanded Themistocles to finally '[apply] himself to the Hellenic problem'.[2]

To lead a fighting force against Athens and the very navy that Themistocles built himself was a bridge too far for the exiled statesman. Now sixty-five years old, he had little interest in doing anything to destroy his legacy and the great Athenian empire he had created. Of course, he also had little interest in being executed by the Persians for rejecting the king's orders. The *Letters of Themistocles* articulated his internal conflict:

But now something even worse has happened – the King Artaxerxes has named me as commander of the Persian army destined to fight against Athens. While many other things will come to pass, this will never happen![3]

Compounding matters was the clear fact that this was to be the first step in Themistocles's military engagement with Greece. After granting him a decade of peaceful governance of Persian cities, Artaxerxes's expectation was for Themistocles to use the siege of Memphis as a springboard to advise Artaxerxes on the invasion of Greece. Artaxerxes was determined to succeed where his father and grandfather had failed: in taking all of the Greek lands, and that path passed directly through the Athenian navy.

Battling through his inner turmoil, Themistocles agreed to fight against his kinsmen the Athenians. He did, however, make a request of King Artaxerxes in return for his participation. This was an enormously bold move, considering the many mercies shown to Themistocles and Persia's penchant for executing those who did not show the Great King due reverence and submission. Themistocles relied on the same courageous rhetoric that had colourized his entire career and won him a place in the Persian empire to begin with. His request of the king was simple: that Artaxerxes make a solemn oath that he 'would not march against the Greeks without Themistocles'.[4]

Such an oath was no small thing. If the king broke the oath, it would be a terrible dishonour on his person and his position. And so, when Artaxerxes agreed to never invade Greece without Themistocles personally accompanying him, Themistocles resolved to end the matter on his own terms.

While he outwardly made preparations to send his military to Egypt, Themistocles invited all of his family and friends to a dinner party at his home in Magnesia. After a night of feasting and partying, he hugged each of them closely and showed them the affection and kindness reserved only for the most vulnerable moments in one's life. After giving his deepest regards to his loved ones, Themistocles made the request for a bull to be brought to the party to serve as a sacrifice. This was not particularly unusual on its face, but Themistocles rarely employed public religious practices without an ulterior motive. On this night, it was his final act of trickery.

Themistocles sacrificed the bull to the gods and then drained some of the blood of the bull into a cup. He then took the cup, said a short prayer, and drank it. Within minutes, he was dead. Themistocles, the great Athenian statesman and general, died of suicide instead of slaughtering his countrymen of Athens. He died in 459 BCE at the age of sixty-five, having ruled Magnesia for a decade and been exiled from Athens for about a dozen years.

Plutarch describes his death as a heroic sacrifice by a Greek patriot, loyal until the bitter end:

> neither embittered by anything like anger against his former fellow-citizens, nor lifted up by the great honour and power he was to have in the war, but possibly thinking his task not even approachable…yet most of all out of regard for the reputation of his own achievements and the trophies of those early days; [Themistocles] decided that his best course was to put a fitting end to his life.[5]

Similarly, the historian Diodorus Siculus exalts Themistocles's death as a passionate expression of his love for Athens and desire to never do her harm: 'Themistocles by his voluntary death left the best possible defence that he had played the part of a good citizen in all matters affecting the interests of Greece.'[6] On hearing the news of Themistocles's passing, Artaxerxes respected Themistocles even more. He did not take it as a betrayal to Persia, but instead as a heroic sacrifice for one's country, something he demanded of his own soldiers. Artaxerxes allowed Themistocles's son Archeptolis to succeed him as governor of Magnesia, a promotion that would never occur if Themistocles's death had been interpreted as disloyalty.

As to the specific cause of his death, the drinking of bull's blood was a relatively common method for poisoning in Classical Greek writing. The obvious historical issue with this is that bull's blood is not actually poisonous for humans to ingest. Because it congeals quickly, it appeared to the ancient Greeks that this would cause congealing in the blood and vital organs and cause a quick death. Because of this, bull's blood was also seen as the most heroic and courageous method of taking one's own life. If Themistocles did indeed die this way, he must have poisoned the bull's blood with actual poison. In his play *The Knights*, just three decades after Themistocles's death, Aristophanes referenced the death of Themistocles and characterized the glory of his sacrifice for Greece:

Demosthenes: Let me think, what is the most heroic?

Nicias: Let us drink the blood of a bull; that's the death Themistocles chose.[7]

There is some controversy surrounding Themistocles' motive and manner of death. In a later biography on Cimon, Plutarch presents Themistocles's death as a pragmatic avoidance of dealing with his ambitious promises of delivering Greece to Persia and the superior military power of Athens. But, just like he lionized Themistocles in his biography, Plutarch does the same to Cimon, stating that Themistocles's death was 'most of all due to Themistocles' despair of his Hellenic undertakings, since he could not eclipse the good fortune and valour of Cimon.'[8]

Thucydides takes a more clinical approach and removes all the romantic drama of his death, saying that Themistocles died of natural causes. He does acknowledge the possibility of Themistocles hoping to avoid disappointing Artaxerxes but dismisses it as hearsay. Cornelius Nepos follows suit and takes the same position.

In all likelihood, Themistocles's death was mobilized as propaganda for both the populist politicians in Athens, who used it to illustrate the heroism of their movement, and by the aristocratic supporters of Cimon, who used it to show that the populist Themistocles died a failure.

*   *   *

No matter how his death was mythologized, either to support his legacy in Athens or to support that of Cimon's, Themistocles's story does not quite end with his death. Like the fierce fighting over the body of Achilles after he fell in battle, Themistocles's descendants went to great lengths to properly honour his remains. Despite given royal honours on his death in Magnesia, where a grand temple in his honour was constructed that stood for hundreds of years after his death, Themistocles had apparently arranged for his remains to be taken home to Athens. He requested this of his family members, impressing upon them the importance of his ancestral home and allowing his bones to forever stay in his beloved Athens.

Apart from the logistical problems of Themistocles's exiled sons or grandsons (now Persian citizens and actively at war with the Athenians and the Delian League) actually getting into Athens, fulfilling Themistocles' final request was challenging because Athens expressly forbid the burial of traitors on Athenian soil. While Themistocles's ostracism did not qualify him as a traitor, his conviction at the Congress at Corinth shortly after that exile had resulted in a formal charge of treason. This meant that even if Themistocles's bones reached Athens again, they would need to remain unmarked or else risk being destroyed by the Athenians.

But Themistocles's boldness must have been hereditary, as his descendants constructed an entire tomb on a small peninsula near the harbour of Piraeus and then proudly posted a sign above its doors proclaiming:

> Thy tomb is mounded in a fair and sightly place;
> The merchantmen shall ever hail it with glad cry;
> It shall behold those outward, and those inward bound,
> And all the emulous rivalry of racing ships.[9]

Richard Cumberland transformed this eulogy from Plutarch into a more energetic and readable edition in his eighteenth century commentaries on the classical world, *The Observer*:

> By the sea's margin, on the watery strand,
> Thy monument, Themistocles, shall stand:
> By this directed to thy native shore,
> The merchant shall convey his freighted store;
> And when our fleets are summoned to the fight
> Athens shall conquer with thy tomb in sight.[10]

Plutarch goes on to criticize the historical writing of those ancients who give any credit to this eulogy, going as far as to say that the story emerged solely as a political tool 'to incite the oligarchs against the people'.[11] He further attacks the construction of a tomb in Athens and dismisses it as populist nonsense meant to romanticize a fallen champion.

Some scholars proclaim that Themistocles's tomb has been found in a set of recently discovered ruins on a former industrial plant near Piraeus named Drapetsona. Although the dating works well, there is scant evidence that it belonged to Themistocles himself. But no matter the historical reality of Themistocles's final resting place, it is clear that Themistocles's descendants carried on his legacy. His son Archeptolis took the reins in

Magnesia and continued its prosperity. Archeptolis further continued the coin minting that Themistocles had begun, with coins bearing his own name, the name of Themistocles, and even – astonishingly – the Athenian owl emblem. Perhaps no pithier example of the ironically overlapping world exists than Persian coins bearing the owl of Athens.

Archeptolis continued his father's dynasty, ruling with Greek style and substance but nevertheless dutifully paying tribute to the Persian king. Archeptolis ruled in Magnesia from 459 BCE, after Themistocles's death, until possibly 412 BCE. If he ruled for that long, then he would have seen the tensions between Athens and Sparta boil over into the three decade long Peloponnesian War, ripping apart Greece and ultimately, due to mismanagement of their naval empire and Persian interference, destroying Athens' Golden Age. Magnesia never felt the impact, continuing to flourish and grow in influence. Its greatest days would come during the Hellenistic era, where it became a vital city along the coast for the kingdom of Pergamon, established by one of Alexander the Great's successors. Magnesia transitioned easily to Roman rule, continuing to prosper until later in the empire. Their continued success was in large part due to the modernization that Themistocles initiated.

Some of Themistocles's descendants, perhaps his own sons or the sons of Archeptolis, made their way home to Athens. The Persians tightened their grip on Ionian Greeks at the turn of the fourth century BCE, and it is likely many of Themistocles's descendants returned to Athens as they no longer benefited from their links to the great statesman. Plutarch recounts meeting a descendant of Themistocles in the first century AD, also known as Themistocles. That Themistocles admitted that he and his family were still collecting revenues from Magnesia nearly six hundred years later. By this point, as well, Themistocles's image had become something of a cult since the aristocratic-populist tensions were long forgotten, which meant that Themistocles's descendants had created their own nobility. It was a far cry from the meagre upbringing that Neocles had offered Themistocles.

Those same descendants sought to memorialize Themistocles in one more final and dramatic homage. Pericles, the son of Xanthippus, had gone on to lead Athens during the apogee of its influence and constructed, with Delian League funds, the famous temple known as the Parthenon. The most phenomenal example of Greek architecture, the Parthenon was the physical representation of the height of Athenian prosperity and culture. Although built after Themistocles's death, it was nevertheless the culmination of his life's work and ambition.

Themistocles's family knew that the Parthenon and the Athenian empire were built on the back of Themistocles, and they honoured him with a painting on the friezes of the Parthenon. The geographer Pausanias saw this painting still present in second century AD, writing: 'The children of Themistocles certainly returned and set up in the Parthenon a painting, on which is a portrait of Themistocles.'[12]

It was a fitting elegy for Themistocles, the man who exhibited all the greatness and ingenuity of Greece. He channelled the best of Greek literature and culture into all of his actions, both those palatable and those unpalatable to modern society.

* * *

The legacy of Themistocles is both complicated and subtle. He cultivated a reputation as a cunning hero who – often through trickery and extreme measures – earned victory for his nation, consequences be damned. Yet despite the magnitude of his achievements and the impact of his life, his contributions are mostly distilled into his military victory at Salamis and his ostracism. Yet, if we look with Greek eyes, we can see quite clearly that Themistocles was far more important to Athens, Greece and the West than as a mere military tactician. He remains the closest embodiment of the mythological and Homeric hero, a man who grasped control of his own destiny and used every iota of talent and strength to accomplish phenomenal things and transform his world.[13]

Plutarch wrote at length about Themistocles as this embodiment of a truly Greek and Homeric hero, saying, 'Themistocles, who was called another [Odysseus] for his wisdom.'[14] Themistocles skyrocketed to success by exhibiting unprecedented *arete* – effectiveness in all aspects of life and achieving the highest human potential. In all fields he pursued, Themistocles was relentlessly effective above all else. Like Achilles, Odysseus, and even Jason and Theseus, Themistocles displayed such virtue and talent that he was simply superior to mortal men, seizing his destiny and defeating great monsters and villains and forcibly etching his name among the great Greek gods and heroes.[15] For Themistocles, grasping his destiny was not just an option, it was a fulfilment of divine prophecy.

Plutarch even zealously guards Themistocles's status as a hero, chastising Herodotus for not emphasizing Themistocles's cunning enough: 'If we have, as some say, antipodes inhabiting the other hemisphere, I believe that they also have heard of Themistocles and his counsel, which he gave to the Greeks, to fight a naval battle before Salamis.'[16] In short, Themistocles had a level of *kudos* among the Greeks that rivalled the great Homeric and mythological heroes. And as time passed further, and less primary sources survived, that mythos became something akin to historical reality.

And Themistocles even experienced the tragic fall of the Homeric hero. Just like the heroes of myth and legend, he fiercely protected his reputation at all costs yet that could not keep him from a downfall. Achilles may have died in the glory of war, but he died in a rather mundane manner, from an arrow to his heel, and without leading his side to victory in the definitive war of his lifetime. Odysseus died at the hands of his own son, through his relationship with the witch Circe, though neither one knew the other was a blood relative at the time. Theseus was thrown off a cliff on Skyros after declining in popularity in his beloved Athens. And Themistocles, despite the romanticism of his self-sacrifice, died in relative obscurity as governor of a second-tier Persian city, a far cry from dominating the politics of the pre-eminent Mediterranean power of Athens.

In Homeric literature, the great heroes are typically accompanied by an epigraph listing their great accomplishments; 'godlike,' 'horse-taming,' 'great spearman,' 'beloved of Ares,' and 'noble' are among the most common. Although such epigraphs don't often exist outside of literature, Themistocles nevertheless established himself as such a force of personality and *arete* that the entire Greek and Persian world had heard of him before he even arrived. The mythos of Themistocles, regardless of historical precision given the relatively scant sources, reconfigured Athens and Greece. Themistocles became immortalized as a legendary figure, a foil for all future politicians and generals. Like Achilles and Odysseus, Themistocles epitomized the rubric of Greek heroism and virtue. But unlike Achilles and Odysseus, Themistocles's mythology was based on enough historical reality for it to be believable and inspirational for the Greeks. His heroism was tangible and relatable, and his enduring impact is directly related to the mythos surrounding his adventurous, unpredictable, and highly effective life.

The ancients saw Themistocles in this very way, even if we do not today. Thucydides showered more praise on him than any other character in his history of Greece. In a return to the opening words of our narrative of the life and work of Themistocles, Thucydides wrote:

> For Themistocles was a man who exhibited the most indubitable signs of genius; indeed, in this particular he has a claim on our admiration quite extraordinary and unparalleled. By his own native capacity, alike unformed and unsupplemented by study, he was at once the best judge in those sudden crises which admit of little or of no deliberation, and the best prophet of the future, even to its most distant possibilities. An able theoretical expositor of all that came within the sphere of his practice, he was not without the power of passing an adequate judgment in matters in which he had no experience. He could also excellently divine the good and evil which lay hid in the unseen future. In fine, whether we consider the extent of his natural powers, or the slightness of his application, this extraordinary man must be allowed to have surpassed all others in the faculty of intuitively meeting an emergency.[17]

Diodorus Siculus does the same several hundred years later, through the lens of the Roman Empire and with full knowledge of the many Greek politicians and leaders:

> We have come to the death of one of the greatest of the Greeks, about whom many dispute whether it was because he had wronged his native city and the other Greeks that he fled to the Persians, or whether, on the contrary, his city and all the Greeks, after enjoying great benefits at his hands, forgot to be grateful for them but unjustly plunged him, their benefactor, into the uttermost perils. But if any man, putting envy aside, will estimate closely not only the man's natural gifts but also his achievements, he will find that on both counts Themistocles holds first place among all of whom we have record. Therefore one may well be amazed that the Athenians were willing to rid themselves of a man of such genius.[18]

And even during Themistocles's own lifetime, his image in Athens rehabilitated the longer he was gone. As the conflict with Sparta intensified and led into a gruelling war, Themistocles once again came to represent the patriotic hero of Athens, remembered far more for Salamis than for his ostracism. The playwright Aristophanes included in *The Knights* a harsh criticism of Cleon, a successor to Cimon as hegemon over Athenian politics:

> You dare to compare yourself to Themistocles, who found our city half empty and left it full to overflowing, who one day gave us the Piraeus for dinner, and added fresh fish to all our usual meals. You, on the contrary, you, who compare yourself with Themistocles, have only sought to reduce our city in size, to shut it within its walls, to chant oracles to us. And Themistocles goes into exile, while you gorge yourself on the most excellent fare.[19]

Themistocles's historical footprint extends far further than the Persian Wars, further than the Athenian empire, and further even than Classical history. The mythos of Themistocles and his status as a type of incarnated Homeric hero directly created the rubric for the successful Greek statesman, general, and citizen.

He was the forerunner of the successful Athenian politician. He was the first to navigate a democratic system and was the first to pull its levers and manipulate its strengths and weaknesses to his own advantage, and the first to accumulate power from the non-aristocratic classes. Themistocles forged the model for political leadership followed by the most famous Athenian statesmen. For the rest of the fifth century, Pericles, Alcibiades and the other leaders of Athens all directly continued Themistocles's vision for Athens: a strong navy, a merciless imperialism in foreign policy, fortification of the harbours and the walls of the city itself, and long term preparations for war with Sparta, Persia and whoever else might rise against Athens.

Pericles, in particular, leaned heavily on the Themistoclean model. Pericles became the pre-eminent politician of Athens, ruling over it for nearly the entire so-called Golden Age of Athens. He built on the bedrock laid by Themistocles for economic and logistic flourishing in the Athenian Golden Age. He lowered taxes on merchants and foreigners. He manipulated the poets, philosophers, teachers and playwrights to present a strong vision of Athens and of himself. He continued Themistocles's naval vision for Athens, constructing massive amounts of triremes each year to guarantee Athenian dominance of the Mediterranean. This also included Themistocles's trick of earning lower class voting support, and by lucratively employing lower class citizens to man all of those ships, Pericles earned annual re-election to the office of *strategos* for virtually his entire career. He continued the *stasis* between the populists and the aristocrats, siding with the commoners and making innovative and fanciful promises to them in exchange for continued power. He also, of course, utilized the Odysseus-like rhetoric and penchant for blackmail and bribery that Themistocles had perfected in the world's first democracy.

By 430 BCE, Pericles built Athens into the dominant and powerful city-state that Themistocles had envisioned, and did so against the backdrop of a decades-long tension with Sparta. Like Themistocles, Pericles spent much of his career sounding the alarm about a powerful enemy and pumping money and resources into properly preparing Athens for the looming war. In response to the Spartan threat, he continued Themistocles's wall building project by creating the Long Walls, a massive construction project linking the urban centre of Athens with the port of Piraeus.

The Long Walls made the entirety of Athens a fortress and completely neutralized the Spartan land supremacy. They saved Athens from a quick destruction – much like Themistocles had done in constructing the Themistoclean Wall immediately after the Persian Wars. It was therefore Themistocles who singularly prepared Athens for its two great rivals of the fifth century, Persia and Sparta. He shaped the political infrastructure and worldview of Athens for the entirety of that century.

Pericles's nephew Alcibiades, the grandson of Xanthippus, extended Themistocles's political legacy further after pairing political effectiveness with theatrical flair and a magnetic personality. Alcibiades, like Themistocles, knew the power of messaging and showmanship, but also the prudence of silence. Alcibiades led Athens during the next great war, the Peloponnesian War against Sparta which began in earnest after Pericles's death in 429 BCE. Alcibiades's career was similarly fraught with incredible achievements and astonishing collapses. He rose quickly through the ranks of Athenian democracy until he influenced every cultural, political and military aspect of the city-state. He was a divisive leader beloved by commoners and either reviled or adored by the aristocrats. His bold stratagems shocked the enemy and inspired his countrymen, until they suddenly did not. Alcibiades advised a foolish invasion of Sicily that decimated the peerless navy and began Athens' slow descent from its Golden Age.

Alcibiades learned again from Themistocles's model of skirting ostracism, a threat he faced virtually non-stop in Athens. He engaged with similar propaganda campaigns, but Alcibiades pushed even further when he figured out that allying with an opponent would allow them to combine forces and ostracize a third person. Alcibiades, in so doing, essentially broke the ostracism system in Athens. Clever manipulation of Athenian democracy – to the point that the system was bent by one man exclusively – became the mantle that Alcibiades took up from Themistocles.

And as a penalty for the magnitude of his influence and the divisions sparked by his leadership, Alcibiades also went on his own Homeric odyssey after an informal ostracism from Athens, although it took a few more twists and turns than his predecessor Themistocles. Alcibiades followed the Themistoclean model of joining one's sworn enemy and partnered with the Spartans to advise them to defeat the Athenians. But Alcibiades had little self-control when it came to romance, and he was forced to flee from Sparta when he was caught in the midst of an affair with the Spartan queen. Alcibiades then joined the other great Athenian rival, and medised. He was seduced by the gifts and honours bestowed on his predecessors in medising, like Themistocles, and advised to drive the wedge further between Athens and Sparta. The Persians placed him in charge of the negotiations with Athens and the Delian League, an opportunity he used to pull yet another cunning manoeuvre when he re-joined the Athenians who welcomed him back home in desperation to save their declining empire. He was subsequently exiled, again informally, and advised all parties of the war – Athenian, Persian, and Spartan – before the Spartans finally defeated Athens in a naval battle. In that battle at Aegospotami, the Spartans followed Alcibiades's advice and borrowed Persian gold to build triremes that finally crushed the vaunted Athenian navy. Themistocles's navy was at long last undone by his own political heir.

Themistocles created the format for the successful democratic politician – one copied again and again throughout history. The *stasis* between aristocrats and commoners still drove Athenian politics after Themistocles's exile. The champions of each party continued the political duel that Themistocles and Aristides fought. Themistocles, the populist, and Aristides, the traditionalist aristocrat, had inherited their own *stasis* from Cleisthenes and Isagoras and that custom continued as Themistocles gave way to the populist Ephialtes who fought against the aristocrat Cimon, which gave way to the populist Pericles who duelled against the aristocrat Cleon, and continued through to the populist Alcibiades struggling against the traditionalist Nicias. The *stasis* ended only after Alcibiades essentially played both sides and helped the Athenian empire crumble apart, and much of its democratic system along with it.

In so doing, Themistocles colourized the gritty reality of democracy and defined what it meant to truly be an Athenian – the good, the bad and the ugly. Themistocles forged the version of democracy, with its equal capacity for ingenuity and vice, that the great Greek philosophers analyzed and based their political philosophies on. Socrates and Plato may never have rejected democracy had Themistocles not learned to manipulate it.

While Pericles left behind the majestic Parthenon as a manifestation of his many contributions to Athens, the hastily constructed Themistoclean Wall is a more apt depiction of Themistocles's legacy. The beauty and splendour of Athens had turned to ruins after the Persian invasion, yet Themistocles was able to cobble it together to form something entirely new and strong enough to not just survive but prosper. His wall, not beautiful yet highly effective, received little credit both at the time and even today, yet it was what directly allowed Athens to transform itself into the most influential civilization in history.

In short, the entirety of Athens' success and contributions to the modern world are directly the product of the unique talents and foresight of Themistocles. He is of course not alone in this, yet his overshadowing in the Classical world is lamentable. His rags-to-riches story and political subterfuge are not completely unique nor was he the first to make that journey, but he was critically the first to accomplish it in a democracy. This makes him the first politician to heavily influence the unique intersection of government, public policy, military, the institution of reforms, information control and culture-building that democracy offers – something that still exists today.

By transforming ancient Greece, Themistocles shaped the world we live in now. Western civilization has inherited the Classical emphasis on individual liberty and democratic ideals. And many leaders throughout history have, intentionally or not, channelled Themistocles's model of democratic manipulation, naval imperialism, and flexible patriotism.

Beyond Classical Athens, the great Hellenistic and Roman leaders mobilized these Themistoclean ideals and built upon them. Throughout history, many rulers seized power despite their humble origins in the working class. The Roman emperor Diocletian rose to power from obscurity through sheer competence and talent, instituted widespread reforms to consolidate power, identified a major rival to the empire (the Christians) that he dedicated the state to defeating, and then died in a [self-imposed] exile far from the centres of power. Many other leaders, like Napoleon or James II of England, went through similar story arcs of falling from grace after impressive conquests and then either returning triumphantly from exile or succumbing to ostracism and fading off into the ether.

With the restoration of democracy in the United States and the French Revolution and spread of democratic ideals, the West rediscovered their Classical roots. Early American leaders like Alexander Hamilton and Thomas Jefferson took up the mantle of merciless political manoeuvring and conglomerating hegemonic influence in a democracy. Later American politicians took up the less valiant aspects of Themistocles's *arete,* such as Andrew Jackson or Richard Nixon. The democratic tradition of leveraging political power through blackmail, bribery and propaganda was one first navigated by Themistocles and inherited by the American, and then later Western, democracies. The Cold War between the Soviet Union and the United States is historically compared to the Peloponnesian War between Athens and Sparta, and the disinformation and propaganda weaponized by both states had their roots in the type of empire-building Themistocles began in Athens.

But perhaps the most striking parallel to Themistocles is the British Prime Minister Winston Churchill. Both used cunning ruses and an ironclad grip on the nation's systems of military and political power to defeat a powerful enemy at all costs. Both also advanced the blueprint for spycraft and subterfuge in warfare. Churchill's spy service, dubbed the 'Ministry of Ungentlemanly Warfare' is a perfect description of the type of warfare and political subterfuge that Themistocles honed in the ancient world. Perhaps the best modern example is D-Day and the Allied invasion of Europe, and how Operation Overlord tricked all parties – including most Allied troops – into thinking that the invasion would be at Calais. Cunning ruses were abundant in the strategies of World War II, and the Allies used everything from fake spies to inflatable tanks to parachuting dummies to tinfoil dropped from planes that confused enemy radar. If Themistocles had inflatable tanks and parachuting dummies at his disposal, he would surely have found a clever use for them against the Persians, but he was confined to false betrayals, blackmailing his allies and disregarding the orders of his superiors in the Hellenic League.

But like the old adage about Churchill, Themistocles was a great leader for wartime in his ability to singularly lead his nation to victory with undaunting effectiveness and willpower, but was not exactly ideal for peacetime. Once the pariah of Nazi Germany or Persia was defeated, Churchill and Themistocles faced the reality of a nation ungrateful for the cost of victory. Churchill was voted out of leadership while Themistocles was ostracized.

The narrative of Themistocles ultimately explains the Classical origins of our modern world. Themistocles epitomizes the romantic potential of any citizen in a democracy to effect national change, he lays bare the tainted underbelly of democratic ideals, he illustrates the great distance between a Homeric hero – one who changes the world no matter the cost – and a modern hero – one whose alleged virtue and nobility extend to all aspects of their life. Themistocles was not a virtuous man nor a good man, but he was an effective man who achieved excellence at everything he pursued. He transformed democracy, redesigned military strategy, organized an empire, weaponized the arts, modelled hegemonic influence, and left an enduring footprint on our modern world. He was a hero worthy of Homer and the Greek myths, and his story remains worth telling.

Diodorus Siculus succinctly phrased the legacy of Themistocles after covering his incredible narrative at length:

Now on the subject of the high merits of Themistocles, even if we have dwelt over-long on the subject in this digression, we believed it not seemly that we should leave his great ability unrecorded.[20]

Glossary

Arete – Translated as virtue, it more precisely means excellence of all kinds and being highly effective at everything a human being can pursue. It is the defining characteristic of a hero in the epic poetry of Homer, and therefore shaped the Greek worldview.

Areopagus – The council of former *archons* in Athens. Meeting on the 'Rock of Ares' (making this the famous Mars Hill from the Bible), the *areopagus* often consisted of aristocrats vying for more power. Themistocles and other populist politicians worked to limit the *areopagus*'s influence.

Aristeia – The 'great moment' of a hero, where they earn their glory and reputation for all of history. For Achilles, this was defeating Hector in combat. For Odysseus, it was capturing Troy with the Trojan Horse or winning back his home from the suitors.

Aristoi – The 'best men' of a Greek society and the root word for aristocrats. Historically, this meant the nobility.

Choregos – The wealthy patron of a Greek theatre production. Responsible for the funding and executive producing of the play, they wielded significant influence over the public's perception of the play and its success in a theatre competition such as the Dionysia.

Deme – A population group in Athenian democracy and a subset of the larger tribes. They were the building block for the democratic reforms of Cleisthenes. Themistocles was from the relatively unremarkable *deme* of Phrearrhi.

Democracy – A government system in which the people have the political authority to decide policy and hold office. It was first invented in Athens after the reforms of Cleisthenes in 508 BCE.

Diekplous – A military tactic in trireme warfare when one trireme slices through the line of the enemy and then immediately turns about-face with the intent of ramming one of the opposing ships. Translated as 'sailing out through', the intent was to break the enemy lines as Themistocles and Eurybiades did at Artemisium and Salamis.

Eponymous archon – The chief magistrate of Athens elected to a year-long term by the voting assembly. Themistocles served as *eponymous archon* from 493–492 BCE.

Homeric – Pertaining to the epic poems of Homer, *The Iliad* and *The Odyssey*. Homer's poems shaped the Greek worldview and cultivated their understanding of virtue and heroism.

Hoplite – Heavy infantry soldiers from Classical Greece. Armed with an eight to ten foot long spear, forty to fifty pounds of heavy armour, a short sword and a shield, they were a unique development in Greece and were highly successful against the faster and lighter Persian infantry.

Kudos – A good reputation for honour, intellect, and effectiveness. An essential trait for a Homeric hero, one's *kudos* often determined one's success in politics.

Medize – To depart Greece and join forces with the Persian empire. The Persians actively recruited turncoats among the populations they targeted for conquest and offered Greek city-state or accomplished individuals money and status to medize.

Oligarchy – Rule by a few elite individuals. Oligarchy was a common form of government in ancient Greece, and Athenian democracy emerged from a long struggle in Athens against tyranny and oligarchy

Ostrakon – A piece of broken pottery used to write the name of an Athenian one wished to ostracize. These were collected into piles and counted, and if one person garnered 6,000 votes then they were exiled from Athens. Plural: *Ostraka*

Paidagōgos – A tutor and teacher to young boys, often a slave in a wealthier household with a position of honour.

Phalanx – A military formation of hoplites in closely arrangement with interlocking shields to guard your allies. The *phalanx* formed a shield wall and could attack an opponent with its eight to ten foot long spears strategically arranged to complement the shields. It was the standard of Classical Greek warfare and won many battles against the Persians during the Persian Wars.

Scolia – A drinking or praise song that has become culturally popular and publicly performed. They are often political in nature and were used as a political tool by poets like Timocreon and Simonides.

Stasis – Meaning a 'standing still', *stasis* described the constant political struggle between the aristocrat classes and the commoners in Athens. It became a hallmark of the Athenian political world, and each side had champions for their cause in holding political offices.

Strategos – The name of one of the ten Greek generals, elected annually by each of the ten tribes. The *strategos* shaped military strategy and held significant political influence. Many successful politicians began as *strategos*, including Themistocles, Miltiades, Pericles, and Xanthippus.

Thalassocracy – A naval-based empire such as the Athenian empire of the 5th century BCE.

Thete – A rower on a Greek trireme, typically from the lower or middle classes. It held a stable income and respect in Athenian society and, grouped as 180 rowers on each ship, the *thetes* became an influential political group courted by democrats like Themistocles.

Trireme – A three-storied warship in the ancient world built for fast travel and ramming opponents. Triremes had about 180 rowers and were the gold standard for naval warfare during the Persian Wars, on both sides.

Tyranny – A government form where one ruler seizes control. It was the most common form of government in ancient Greece.

Xenia – The Greek word for hospitality and respect given to guests and to hosts. It was a major Greek virtue and has special emphasis in the poems of Homer, particularly Odysseus in *The Odyssey*.

Character List

Achilles – The main hero from Homer's epic poem *The Iliad*, he was the world's greatest fighter and the hero of the Trojan War. His impact on the Greek worldview cannot be overstated as his effectiveness in combat and glory inspired the Greeks for generations.

Aeschylus – An Athenian playwright, poet, and veteran of the major battles of the Persian Wars. He wrote *The Persians* and many other famous plays based on his experiences on the battlefield at Salamis.

Aminias – An Athenian trireme captain and warrior, and the brother of the playwright Aeschylus. He won honours at Salamis for his valour and performance.

Archeptolis – The son of Themistocles who ruled Magnesia on the Meander after the death of Themsitocles. Although not as successful as his father, he inherited Themistocles's gift for politics and foresight.

Aristides the Just – Themistocles's main rival early in his political career. A champion of the aristocrats and renowned for his honour and justice, he was the most trustworthy man in Athens. Themistocles arranged his ostracism from Athens as a political ploy, but then also arranged his triumphant return from exile to help lead the Greeks to victory in the Persian Wars.

Artemisia – The queen of Halicarnassus and the only female admiral in Xerxes the Great's invasion force. She was crafty, wise, and brutally effective.

Artaxerxes the Great – The king of Persia after his father Xerxes's death. He ruled from 465–424 BCE and was a successful king despite facing many internal conflicts. He was the king who welcomed Themistocles to the Persian court.

Cimon – An Athenian politician and general who was a rival to Themistocles during Themistocles's later career in Athens. He was closely allied with the Spartans during the rising tensions between Athens and Sparta after the Persian Wars.

Cleisthenes – The 'Father of Democracy' who first instituted the major democratic reforms in Athens in 508 BCE. His reforms led to the emergence of the first democracy.

Congress at Corinth – A meeting of the Greek city-states at the Isthmus of Corinth in 481 BCE to strategize for the invasion of Xerxes the Great's massive Persian army. The Spartans led the Congress but Themistocles led the Athenian delegation in his first foray beyond Athenian politics.

Cyrus the Great – The first King of Kings in Persia, conquering a massive empire from 559–530 BCE, including Ionian Greece and most of modern-day Turkey. Cyrus's rule was characterized by the kind treatment of conquered people and his impressive diplomacy.

Darius the Great – The most successful King of Kings in Persia, ruling from 522 to 486 BCE. He was a talented administrator, skilled economist, and expanded Cyrus's empire significantly. He ordered the first Persian invasion of Greece which was repelled at Marathon. He made subsequent plans to reinvade but died before executing them. His son Xerxes succeeded him.

Delian League – The Athenian-dominated alliance of Greek city-states after the Persian Wars. The Delian League was dedicated to protection against lingering Persian attacks and to eliminating the Persian presence in the Aegean. Athens led the league with an iron fist and effectively converted it into an Athenian empire.

Demaratus – The former king of Sparta who fled his post and was one of the first major Greeks to medize and join the Persian empire. He advised Xerxes during the second Persian invasion and was one of the most esteemed Greeks serving in the Persian court, eventually alongside Themistocles.

Diodorus Siculus – A first century AD Roman historian of Greek heritage. Diodorus Siculus, meaning 'of Sicily', wrote a comprehensive history of the Greco-Roman world that compiled and quoted many sources now lost to history.

Eurybiades – A Spartan admiral and leader of the Hellenic League's navy during the second Persian invasion of Greece. A competent and honourable leader, he nevertheless often deferred to Themsitocles as the war continued.

Ephialtes (of Athens) – An Athenian politician and populist leader who led a series of reforms that stripped power from the oligarchs in the *areopagus*. According to Aristotle, he partnered with Themistocles to do this in the waning years of Themistocles's days in Athens. He succeeded Themistocles as the populist champion in Athenian democracy.

Hellenic League – The alliance of independent Greek city-states formed at the Congress at Corinth in 481 BCE whose sole mission was to defend Greece from the Persian invasion. The Hellenic League was eventually succeeded by the Delian League after the Greeks' victory in the war.

Herodotus – The 'Father of History' who first wrote a detailed narrative of the world as he knew it. He was most famous for the history of the Persian Wars that he wrote after allegedly travelling to Persia, Babylon, and Egypt and interviewing witnesses from about 445 to 430 BCE.

Hector – The great Trojan hero from Homer's epic poem *The Iliad*, Hector was a brave and honourable warrior killed in combat by the only warrior greater than him: Achilles.

Hippias – The final tyrant of Athens, Hippias was exiled from Athens around 510 BCE after which Cleisthenes created the Athenian democratic system. Hippias fled to Persia, allied with Darius the Great, and advised the Persians on their first invasion which failed at Marathon. Had the Persians won at Marathon, he would have led Athens and potentially all of Greece as Persia's governor.

Homer – The blind poet who authored the most formative texts of the Classical and ancient worlds: *The Iliad* and *The Odyssey*. His works, in tandem with the Greek myths, were responsible for shaping the Greek definition of virtue and heroism in the age of Themistocles.

Leonidas – A king of Sparta during the second invasion of Greece. He famously led the Spartan hoplites in their dramatic – and doomed – final stand at the Battle of Thermopylae and wrote himself into Greek mythology and legend as a result.

Mardonius – The greatest Persian general in both invasions of Greece. He was a close ally of Darius the Great and continued as second-in-command to Xerxes the Great. He led the Persian invasion after Xerxes departed following the loss at Salamis.

Miltiades – An Athenian general and politician who engineered the great victory at the Battle of Marathon in 490 BCE. He had originally worked for the Persians as a medized Greek but came to his ancestral home of Athens after the Athenians fought against the Persians in the Ionian Revolt.

Mnesiphilus – An early Athenian politician active in the late sixth century BCE, little is known of him apart from his close mentoring of Themistocles and his political survival skills as he skirted ostracism on several occasions.

Neocles – The father of Themistocles. An unremarkable man who most likely worked as a ship's captain, he advised Themistocles to never enter politics or else Themistocles would end up like the ruined triremes they saw daily on the beaches of the small part of the city called Phrearrhi.

Pausanias – A Spartan general and regent who led the Greeks to victory in the Battle of Plataea, the final battle that vanquished Persians from the mainland of Greece. Pausanias soon set himself up as a Persian-style tyrant and attempted to join the Persian empire, for which he was repeatedly arrested and eventually killed. He had a dubious relationship with Themistocles, and many thought the two to be in cahoots.

Plutarch – A second century AD Roman historian of Greek heritage. He wrote a famous set of biographies called *Parallel Lives* that chronicled the great figures of Greece and Rome. He included Themistocles, Aristides the Just and Cimon among those biographies.

Odysseus – The hero of Homer's epic poem *The Odyssey* and a main character in its forerunner *The Iliad*, Odysseus represented the cunning resourcefulness, clever manoeuvring, and ruthless effectiveness that the Greeks valued in a true hero.

Sicinnus – The slave and *paidagōgos* of Themistocles and his most loyal servant. Themistocles trusted Sicunnus more than any other person alive and used Sicinnus as the mediator for his messages to the Persian king Xerxes.

Simonides – A renowned poet from the island of Ceos, he was famous for his epitaphs for famous heroes, such as the famous memorial for the Battle of Thermopylae. He was a bitter rival of other poets of the day, such as Pindar and Timocreon, and was employed by Themistocles for publicity purposes.

Themistocles – An Athenian statesman and general who lived from 524–459 BCE. He was among the very first populist politicians to operate in a democracy, he embodied the rags-to-riches potential of a democracy, he led the Greeks to victory over the invading Persians, he ushered Athens into its Golden Age, he was ostracized from his beloved Athens and he fled to his former rival Persia where he garnered even more fame and glory.

Thucydides – An Athenian general and historian, he wrote *The History of the Peloponnesian War* chronicling the narrative of the great war between Athens and Sparta, which Themistocles helped prepare the Athenians for. His history writing is more measured than Herodotus's, and he quotes many historians whose work has been destroyed.

Timocreon – A playwright and poet from Rhodes who made his home in Athens shortly after the Persian Wars. He was famous for his drinking songs and his elbow-rubbing with many aristocrats and kings, including the Great King of Persia. Timocreon had a personal grudge against Themistocles and penned songs insulting him.

Xanthippus – An Athenian aristocrat and politician from a powerful noble family, Xanthippus was a rival of Themistocles in the 480s until Themistocles engineered his ostracism. Xanthippus, along with Aristides the Just, was recalled from exile by Themistocles to fight in the Persian Wars where he distinguished himself in leadership.

Xerxes the Great – The King of Kings of Persia, he inherited the empire after his father Darius the Great died in 486 BCE. He fulfilled his father's vision of a great invasion of Greece to get vengeance on Athens. Despite conquering much land and even burning Athens, the Persian invasion failed due to Themistocles's leadership at the Battle of Salamis and the subsequent defeat at Plataea.

Notes

Introduction

1. Thucydides, *The History of the Peloponnesian War*, trans. Richard Crawley (Cambridge: Harvard University Press, 1874), 1.137.
2. For good measure, he also saved Athens once more – but from fellow Greeks. He convinced the Athenians to properly prepare to fight Sparta from the moment the war ended. His construction of the Long Walls to guard Athens were especially critical as they protected the city from Spartan hoplites and allowed the Athenian navy to do the fighting
3. Fry, Stephen. *Heroes*. (London: Random House, 2018), 1
4. Homer, *The Iliad*. trans. Samuel Butler (London: A. C. Fifield, 1914), Book I ll.1–3
5. Longinus, *On the Sublime*, trans. H.L. Havell, (London: Macmillan Publishers, 1890), 9.7.
6. Plutarch. *Parallel Lives*. 'Life of Themistocles,' trans. Bernadotte Perrin (Loeb Classical Library. Cambridge: Harvard University Press, 1914), 31.5.
7. Robert Lenardon argues this most persuasively in *The Saga of Themistocles*, where the entire book is organized around the epic hero's journey. Lenardon, Robert J. *The Saga of Themistocles* (London: Thames & Hudson Press, 1978)
8. Hamilton, Edith. *The Greek Way*. (1930; repr., New York: W.W. Norton, 2010), 31, 137–8.
9. M. Tullius Cicero. *The Orations of Marcus Tullius Cicero*. 'For Archias.' trans C. D. Yonge (London: Henry G. Bohn, 1856), 9.20.
10. Thucydides, *The History of the Peloponnesian War* 1.138.6

Chapter 1: From Obscurity to Marathon

1. Herodotus does not give the exact number of Persian troops. Most later historians of the ancient world number it at 100,000 to 200,000 or even more. However, modern historians have settled on approximately 25,000 Persians
2. Herodotus, *The Histories* trans. A. D. Godley (Loeb Classical Library. Cambridge: Harvard University Press, 1920), 7.218.3.
3. Herodotus, *The Histories* 6.94
4. Herodotus, *The Histories* 7.133
5. The Spartans, of course, had two kings at once but their power was far from absolute or autocratic and Sparta is more generally considered an oligarchy
6. Herodotus, *The Histories* 6.112
7. Herodotus, *The Histories* 6.113
8. Pausanias, *Description of Greece* trans. W.H.S. Jones and H.A. Ormerod. (Cambridge: Harvard University Press and London, William Heinemann Ltd, 1918), 1.32.4
9. Plutarch, *Themistocles* 1.1

10. Plutarch, *Moralia* 'How to Profit by One's Enemies' 9 as cited in Stadter, Philip A. 'Notes and Anecdotes: Observations on Cross-Genre *Apophthegmeta*' in Nikolaidis, Anastasios, ed. *The Unity of Plutarch's Work: 'Moralia' Themes in the 'Lives', Features of the 'Lives' in the 'Moralia'* (Berlin & Boston: De Gruyter, 2008), 60

11. Herodotus, *The Histories* 2.1

12. Plutarch, *Themistocles* 2.1–2

13. Plutarch, *Themistocles* 2.2

14. Plutarch, *Themistocles* 2.3

15. Plutarch, *Themistocles* 2.4

16. Plutarch says other ancient biographers falsely identified Themistocles's mentor. But his inclusion in Herodotus's account is a good indicator of his historicity, and with the limited sources on Themistocles's early life it is safe to believe Mnesiphilus was a formative figure for Themistocles

17. Plutarch, *Themistocles* 2.5

18. Plutarch, *Themistocles* 2.6

19. Plutarch, *Themistocles* 1.1

20. Plutarch, *Moralia* 'Sayings of Kings and Commanders' trans. E. Hinton, ed. by William W. Goodwin (Boston: Little, Brown, and Co., 1878), 39

Chapter 2: The Rise of the Subtle Serpent of Athens

1. Herodotus, *The Histories* 5.78

2. Plutarch, *Themistocles* 5.4

3. Plutarch, *Themistocles* 5.5

4. Plutarch, *Moralia*, 'Sayings of Kings and Commanders' 39

5. Plutarch, *Moralia*, 'Sayings of Kings and Commanders' 39

6. Plutarch, *Themistocles* 5.4

7. Strauss, Barry. *The Battle of Salamis: The Naval Encounter that Saved Greece – And Western Civilization* (New York: Simon & Schuster, 2005), 132–3

8. Herodotus, *The Histories* 6.21

9. Diodorus Siculus. *Library of History, Volume XI: Fragments of Books 21–32*, trans. Francis R. Walton (Loeb Classical Library 409. Cambridge: Harvard University Press, 1957), 11.41.4

10. Diodorus Siculus, *Library of History* 11.41.3

11. Diodorus Siculus, *Library of History* 11.43.2

12. Diodorus Siculus, *Library of History* 11.43.2

13. Diodorus Siculus, *Library of History* 11.43.3

14. Plutarch, *Themistocles* 3.3–4

15. Herodotus, *The Histories* 7.133

16. Plutarch, *Themistocles* 4.2

17. Cicero, *Letters to Atticus, Vol. II* trans. E.O. Winstedt. (London: William Heinemann 1921), 10.8.4

18. Aristotle, *The Constitution of Athens*, trans. Sir Frederic G. Kenyon (London: G. Bell, 1891), 22.7

19. Plutarch, *Themistocles* 4.3

20. Plutarch, *Themistocles* 4.3

21. Xenophon, *The Memorabilia: Recollections of Socrates* trans. by H. G. Dakyns. (New York: Macmillan and Co., 1897), 2.6

Chapter 3: Of Rivalries and Ostracisms

1. Herodotus, *The Histories* 8.79.1
2. Plutarch. *Parallel Lives*. 'Life of Aristides,' trans. Bernadotte Perrin (Loeb Classical Library. Cambridge: Harvard University Press, 1914), 2.1
3. Plutarch, *Moralia*, Vol. I. 'How a Young Man Should Study Poems' trans. Simon Ford, ed. William W. Goodwin (Boston: Little, Brown, and Co., 1878), 83. A similar version is found in Aeschylus, *The Persians*
4. Plutarch, *Aristides* 2.5
5. Plutarch, *Themistocles* 3.2
6. Plutarch, *Aristides* 2.1–2
7. Plutarch, *Aristides* 4.2
8. Plutarch, *Aristides* 4.3
9. Plutarch, *Aristides* 4.4–5
10. Plutarch, *Aristides* 3.2
11. Plutarch, *Aristides* 3.2
12. Diodorus Siculus, *The Library of History* 11.55
13. Diodorus Siculus, *The Library of History* 11.55.3
14. Aristotle, *The Constitution of Athens* 28
15. Aristotle, *The Constitution of Athens* 22.5
16. Asmonti, Luca. *Athenian Democracy: A Sourcebook*. London: Bloomsbury Academic, 2014, pg. 94
17. Plutarch, *Aristides* 7.1
18. Plutarch, *Aristides* 7.1
19. Plutarch, *Aristides* 7.5–6
20. Plutarch, *Aristides* 7.2
21. Plutarch, *Aristides* 2.4
22. Homer, *The Odyssey* 20.17

Chapter 4: The Persian Invasion & the Hellenic League

1. Herodotus, *The Histories* 7.8
2. Herodotus, *The Histories* 7.133
3. Aeschylus, *The Persians* in *Four Plays of Aeschylus*. trans. G. M. Cookson. (Blackwell Publishing: Oxford, 1922), 88
4. Herodotus, *The Histories* 7
5. This is Herodotus's account, yet the fact that Miltiades served Persia for another decade and a half suggests that it may not be especially reliable.
6. Aeschylus, *The Persians* 91
7. Herodotus, *The Histories* 7.24
8. Plutarch. Parallel Lives. 'Life of Theseus,' trans. Bernadotte Perrin (Loeb Classical Library. Cambridge: Harvard University Press, 1914), 25.3
9. Plutarch. Parallel Lives. 'Life of Theseus,' trans. Bernadotte Perrin (Loeb Classical Library. Cambridge: Harvard University Press, 1914), 25.3
10. Herodotus, *The Histories* 7.138
11. Herodotus, *The Histories* 7.147
12. Herodotus, *The Histories* 7.132
13. Herodotus, *The Histories* 7.220
14. Herodotus, *The Histories* 7.220
15. Herodotus, *The Histories* 7.145

16. Herodotus, *The Histories* 7.140
17. Herodotus, *The Histories* 7.141, trans. George Rawlinson
18. Herodotus, *The Histories* 7.143
19. Herodotus, *The Histories* 8.2
20. Herodotus, *The Histories* 5.97
21. Plutarch, *Themistocles* 7.3
22. Herodotus, *The Histories* 7.132

Chapter 5: Artemisium: The Cornerstone of Democracy

1. Herodotus, *The Histories* 7.220
2. The Troezen Decree. Translation my own. Greek text from Lenardon, Robert J. *The Saga of Themistocles* (London: Thames & Hudson Press, 1978), 129
3. Plutarch, *Themistocles* 10.1
4. Plutarch, *Themistocles* 10.2
5. The Troezen Decree. Translation my own
6. Plutarch, *Themistocles* 10.5
7. The Troezen Decree. Translation my own
8. Plutarch, *Themistocles* 11.1
9. Plutarch, *Aristides* 8.1
10. Plutarch, *Themistocles* 10.5.
11. Herodotus, *The Histories* 8.5
12. Green, Peter. *The Greco-Persian Wars* (Berkeley: University of California Press, 1996), 131
13. Diodorus Siculus, *The Library of History* 11.12.4
14. Plutarch, *Themistocles* 7.5
15. Herodotus, *The Histories* 8.10
16. Herodotus, *The Histories* 7.147
17. Herodotus, *The Histories* 8.11
18. Herodotus, *The Histories* 8.10
19. Diodorus Siculus, *The Library of History* 11.13.4
20. Plutarch, *Themistocles* 8.2
21. Herodotus, *The Histories* 8.53

Chapter 6: Engineering Salamis: The Final Stand of Greece

1. Herodotus, *The Histories* 8.22
2. Herodotus, *The Histories* 8.22
3. Herodotus, *The Histories* 8.57
4. Cornelius Nepos, Lives of Eminent Commanders, trans. Rev. John Selby Watson in Justin, Cornelius Nepos, and Eutropius: Literally Translated, with Notes and a General Index (London: Henry G. Bohn, 1853), 2.4
5. Herodotus, *The Histories* 8.59, trans. A. D. Godley
6. Herodotus, *The Histories* 8.59, trans. A. D. Godley
7. Plutarch, *Themistocles* 11.3, paraphrased
8. Herodotus, *The Histories* 8.60
9. Herodotus, *The Histories* 8.62
10. Herodotus, *The Histories* 8.68
11. Herodotus, *The Histories* 8.75
12. Plutarch, *Themistocles* 12.4

13. Plutarch, *Aristides* 8.5
14. Diodorus Siculus, *The Library of History* 11.17.4
15. Plutarch, *Aristides* 8.6
16. Herodotus, *The Histories* 7.141, trans. George Rawlinson

Chapter 7: The *Aristeia* at Salamis

1. Plutarch, *Themistocles* 13.3
2. Herodotus, *The Histories* 8.83
3. Plutarch, *Themistocles* 14.2
4. Strauss, *The Battle of Salamis*, 133
5. Plutarch, *Themistocles* 14.2
6. Aeschylus, *The Persians* 76
7. Diodorus Siculus, *The Library of History* 11.18.6
8. Plutarch, *Themistocles* 14.2
9. Plutarch, *Themistocles* 14.2
10. Plutarch, *Themistocles* 14.3
11. The timing of this duel is a bit unclear across the accounts of Herodotus, Diodorus Siculus, and Plutarch. This is potentially the same Persian commander killed by Aminias at the battle's onset, For this narration, I have interpreted it as two separate events occurring at separate points in the battle
12. Herodotus, *The Histories* 8.86
13. Herodotus, *The Histories* 8.90
14. Aeschylus, *The Persians* 76–77
15. Herodotus, *The Histories* 8.92
16. Herodotus, *The Histories* 8.92
17. Ctesias, *Persica* from Photius. *Bibliotheca* or *Myriobiblon*. trans. by J.H. Freese and transcribed by Roger Pearse (Ipswich, UK: Tertullian.org, 2002), 30
18. Ctesias, *Persica* 30
19. Diodorus Siculus, *The Library of History* 11.19.4
20. Herodotus, *The Histories* 8.97
21. Herodotus, *The Histories* 8.100
22. Herodotus, *The Histories* 8.88
23. Herodotus, *The Histories* 8.110
24. Herodotus, *The Histories* 8.108
25. Herodotus, *The Histories* 8.109
26. Herodotus, *The Histories* 8.109
27. Herodotus, *The Histories* 8.110
28. Cornelius Nepos, *Lives of Eminent Commanders* 2.4
29. Xenophon, *Memorabilia* 2.6

Chapter 8: A Defeated Persia, A Wounded Themistocles

1. Herodotus, *The Histories* 8.94
2. Herodotus, *The Histories* 8.111
3. Plato, *Timaeus* trans. Benjamin Jowett (Oxford: Oxford University Press, 1892), 48.
4. Simonides. *Fragments of Simonides* 37.1.27 as cited in Plato, *Protagoras* 345d in *Plato in Twelve Volumes, Vol. III*. trans. by W.R.M. Lamb. (Cambridge: Harvard University Press, 1967)
5. Herodotus, *The Histories* 8.111

6. Herodotus, *The Histories* 8.112
7. Diodorus Siculus, *The Library of History* 11.27.3
8. Herodotus, *The Histories* 8.124
9. Thucydides, *The History of the Peloponnesian War* 1.74.2
10. Herodotus, *The Histories* 8.124
11. Plutarch, *Themistocles* 17.2
12. Plato, *The Republic* 329e-330a
13. Herodotus, *The Histories* 8.125
14. Diodorus Siculus, *The Library of History* 11.42.4
15. Diodorus Siculus, *The Library of History* 11.27.3
16. Herodotus, *The Histories* 8.136
17. Herodotus, *The Histories* 8.140
18. Herodotus, *The Histories* 8.143
19. Plutarch, *Aristides* 10.8

Chapter 9: Sparta Provoked

1. Plutarch, *Aristides* 22.2
2. Diodorus Siculus, *Library of History* 11.44.3–4
3. Thucydides, *The History of the Peloponnesian War* 1.128.7
4. Thucydides, *The History of the Peloponnesian War* 1.90.2
5. Plutarch. *Parallel Lives.* 'Life of Lycurgus' trans. Bernadotte Perrin (Loeb Classical Library. Cambridge: Harvard University Press, 1914), 19.2
6. Plutarch, *Moralia*, Vol. III. 'Sayings of the Spartans', trans. Frank Cole Babbitt. (Loeb Classical Library. Cambridge: Harvard University Press, 1931), ll. 2.29
7. Thucydides, *The History of the Peloponnesian War* 1.93.1
8. Thucydides, *The History of the Peloponnesian War* 1.90.4
9. Thucydides, *The History of the Peloponnesian War* 1.91.1
10. Thucydides, *The History of the Peloponnesian War* 1.90.4–7
11. Cornelius Nepos, *Lives of Eminent Commanders* 8
12. Thucydides, *The History of the Peloponnesian War* 1.92.1
13. Thucydides, *The History of the Peloponnesian War* 1.93.7
14. Diodorus Siculus, *Library of History* 11.41.2
15. Diodorus Siculus, *Library of History* 11.42.4
16. Diodorus Siculus, *Library of History* 11.42.6
17. Diodorus Siculus, *Library of History* 11.43.2
18. Thucydides, *The History of the Peloponnesian War* 1.93.6
19. Thucydides, *The History of the Peloponnesian War* 1.93.5
20. Plutarch, *Themistocles* 20.4
21. Plutarch, *Themistocles* 20.4
22. Thucydides, *The History of the Peloponnesian War* 1.23.6

Chapter 10: A Reckoning in the Athenian Golden Age

1. Plutarch, *Themistocles* 2.3
2. Plutarch, *Moralia*. 'Sayings of Kings and Commanders' 39
3. Plutarch, *Moralia*. 'Sayings of Kings and Commanders' 39
4. Plutarch, *Themistocles* 18.1
5. Plutarch, *Themistocles* 18.2

6. Plato, *Hippias Minor* in *Plato in Twelve Volumes, Vol. IX.* trans. by W.R.M. Lamb (Cambridge: Harvard University Press, 1925), 365b
7. Aelian. *Various Histories.* trans. by Thomas Stanley. (London: Thomas Dring. 1665), 49
8. Plutarch, *Themistocles* 5.4
9. Plutarch. *Parallel Lives.* 'Life of Cimon' trans. Bernadotte Perrin (Loeb Classical Library. Cambridge: Harvard University Press, 1914), 4.4
10. Plutarch, *Cimon* 5.4
11. Plutarch, *Themistocles* 5.3
12. Plutarch, *Themistocles* 21.2–3, this middle stanza from Plutarch, *Plutarch's Lives*, Vol. 12. 'Life of Themistocles', trans. John Dryden and Arthur Hugh Clough. (New York: P.F. Collier & Son, 1909), 21.2–3
13. Plutarch, *Themistocles* 21.2–3
14. Athenaeus, *The Deipnosophists* 11.9. Translation my own. Greek text from *Athenaeus V: The Learned Banqueters: Books 10.420e-11.* trans. S. Douglas Olson. Cambridge: Harvard University Press, 2009
15. *Palatine Anthology* 13.31. Translation my own. Greek text from *Palatine Anthology* from the University of Heidelberg Digital Library, Cod. Pal. graec. 23 — Konstantinopel, 2. Hälfte 9. Jh. und 1. Hälfte 10. Jh.https://digi.ub.uni-heidelberg.de/diglit/cpgraec23/0011
16. Aristophanes, *Peace* in *The Complete Greek Drama, Vol II.*, trans. Eugene O'Neill (New York: Random House, 1938), 695
17. Aeschylus, *The Persians* 68
18. Aeschylus, *The Persians* 76
19. Plutarch, *Themistocles* 25.1
20. Plutarch, *Moralia.* 'Sayings of Kings and Commanders' 39
21. Aristotle, *The Constitution of Athens* 25. Some historians count Themistocles's involvement here as anachronistic, and argue that these reforms should be attributed to Ephialtes alone or perhaps to Pericles (to whom Plutarch attributes the reforms).
22. Aristotle, *The Constitution of Athens* 25

Chapter 11: The Ostracism of the Saviour of Athens
1. Plutarch, *Themistocles* 25.1
2. Plutarch, *Themistocles* 25.1
3. Plutarch, *Moralia*, Vol. II. 'How to Profit by One's Enemies', trans. Frank Cole Babbitt. (Loeb Classical Library. Cambridge: Harvard University Press, 1928), 6.1
4. Thucydides, *The History of the Peloponnesian War* 1.135.3
5. Diodorus Siculus, *The Library of History* 11.55.8
6. Plutarch, *Moralia*, 'On the Malice of Herodotus' trans. John Thomson, ed. William W. Goodwin (Boston: Little, Brown, and Co., 1878), Bk. 14
7. Plutarch, *On the Malice of Herodotus* 14
8. Plutarch, *Themistocles* 22.7
9. Inscription C from Easterling and Handley, Eds. *Greek Scripts. An Illustrated Introduction* (London: Society for the Promotion of Hellenic Studies, 2001)
10. Brenne, Stefan. T1/147 as cited in Forsdyke, Sara. *Exile, Ostracism, and Democracy: The Politics of Expulsion in Ancient Greece* (Princeton University Press, 2009), p. 155

11. Brenne, Stefan. T1/150 as cited in Forsdyke, Sara. *Exile, Ostracism, and Democracy: The Politics of Expulsion in Ancient Greece* (Princeton University Press, 2009), p. 155. A more precise translation would be the one penetrated in anal intercourse, an insulting term for an adult male Athenian

12. Plutarch, *Moralia*. 'The Roman Questions' 25

13. Plutarch, *Aristides* 25.7

14. A likely reference to Plato, *Gorgias* 526b although Themistocles, Cimon and Pericles are not mentioned by name in the passage

15. Plutarch, *Aristides* 25.6

16. Plutarch, *Themistocles* 21.4–5

17. Plutarch, *Themistocles* 21.4–5

18. Diodorus Siculus, *The Library of History* 11.55.4

19. Plutarch, *Themistocles* 23.3

20. Plutarch, *Themistocles* 23.4

21. *The Letters of Themistocles* 2, 'To Pausanias.' Translation my own. Greek text from Hercher, Rudolf. 'Themistoclis Epistolae' in *Epistolographoi Ellēnikoi*. Parisiis: Didot, 1871, pp. 741–762

22. Plutarch, *Themistocles* 23.2

23. Diodorus Siculus, *The Library of History* 11.55.6

24. Thucydides, *The History of the Peloponnesian War* 1.136.1

25. *The Letters of Themistocles* 20, 'Themistocles greets Polygnotus.' Translation my own.

26. *The Letters of Themistocles* 4, 'Themistocles greets Habronichus.' Translation my own.

27. Plutarch, *Themistocles* 24.2

28. Thucydides, *The History of the Peloponnesian War* 1.136.4

29. *The Letters of Themistocles* 5, 'Themistocles greets Temenidas.' Translation my own.

30. Plutarch, *Themistocles* 24.4

31. Plutarch, *Themistocles* 25.1

32. *The Letters of Themistocles* 20, 'Themistocles greets Polygnotus.' Translation my own.

33. Plutarch, *Themistocles* 25.2

Chapter 12: Themistocles of Persia

1. Royal Collection Trust, *Letter of surrender from Napoleon to the Prince Regent*, 13 July 1815. www.rct.uk RCIN 452438.d

2. Diodorus Siculus identifies the Persian aristocrat who sheltered Themistocles and arranged his connection to the Persian king as Lysitheides. The overall narrative remains similar

3. Plutarch, *Themistocles* 26.2

4. Plutarch, *Themistocles* 26.2–3

5. Thucydides, *The History of the Peloponnesian War* 1.137.4

6. *Letters of Themistocles* 8, 'Themistocles to Leager.' Translation my own.

7. Aristotle, *Politics*, trans. Benjamin Jowett (Oxford, Clarendon Press, 1885), 5.131

8. Ctesias, *Persica* 20

9. Plutarch, *Themistocles* 27.3

10. Plutarch, *Themistocles* 27.4

11. Plutarch, *Themistocles* 27.5

12. Herodotus, *The Histories* 5.105

13. Plutarch, *Themistocles* 28.1–2

14. Plutarch, *Themistocles* 28.3
15. Plutarch, *Themistocles* 29.1
16. Plutarch, *Themistocles* 29.3
17. Diodorus Siculus, *The Library of History* 11.57.4
18. Thucydides, *The History of the Peloponnesian War* 1.138.2
19. Plutarch, *Themistocles* 29.4
20. Xenophon, *Memorabilia* 3.6
21. Diodorus Siculus, *The Library of History* 11.58.1
22. Plutarch, *Themistocles* 25.3
23. Plutarch, *Themistocles* 29.6
24. Plutarch, *Themistocles* 30.1
25. Cahn, Herbert A., and Dominique Gerin. 'Themistocles at Magnesia.' *The Numismatic Chronicle* (1966–) 148 (1988): 18. Accessed February 18, 2020. www.jstor.org/stable/42668124
26. *The Letters of Themistocles* 20, 'Themistocles greets Polygnotus.' Translation my own

Conclusion: The Legacy of Themistocles

1. Cicero, *de Finibus* in *The Academic Questions: Treatise de Finibus and Tusculan Disputations of M. T. Cicero*. 'de Finibus.' trans. C. D. Yonge. (London: George Bell and Sons, 1875), 2.32.104
2. Plutarch, *Themistocles* 31.3
3. *The Letters of Themistocles* 20, 'Themistocles greets Polygnotus.' Translation my own.
4. Diodorus Siculus, *The Library of History* 11.58.2
5. Plutarch, *Themistocles* 31.4
6. Diodorus Siculus, *The Library of History* 11.58.3
7. Aristophanes, *The Knights* in *Aristophanes: The Eleven Comedies*. trans. The Athenian Society (London: The Athenian Society, 1912), 79–86
8. Plutarch, *Cimon* 18.6
9. Plutarch, *Themistocles* 32.5
10. Cumberland, Richard. *The Observer Vol. III*. (London: J. Richardson and Co, 1822), 270. A paraphrasing of Plutarch, *Themistocles* 32.5
11. Plutarch, *Themistocles* 32.3
12. Pausanias, *Description of Greece* 1.1.2
13. Paraphrase of Fry, Stephen. *Heroes*. (London: Random House, 2018), 1
14. Plutarch, *On the Malice of Herodotus* 14
15. Paraphrase of Fry, Stephen. *Heroes*. (London: Random House, 2018), 1
16. Plutarch, *On the Malice of Herodotus* 14
17. Thucydides, *The History of the Peloponnesian War* 1.138.3–4
18. Diodorus Siculus, *The Library of History* 11.58.4
19. Aristophanes, *The Knights* 815–819
20. Diodorus Siculus, *The Library of History* 11.59.4

References

Primary Sources
All translations are public domain unless otherwise noted.

Aelian. *Various Histories*. Translated by Thomas Stanley. London: Thomas Dring, 1665.

Aeschylus, *The Persians in Four Plays of Aeschylus*. Translated by G. M. Cookson. Blackwell Publishing: Oxford, 1922.

Aristophanes, *Peace in The Complete Greek Drama, Vol II*. Translated by Eugene O'Neill. New York. Random House. 1938.

Aristophanes, *The Knights* in *Aristophanes: The Eleven Comedies*. Translated by The Athenian Society. London: The Athenian Society, 1912.

Aristotle. *The Constitution of Athens*. Translated by Sir Frederic G. Kenyon. London: G. Bell, 1891.

Aristotle. *Politics*. Translated by Benjamin Jowett. Oxford, Clarendon Press, 1885.

Athenaus, *The Deipnosophists*. My own translation from the Greek text in *Athenaeus V: the Learned Banqueters: Books 10.420e-11*. Translated by S. Douglas Olson. Cambridge: Harvard University Press, 2009.

Cornelius Nepos. *Lives of Eminent Commanders*. Translated by Rev. John Selby Watson. In *Justin, Cornelius Nepos, and Eutropius: Literally Translated, with Notes and a General Index*. London: Henry G. Bohn, 1853.

Diodorus Siculus. *Library of History, Volume XI: Fragments of Books 21–32*. Translated by Francis R. Walton. Loeb Classical Library 409. Cambridge: Harvard University Press, 1957. Published with notice but copyright was not renewed.

Hamilton, Edith. *The Greek Way*. 1930. Reprint, New York: W.W. Norton, 2010.

Hamilton, Edith. *The Roman Way*. 1932. Reprint, New York: W.W. Norton, 2017.

Hercher, Rudolf. 'Themistoclis Epistolae' in *Epistolographoi Ellēnikoi*. Parisiis: Didot, 1871.

Herodotus. *The Histories*. Translated by A. D. Godley. Loeb Classical Library. Cambridge: Harvard University Press, 1920.

Herodotus. *The Histories*. Translated by George Rawlinson. New York: Charles Scribner's Sons, 1897.

Homer. *The Iliad*. Translated by Samuel Butler, London: A. C. Fifield, 1914.

Homer. *The Odyssey*. Translated by Samuel Butler, London: A. C. Fifield, 1900.

Longinus. *On the Sublime*. Translated by H.L. Havell, London: Macmillan Publishers, 1890.

M. Tullius Cicero, *Letters to Atticus, Vol. II*. Translated by E.O. Winstedt. London: William Heinemann 1921.

M. Tullius Cicero. *The Academic Questions: Treatise de Finibus and Tusculan Disputations of M. T. Cicero*. 'de Finibus.' Translated by C. D. Yonge. London: London: George Bell and Sons, 1875.

M. Tullius Cicero. *The Orations of Marcus Tullius Cicero.* 'For Archias.' Translated by C. D. Yonge. London: Henry G. Bohn, 1856.

Palatine Anthology from the University of Heidelberg Digital Library, Cod. Pal. graec. 23 — Konstantinopel, 2. Hälfte 9. Jh. und 1. Hälfte 10. Jh.https://digi.ub.uni-heidelberg. de/diglit/cpgraec23/0011.

Pausanias, *Description of Greece.* Translated by W.H.S. Jones and H.A. Ormerod. Cambridge: Harvard University Press and London, William Heinemann Ltd, 1918.

Photius. *Bibliotheca or Myriobiblon.* Translated by J.H. Freese and Transcribed by Roger Pearse. Ipswich, UK: Tertullian.org, 2002.

Plato, *Hippias Minor* in *Plato in Twelve Volumes, Vol. IX.* Translated by W.R.M. Lamb. Cambridge: Harvard University Press, 1925.

Plato, *Protagoras* in *Plato in Twelve Volumes, Vol. III.* Translated by W.R.M. Lamb. Cambridge: Harvard University Press, 1967.

Plato, *The Republic.* Translated by Benjamin Jowett. Oxford: Oxford University Press, 1888.

Plato, *Timaeus.* Translated by Benjamin Jowett. Oxford: Oxford University Press, 1892.

Plutarch, *Moralia* 'How a Young Man Should Study Poems' Translated by Simon Ford, D.D. Edition by William W. Goodwin, Boston: Little, Brown, and Co., 1878.

Plutarch, *Moralia*, Vol. II. 'How to Profit by One's Enemies.' Translated by Frank Cole Babbitt. Loeb Classical Library. Cambridge: Harvard University Press, 1928.

Plutarch, *Moralia* 'On the Malice of Herodotus' Translated by John Thomson. Edition by William W. Goodwin, Boston: Little, Brown, and Co., 1878.

Plutarch, *Moralia* 'Sayings of Kings and Commanders' Translated by E. Hinton. Edition by William W. Goodwin, Boston: Little, Brown, and Co., 1878.

Plutarch, *Moralia*, Vol. III. 'Sayings of the Spartans.' Translated by Frank Cole Babbitt. Loeb Classical Library. Cambridge: Harvard University Press, 1931.

Plutarch, *Moralia*, Vol. IV. 'The Roman Questions' Translated by Frank Cole Babbitt. Loeb Classical Library. Cambridge: Harvard University Press, 1936.

Plutarch. *Parallel Lives.* 'Life of Aristides.' Translated by Bernadotte Perrin. Loeb Classical Library. Cambridge: Harvard University Press, 1914.

Plutarch. *Parallel Lives.* 'Life of Cimon.' Translated by Bernadotte Perrin. Loeb Classical Library. Cambridge: Harvard University Press, 1914.

Plutarch. *Parallel Lives.* 'Life of Lycurgus.' Translated by Bernadotte Perrin. Loeb Classical Library. Cambridge: Harvard University Press, 1914.

Plutarch. *Parallel Lives.* 'Life of Themistocles.' Translated by Bernadotte Perrin. Loeb Classical Library. Cambridge: Harvard University Press, 1914.

Plutarch. *Parallel Lives.* 'Life of Theseus.' Translated by Bernadotte Perrin. Loeb Classical Library. Cambridge: Harvard University Press, 1914.

Plutarch, *Plutarch's Lives*, Vol. 12. 'Life of Themistocles.' Translated by John Dryden and Arthur Hugh Clough. New York: P.F. Collier & Son, 1909.

Royal Collection Trust, *Letter of surrender from Napoleon to the Prince Regent*, 13 July 1815. www.rct.uk RCIN 452438.d

Thucydides. *The History of the Peloponnesian War.* Translated by Richard Crawley. Cambridge: Harvard University Press, 1874.

Xenophon, *The Memorabilia: Recollections of Socrates* 2.6. Translated by H. G. Dakyns. New York: Macmillan and Co., 1897.

Secondary Sources

Asmonti, Luca. *Athenian Democracy: A Sourcebook*. London: Bloomsbury Academic, 2014.

Brenne, Stefan. *Ostrakismos und Prominenz in Athen: Attische Bürger des 5. Jhs. v. Chr. auf den Ostraka*. A. Holzhausens Nfg., 2001

Cahn, Herbert A., and Dominique Gerin. 'Themistocles at Magnesia.' *The Numismatic Chronicle* (1966–) 148 (1988): 13–20. Accessed February 18, 2020. www.jstor.org/stable/42668124.

Cumberland, Richard. *The Observer Vol. III*, London: J. Richardson and Co, 1822.

Easterling and Handley, eds. *Greek Scripts. An Illustrated Introduction*. London: Society for the Promotion of Hellenic Studies, 2001.

Forsdyke, Sara. *Exile, Ostracism, and Democracy: The Politics of Expulsion in Ancient Greece*. Princeton: Princeton University Press, 2009.

Fry, Stephen. *Heroes*. London: Random House, 2018.

Green, Peter. *The Greco-Persian Wars*. Berkeley: University of California Press, 1996.

Holland, Tom. *Persian Fire: The First World Empire and the Battle for the West*. New York, New York: Anchor Books, 2007.

Lenardon, Robert J. *The Saga of Themistocles*. London: Thames & Hudson Press, 1978.

Munn, Mark. *The School of History: Athens in the Age of Socrates*. Berkeley: University of California Press, 2000.

Nikolaidis, Anastasios, ed. *The Unity of Plutarch's Work: 'Moralia' Themes in the 'Lives', Features of the 'Lives' in the 'Moralia'* Berlin & Boston: De Gruyter, 2008.

Podlecki, A.J. *The Life of Themistocles: A Critical Survey of the Literary and Archaeological Evidence*. Montreal: McGill–Queen's University Press, 1975.

Stadter, Philip A. 'Notes and Anecdotes: Observations on Cross-Genre Apophthegmata.' In *The Unity of Plutarch's Work*, 53–66. Berlin & Boston: De Gruyter, 2008.

Strauss, Barry. *The Battle of Salamis: The Naval Encounter that Saved Greece – And Western Civilization*. New York: Simon & Schuster, 2005.

Index